MAGGIE BEER'S AUTUMN HARVEST RECIPES brings together over 90 of Maggie's signature autumn recipes, detailed descriptions of her favourite ingredients and inspiring accounts of memorable meals with family and friends.

The recipes highlight Maggie's philosophy of using the freshest and best seasonal produce available in the Barossa Valley, South Australia, and treating it simply, allowing the natural flavours to speak for themselves. Describing herself as a 'country cook', Maggie cooks from the heart and is passionate about instilling in others this same confidence – to use recipes as a starting point, and be guided by instinct and personal taste.

This collection of recipes from one of Australia's best-loved cooks has been taken from *Maggie's Harvest* and is essential for anyone with an appreciation of the pleasures of sourcing, cooking and sharing food.

✦ ✦ ✦

MAGGIE BEER is one of Australia's best-known food personalities. As well as appearing as a guest chef on *MasterChef Australia* and writing books, Maggie devotes her time to her export kitchen in the Barossa Valley, which produces a wide range of pantry items for domestic and international markets. These include her famous verjuice, pâté and quince paste as well as her new ice cream range. Maggie was also recognised as Senior Australian of the Year in 2010 for inspiring joy to many Australians through food.

Maggie is the author of many successful cookbooks: *Maggie's Christmas*, *Maggie Beer (Lantern Cookery Classics)*, *Maggie's Verjuice Cookbook*, *Maggie's Kitchen*, *Maggie's Harvest*, *Maggie's Table*, *Cooking with Verjuice*, *Maggie's Orchard* and *Maggie's Farm*, and co-author of the bestselling *Stephanie Alexander and Maggie Beer's Tuscan Cookbook*.

maggiebeer.com.au

MAGGIE BEER'S
AUTUMN HARVEST
— RECIPES —

Maggie Beer

with photography by Mark Chew

LANTERN

an imprint of
PENGUIN BOOKS

For Colin

CONTENTS

Introduction 1

Almonds   2
Beef   11
Crabapples   21
Fennel   26
Figs   32
Grapes   43
Guinea fowl   52
Hare   59
Mushrooms   66
Olives   74
Partridge   81
Pears   88
Persimmons   97
Pheasant   104
Pomegranates   112
Pumpkin   117
Quinces   124
Rhubarb   135
Verjuice   141
Vinegar   150

Walnuts   159
Wild duck and duck fat   167

Basics   177
Glossary   185
List of sources   187
Bibliography   188
Acknowledgements   191
Index   192

INTRODUCTION

MY PASSION FOR FOOD HAS GIVEN ME SO MUCH IN LIFE – a sense of purpose, a delicious anticipation of each new day, and gifts of a much deeper kind than financial. Harvesting the bounty from living off the land, sharing the harvest with my family and friends, and being part of a community are incredibly rewarding – I wouldn't swap my life for anything!

Maggie's Harvest, a landmark book when it was first published in 2007, was the culmination of a lot of hard work and highlights my philosophy of using the freshest and best seasonal produce available at my doorstop in the Barossa Valley. The cover design was heavy with symbolism as well – the pear tree bearing golden fruit, like the one that stands at the bottom of my garden, are what Kylie Kwong called the 'golden orbs' of my life. And the pheasant on the end of the branch dips the hat to my Colin, whose vision to farm pheasants inspired our move to the Barossa, and thus began this food life of mine.

And while the original *Harvest* edition still lives in its beautifully bound, embroidered cover, for ease of use, what better way to approach each new season than with a paperback edition, exclusively featuring the recipes you'll need for the months ahead. More practical in the kitchen – although you need to know how much I love to see splattered copies of any of my books. These seasonal paperbacks celebrate my love for each season and bounty it brings; accentuating the produce available.

Autumn is about so much produce at its peak. In the orchard there are quinces, pomegranate and persimmon slowly ripening. And there's the game, such as the pheasant and guineafowl. It's a truly magical season.

I love and celebrate each change in the season and the food it brings. I hope you love autumn too and that, in turn, you'll collect each of the four seasons.

ALMONDS

 ALMONDS HAVE A SPECIAL PLACE IN MY BAROSSA LANDSCAPE. The first trees to blossom when the weather is still bitterly cold, they are a sign of the coming spring. The sight of these trees in flower lifts my heart immediately, and I always sacrifice some of the promised fruit by picking blossom for my kitchen table so I can drink in its exquisite perfume.

Did you know that an almond is actually a peach in disguise? I didn't until I opened Louis Glowinski's *Complete Book of Fruit Growing in Australia*. He calls it a dry-fleshed close relative: the similarity lies in the peach seeds, which Glowinski says can be sweet like an almond. I have not eaten many peach seeds, so I can't give an opinion, but can tell you that both trees grow very well here in South Australia.

All almond growers face the same problem each year: how to pick the crop before the birds decimate it. In South Australia's Riverland, where there are vast almond groves, light aircraft are used to move the birds on to another area; here in the Valley shiny pieces of foil are tied to the trees and hawk-shaped kites are flown. It is an ever-increasing problem and one I've almost given up trying to solve, so I usually buy my almonds fully mature from more organised neighbours.

It was in *Stephanie's Australia* that I first read about green almonds (almonds picked early, before the birds can strike). Stephanie Alexander stayed with us for a week while she was writing this book, and I remember well her being on the almond trail, but at that stage I had no trees and so wasn't quite ready to digest the information. We subsequently planted fifteen trees, and it wasn't until cockatoos had attacked and half-eaten every almond for several years in a row that I was reminded by sheer frustration of the culinary benefits of green almonds.

I am so disorganised that even with a note in my diary to pick our almonds in November while they are still green, it is always such a busy time that I only ever get the chance to pinch a basketful for a particular dish before the birds get them. However, there is always next year. As our almond trees surround the property, following the fence line, there is not the same impetus to do something about them as there is with the orchard, which I walk through every day – lucky birds, I say.

It was also Stephanie who, many years ago, introduced me to the books of American food writer Paula Wolfert. So, on Paula's first trip to South Australia to talk about olives and olive oil, I jumped at the chance to look after her for a day. It is difficult to explain how many ideas can be seeded in just one day in the company of women like Paula and Stephanie. It was such a shame I had to drive when I wanted so much to stop and take notes about the many possibilities of our Mediterranean climate, but I made mental notes. In response to my cries of despair about always losing my almond crop, Paula talked a lot more about green almonds, and suggested I look up various Italian references and her book *The Cooking of the Eastern Mediterranean*.

I later found mention of green almonds in *The Fruit, Herbs and Vegetables of Italy* by Giacomo Castelvetro: 'green almonds are not in season long; they are much healthier than hazelnuts and considered to be the noblest nut of all. Many people in Italy, especially in Tuscany, eat them green when the shell is still soft, or cook them like truffles.' With this in mind, I'll now commit myself, in writing, to start picking much earlier, so I'll have more green almonds than I could ever use.

Try pan-frying green almonds in nut-brown butter as an hors d'oeuvre with sea salt flakes, or to serve with pan-fried trout. Toss pan-fried sliced green almonds through pasta with a fruity extra virgin olive oil and lots of Parmigiano Reggiano.

I have often written about the difference between buying new-season almonds and those of anonymous parentage and unknown age. However, I was recently given a bag of almonds from McLaren Vale that were nine months old, yet they were still fresh, crisp and almondy (it may sound crazy but almonds don't always taste so). I was blooded on fresh Barossa almonds twenty-plus years ago, and I have to say that if my palate memory serves me right, wonderful as they were then, these almonds tasted even better.

It seems to me that, at least in South Australia, the almonds of McLaren Vale are an example of terroir – the growing environment. I have never tasted better. At a meeting in Mildura a few years ago, I remember sitting next to a former McLaren Vale almond grower who told me that their operation was moved to the Riverland because it better suited the economies of scale to grow large plots of almonds. The grower said, sadly, that there was nothing to equal the flavour of the almonds from the original grove – the unique combination of soil quality, prevailing weather conditions and position at McLaren Vale had helped to produce such wonderful almonds, and these conditions just couldn't be replicated at the new site. Unfortunately, this has resulted in a compromise in flavour: it's sometimes difficult to get the balance right.

There are two types of almond: the more commonly found sweet almond, and the hard-to-find bitter almond (most of which are imported into Australia from Spain). In Australia most almonds are grown from grafted rootstock, while in Europe the norm is to grow seedling trees. Usually 1–2 per cent of these will turn out to be bitter almonds. The nuts from these trees are not kept separate from the crop in most cases, so almond oil from France, for example, will have a tiny percentage of bitter almonds in it. Bitter almonds are also grown specifically to make confectionery, particularly marzipan, and as the base for the Italian liqueur Amaretto di Saronno.

Bitter almonds add an edge that the sweet almond alone cannot – even two or three bitter almonds ground with 250 g sweet almonds make a startling difference to desserts. A few of these nuts give a quivering blancmange a flavour like no other, as they do ice cream. However, straight from the tree, bitter almonds are high in prussic acid, a poison which is later removed from the oil. Experts at the Botanic Gardens in Adelaide advise me that sixty untreated bitter almonds can kill a human. After eating several untreated nuts while once making marzipan, I doubt that anyone could eat more than two or three in one sitting, but I leave in the warning just in case.

It is possible to buy bitter almonds here, but not without difficulty. The best solution is to find an almond grower, who will usually have a tree or two of the bitter variety. The nuts are often kept aside since bitter almonds have very hard shells and cannot be cracked easily by the equipment designed for the softer sweet almonds.

It was during the autumn of my first year in the Barossa that I realised what a taste sensation fresh almonds are. Ed Auricht, a neighbour then well into his seventies, would crack them at night to sell to the initiated the next day. As much as an almond can tempt me at any time, when the new crop comes in my passion for them is renewed. There is a world of difference in the flavour.

Australian almonds are at times sold in the shell and, as such, keep better than shelled nuts. Happily, the paper-shell almond, which is easier to shell, is now the preference of most growers. Nuts in the shell should feel heavy for their size and have no visible cracks and certainly no mould. If you're buying almonds in the shell, allow twice the weight called for in a recipe using shelled nuts. Because the almond, like the walnut and hazelnut, contains a substantial amount of oil, it turns rancid easily once shelled. For this reason, almonds should be stored away from light, moisture and heat. While it is often suggested that shelled almonds be kept in the refrigerator to control deterioration, as oil-makers do, bitter almonds are actually best kept in the freezer as they tend to be used so sparingly.

I never blanch almonds (I might feel differently if I were a dessert cook, but I doubt it), and I never buy ground almonds as they are invariably stale. If I require ground almonds (also called almond meal), I dry-roast the nuts in a 220°C oven for 6–8 minutes until their aroma is released, then allow them to cool before grinding them in a food processor (a little rosewater or orange-flower water will prevent the nuts from 'oiling'). Better still is to use elbow grease and pound them using a mortar and pestle. The flavour from pre-ground almonds is just not the same. I use freshly ground almonds to make an almond and cumquat tart. Whenever I was lucky enough to have the dried cumquats that my friend Noëlle Tolley made, I would reconstitute them in verjuice and scatter them in the base of the tart – fantastic!

Elizabeth David's writings convinced me that blancmange made with almond milk is eons away from the blancmange I ate in hospital after having my tonsils out as a young child. I also find almond milk a refreshing drink on those autumn days that are surprisingly hot. Somewhere in my reading on early English cooking I came across an unexpected reference to almond milk being mixed with verjuice made from crabapples and used to poach salmon or eel. I have tried this with riverfish with great success. Making almond milk is a simple process: heat 500 ml milk (I sometimes use 1 part buttermilk to 3 parts milk) and then stir in 1 tablespoon castor sugar and pour the mixture over 140 g ground almonds flavoured with a few drops of orange-flower water. Allow the mixture to infuse for 4 hours, then strain the milk into a bowl through muslin (or even a new Chux), squeezing out the last drops, and refrigerate it until required.

I hated marzipan (which has bitter almonds in it) until I made a fresh almond paste myself. Rather than use it as a cake topping, I love to sandwich it between layers of butter cake to make it really moist.

Almonds are a great snack food and are often partnered with dried fruit. If you buy shelled almonds, always take the time to roast them before eating – it makes a huge difference. Put them on a tray in the oven at 220°C for a few minutes or until they pop their skins just a little. To make an adult treat, put a roasted almond inside a pitted prune, then dip in melted dark couverture chocolate. Don't skip the roasting step – the result just won't be the same.

If you like peanut butter, try a different style using almonds. Roast the almonds as above and leave to cool before pulsing in a food processor. Add a drop of cold water or rosewater after two or three pulses, so the oil in the almonds doesn't split, then add room temperature unsalted butter in the same proportion as the nuts. Pulse again until the nuts and butter are incorporated, then roll into a log and wrap in baking paper (it will oxidise if not totally covered) and refrigerate for a few days – don't keep it too long as nuts in any form are subject to rancidity. Spread wholemeal toast with almond butter for breakfast, or smother whole trout with it before cooking, adding a squeeze of lemon juice and freshly ground black pepper.

Figs and almonds are another great combination – especially to serve with coffee. Stuff good dried figs with freshly roasted almonds, skins on.

Almonds are just as good in savoury dishes. Spaghettini with flaked almonds, extra virgin olive oil, flat-leaf parsley and lots of freshly ground black pepper is a meal in a moment; a nutty ripe avocado can be sliced into this dish, too. A friend's clever twist on traditional trout with almonds is to make a flavoured butter using chopped roasted almonds. She greases baking paper or foil heavily with the softened almond butter and then places sliced lemon and dill inside the trout, which is then salted well and wrapped in the foil. The trout parcel is baked in the oven for about 15 minutes at 220°C and is turned halfway through cooking. Each person opens their parcel at the table, so that the wonderful aromas can be savoured.

Almond soup, very much a part of Mediterranean cuisines, is just as good cold as hot. Grind the almonds as for the almond butter on page 5, then stir in a mix of light chicken stock and buttermilk. A good dash of sherry provides the finishing touch. Served chilled with a garnish of fresh sultana grapes (as the version on page 48 is), this soup is perfect for warmer weather. Used as a thickening agent, ground almonds can also be added to a stock-based soup as a winter treat.

AVOCADO, GINGER AND ROASTED ALMONDS WITH PASTA AND FRESH CORIANDER

Serves 6 as an entrée or 3 as a main course

This incredibly refreshing pasta is one where it is essential that the pasta and roasted almonds are piping hot. This dish is also terrific with good-quality dried pasta (use a 500 g packet).

juice of 1 lemon

2 large reed *or* 4 medium hass avocados, peeled and cut into pieces

2 teaspoons finely chopped ginger (or extra to taste in winter)

100 ml extra virgin olive oil

½ cup (40 g) flaked almonds

500 g fresh tagliatelle

1 cup coriander leaves

sea salt flakes and freshly ground black pepper

Bring a large saucepan of water to the boil. Preheat the oven to 200°C.

Squeeze the lemon juice over the cut avocado. Mix the ginger with 1 tablespoon of the olive oil.

Roast the flaked almonds on a baking tray for 5 minutes or until golden brown. Meanwhile, cook the pasta in the boiling water for 3–4 minutes, then drain. Immediately toss the hot pasta with the ginger and olive oil mixture, allowing it to spread amongst the pasta. Quickly add the hot almonds, remaining olive oil, avocado and coriander.

Squeeze over a little more lemon juice to taste, then season with salt and pepper and serve.

PHEASANT WITH ALMONDS AND SHERRY

Serves 4

Ground almonds are often used to thicken sauces in Mediterranean cooking, particularly in Spain. A good friend of mine, whose family has a great food tradition, sent my first book, *Maggie's Farm*, to his sister in Spain. She responded by sending me a recipe she thought I would find interesting as it combined pheasant, almonds and sherry, all of which I have at my fingertips in the Barossa. I changed it to suit my method of cooking pheasant and took from the original Spanish recipe the important mix of ground almonds, sherry and garlic, which I whisked into a stock-based sauce. The result was a wonderful marriage of the nuttiness of the almonds and the sherry with the sweetness of the pheasant.

50 g almonds

juice of 1 lemon

1 × 900 g pheasant

sea salt flakes and freshly ground
   black pepper

1 onion, finely chopped

3 tomatoes, halved

2 sprigs thyme

1 fresh bay leaf

extra virgin olive oil, for cooking

150 ml dry sherry

1 cup (250 ml) jellied pheasant stock
   or reduced Golden Chicken Stock
   (see page 181)

1 clove garlic

Preheat the oven to 220°C. Dry-roast the almonds for 6–8 minutes, then set them aside. Squeeze the lemon juice into the cavity of the pheasant, then season it with salt and pepper. Sweat the onion and tomatoes with the thyme and bay leaf in a little olive oil in an enamelled casserole over low heat for 20 minutes.

Add the pheasant to the casserole and brown very gently on all sides. Deglaze the casserole with half the sherry, then add 100 ml of the stock and cook, covered, over very low heat at just a simmer, with the pheasant on its side, for 10 minutes. Turn the bird onto its other side and simmer for another 5 minutes, adding a little more stock if necessary. Turn the pheasant breast-side down and cook for another 5 minutes, then transfer it to a plate to rest. Using a mortar and pestle, grind the almonds with the garlic and remaining sherry to make a *picada* (paste). Add the remaining stock to the casserole and stir in the almond *picada* to thicken the sauce – turn up the heat to reduce the sauce if necessary.

Season to taste and serve. My favourite accompaniments for this dish are crisp roasted parsnips and braised cavolo nero.

ORCHARD CAKE

Serves 10–12

I first cooked this cake in 1996 for my pâté-making girls, who all had a sweet tooth and were forever trying to foist delicacies on me. I had been given a basic recipe for a Jewish cake, but instead I adapted it with different types and ratios of fruit. What made it so special was that nearly all the ingredients I used – everything except the butter, sugar and spices – came from my own orchard or from theirs. The first time I made it we were so excited that we ate the cake a little warm and it was wonderful. What a joy it is to be able to use your own produce.

This cake can be made with other dried fruit; just ensure it is of top-notch quality. Remember – bitter almonds are poisonous if eaten to excess.

90 g dried figs

90 g dried nectarines

90 g dried apricots

90 g dried peaches

310 ml verjuice

180 g dried currants

60 g almonds

120 g dark-brown sugar

180 g unsalted butter, chopped

4 eggs

180 g self-raising flour

½ teaspoon ground cinnamon

½ teaspoon ground nutmeg

120 g candied lemon peel

or mixed peel

finely grated rind of 1 lemon

ALMOND PASTE

1¼ cups (120 g) almonds

2 bitter almonds

100 g icing sugar

1 egg yolk

Place the figs, nectarines, apricots and peaches in a bowl with 250 ml of the verjuice and soak for at least 1 hour. Strain the fruit, reserving the verjuice, then cut into pieces. Soak the currants in the reserved verjuice for 30 minutes or more, then drain, again reserving the verjuice.

Preheat the oven to 220°C and grease and line a 20 cm round cake tin with baking paper. Dry-roast the 60 g almonds on a baking tray, as well as the 120 g almonds and 2 bitter almonds for the almond paste on a separate baking tray, for 6–8 minutes, then set aside to cool separately. Reset the oven to 180°C.

To make the almond paste, blend the almonds and bitter almonds in a food processor, then add the icing sugar and egg yolk to the processor and pulse to form a stiff paste. Set aside.

Using hand-held electric beaters, cream the brown sugar and butter until pale and fluffy. Beat in the eggs one at a time, adding a spoonful of flour if the mixture curdles. Fold in the flour, spices, drained fruit, almonds and candied peel. Stir the grated lemon rind into the mixture, along with the remaining verjuice, to give a soft batter.

Spoon half the batter into the prepared tin, then spread the almond paste over the mixture and top it with the remaining batter.

Bake for 2½ hours or until a fine skewer inserted into the cake comes out clean. Leave the cake to cool a little in the tin before turning it out.

Orchard cake

ALMOND MACAROONS

Makes 40

Macaroons are a great way of using leftover egg whites.

350 g almonds

few drops of rosewater

4 egg whites

2 teaspoons lemon juice

325 g icing sugar

Preheat the oven to 220°C. Dry-roast the almonds on a baking tray for 6–8 minutes, but don't let the skins blister. Reduce the oven temperature to 170°C. Once cooled, grind the almonds using a mortar and pestle or food processor until fairly fine, adding a drop or two of rosewater.

Beat the egg whites with the lemon juice in a large bowl until soft peaks form, then add the icing sugar bit by bit, beating all the time, until the meringue is stiff. Fold in the ground almonds, then spoon teaspoonfuls of the mixture 5 cm apart onto a baking tray lined with baking paper. Bake for 35 minutes or until lightly coloured, then turn off the oven and allow the macaroons to cool for 20 minutes before removing them to a wire rack. Store the cooled macaroons in an airtight container, where they will keep for a few days.

BEEF

BEEF WAS THE CENTRE OF MY FAMILY'S MEALS WHEN I GREW up, as it was in many Australian households. As much as I love really good beef, I eat far less of it now, given the widening choice of grains and our improved access to really good poultry and fish.

No matter how often we ate beef as a family, we never took it for granted. My mother would only accept her favourite cut and the butcher always knew which pieces to keep aside for us. As a family of five, with my parents running their own business, the closest thing to convenience food was steak, which we often had during the week. We developed quite a rapport with our butcher (a lesson well learnt!).

It wasn't just a steak, though; it was always the dense and juicy 'back cut' of rump from an older animal (that small piece at the end of the rump), often bought as one piece and sliced ourselves. We always preferred our steak thick and juicy. I am sure it was then, too, that I learnt the importance of resting meat. I doubt we ever had fillet steak, even when making carpetbag steak (see page 20), our family's favourite special-occasion dish, as flavour rather than tenderness was our criterion.

There is no foolproof method of finding good beef, as Australia hasn't succeeded in implementing a quality system across the board to assure us that every piece of beef we buy will be tender, yet there are more and more producers taking the care needed. With beef, there are so many potential variations – between breeds, and whether the animal is grass or grain fed – but more influential than anything else is how well the animal has been looked after, the age it is reared to and how it is killed, hung and aged. (I've found dry-aged beef to be the best of all.) And the best beef will inevitably have cost a lot more to rear and will therefore be more expensive. Before I had access to beef producers I trusted, I used to describe my favourite beef as 'station beef', which was always from the more mature animal. I have never liked the young, bright-red meat from yearling beef, though the more I learn the more I realise colour isn't the only guide. You simply get what you pay for, and now I always choose a branded beef I know and trust, so I buy Richard Gunner's Coorong Angus Beef. Richard set out from the beginning to follow the path of excellence. Driven by flavour, he's learnt every bit of the trade, from the growing to the selling, and he's always striving to continually improve his product. He and my daughter Saskia share similar philosophies and know each other well. His beef is hung to tender stretch, which is a way of hanging the animal in its natural conformation. This takes a lot more room to do, so only those dedicated to maximising quality commit to this practice. I've cooked his beef rump, hung to tender stretch, and it is like butter in the mouth – better than any other beef I've eaten and full of flavour, and there are similar examples of such quality in each state.

I have to admit I had always cooked my roast beef at a high temperature and well salted to caramelise the skin before reading Neil Perry's book *The Food I Love*. I followed his advice to cook a Coorong Angus dry-aged rib roast, taking it out of the refrigerator several hours before cooking. I rubbed the fat with lots of sea salt and finely chopped rosemary all held together with a little extra virgin olive oil. I cooked it for 3 hours at 70°C (hastily borrowing a meat thermometer from the export kitchen before deciding that I must have one at home). After 3 hours the meat had reached 53°C and while resting (just as Neil suggested), it went to 55°C. I left it resting for 30 minutes, then slipped out the bones and seared the outer skin of the beef until caramelised. It was the juiciest, pinkest, tastiest beef I have ever had, and gave me a totally different perspective on my roast meats.

The importance of buying top-quality beef was instilled in me at a very early age. When my parents' manufacturing business failed in the 1960s they turned to cooking, first in an RSL club, then leagues clubs and later golf clubs. They never did more than keep their heads above water financially, but in their way they provided amazing food. My father was ahead of his time: even in those days he ordered aged beef (fillet for his customers, if not his family, as it was so much easier to portion than rump). If my memory serves me correctly it came in an early form of vacuum-packaging. He cooked by instinct, not giving a choice of rare, medium or well-done, and I remember that the meat melted in the mouth. Yet it was continually rejected by many of his patrons, who wanted their steaks well-done and not so 'strong'.

Considering we cooked so much offal in our house, it is surprising we rarely used the lesser cuts of beef for slow-cooking. Not so long ago at a family dinner in Sydney, a much-loved aged aunt reminded me of my mother's inability to economise and how she would make a curry with the best rump. Knowing that my mother's enemy was time and that she cooked by 'feel' rather than following recipes, I suspect she would have known that the lesser cuts such as chuck steak are better for long, slow cooking, but with so little time she knew she could cheat by sautéing onion, curry powder and other ingredients and then tossing cubed rump in this mixture for a minute or so with apple and sultanas and a little flour before adding stock, chutney and, if she was very daring, a little coconut; they were always sweet curries! As good a cook as my mother was, she never cooked anything that took loads of time, except tripe and, in summer, brawn. Her quick curry using rump wouldn't stand up to the spicy curries of today, but it seemed pretty exotic then and was always delicious.

I've never had lots of time either, but when the weather gets cooler there is nothing better than long, slow cooking. One favourite dish is chuck steak cooked as a whole piece very, very slowly for 2½ hours or more. I use a heavy-based casserole just large enough to fit the meat and lots of baby onions. I first sear the seasoned meat gently on all sides, then add a dash of stock, some oregano first warmed in a little extra virgin olive oil, and the onions. I cover the casserole tightly and put it into a slow oven (about 160°C), checking that there is enough liquid every 30 minutes or so. I then carve it into chunks to serve.

Brisket, a fatty piece of meat from the lower part of the shoulder, is often boned and rolled, and can be boiled, pot-roasted or corned. The shin (or shank) is usually sold sawn across the bone into slices; if cooked long and slow as in osso buco, the sinews become wonderfully gelatinous and tasty. The shin bones also contain marrow; a specially shaped spoon helps marrow lovers like me locate the prized pieces. And, of course, there is oxtail – slow-cooking meat at its best. I have included a recipe for Oxtail with Orange, Olives and Walnuts (see page 18), a dish that is made for enjoying with people who aren't scared to use their fingers as they suck the sweet meat from the bones.

In the middle years of the Pheasant Farm Restaurant, before the tradition of the five o'clock staff 'lunch' began, our friends the Walls would rescue us every Sunday night and cook for us. Their daughters Eloise and Cressida are very close in age to Saskia and Elli, so it worked remarkably well. Judith or Peter would cook: Judith's favourite cold-weather dish was Elizabeth David's beef and wine stew with black olives from *French Provincial Cooking*. On these nights I would be pretty boisterous for an hour or so, then, after we'd eaten and drunk and listened to great music, the whole week's exhaustion would catch up with me and I would often fall asleep on the couch fairly early in the evening.

Many restaurateurs will tell you that the simple steak (often cooked well-done) is one of their most popular dishes, which I always find a little surprising since it is so easily produced at home. Those restaurants that feature classic French dishes such as *boeuf à la ficelle* (beef on a string – a poached sirloin or fillet served with boiled vegetables and accompanied by sea salt, mustard, horseradish and cornichons or pickles) often have difficulty selling them. Do people only order what they feel comfortable with? What a shame, if that's true! I would hope that going to a restaurant might be seen as a chance to try new things and expand horizons. Huge amounts of time and skill go into creating such complex dishes, and these skills need to be used if we are not to lose them completely – this is a big issue facing the restaurant industry at the moment.

We mustn't become complacent or lazy when it comes to buying beef to cook at home either. Although we all lead busy lives, we owe it to ourselves to seek out a butcher who cares about quality. Word of mouth is a good place to start, and if you can find a butcher really interested in his or her craft, they will have a wealth of knowledge to share with you.

COORONG ANGUS BEEF PIE WITH RED WINE, FENNEL AND GREEN OLIVES

Serves 8

Although I usually make this pie with my Sour-cream Pastry (see page 177), when given the challenge of making it with a luscious gluten-free pastry I couldn't believe just how wonderful it was. As part of the TV series *The Cook and The Chef*, the ABC suggested I test out the pies at Colin's squash club, as they always have supper at the end of competition nights. I might add that as it's the Barossa squash club, the supper is usually quite a different kettle of fish from that served at most other sporting clubs. Many local wine-makers are members, and on the table that night there were at least eighteen bottles of really top-quality red; it was winter, after all, and they had been told I was coming with a beef and shiraz pie.

I made 32 individual pies, half with Choux Pastry-style Gluten-free Pastry (see page 178) and the other half with a cream cheese-based gluten-free pastry. The fascinating thing was the overwhelming support for the choux pastry-style, which absolutely flummoxed me as my own preference was for the crisper, more shortcrust style of the cream cheese version. The players were so enthusiastic that I think they would each have eaten a second one if I'd made enough. It was obvious that the combination of hard exercise, a cold winter's night and the seductive smell of freshly baked pies had great appeal – I think they'll ask me back.

While I slowly braise the meat in a crockpot on its lowest setting, it could easily be cooked in a heavy-based cast-iron casserole over low heat with a simmer mat or in a 120°C oven for a few hours.

plain flour, for dusting

sea salt flakes and freshly ground
    black pepper

1 kg Coorong Angus Beef chuck, or other
    quality beef chuck, cut into 3 cm cubes

extra virgin olive oil, for cooking

400 ml shiraz

1 medium–large fennel bulb,
    trimmed and finely chopped

400 g golden shallots, peeled

4 cloves garlic, chopped

2 cups (500 ml) veal *or*
    Golden Chicken Stock
    (see page 181)

1 sprig rosemary

6 sprigs thyme

2 fresh bay leaves

finely chopped rind of 1 orange

16 green olives, pitted

1 × quantity Sour-cream Pastry
    (see page 177)

1 egg, beaten

Coorong Angus beef pie with red wine, fennel and green olives

Season the flour with salt and pepper, then toss the meat in the seasoned flour, shaking off any excess. In a large deep frying pan, seal the meat in olive oil over high heat in small batches until all the meat is browned.

Heat a crockpot to its highest setting, then transfer the sealed meat to it. Deglaze the frying pan with the wine, reducing it by three-quarters over high heat, then add the wine to the crockpot. Return the frying pan to the stove, then add more olive oil and sauté the fennel and shallots over medium heat for 6–8 minutes or until soft. Add the garlic and continue to sauté for another 5 minutes.

Transfer the vegetables to the crockpot, then add stock to the frying pan, bring to a rapid boil over high heat then add it to the crockpot with the herbs. Cook on the highest setting for 30 minutes, then turn to the lowest setting and cook at this low temperature for about 6 hours (or even overnight), until the meat is melt-in-the-mouth tender, adding the orange rind and olives in the last 20 minutes. Let the beef mixture cool.

Meanwhile, make and chill the pastry as instructed.

To assemble the pies, roll pastry to a 5 mm thickness and cut to fit the bases of 8 individual pie tins (you can buy standard-sized disposable foil pie tins from the supermarket). Make sure the pastry bases overhang the lips of the pie tins, and brush the bases with beaten egg, to help seal in the juices. Cut out the pastry tops.

Divide the beef mixture among the pie tins and cover with the pastry tops. Fold the edges of the pastry to seal, then brush the tops of the pies with beaten egg. Return the pies to the refrigerator for the pastry to really set; about 15 minutes.

Preheat the oven to 220°C. Place the pie tins on a baking tray and bake for 20 minutes or until golden brown.

SLOW-BRAISED BEEF CHEEKS IN BAROSSA SHIRAZ *Serves 12*

The late Maurice de Rohan, the Agent General in London for many years, persuaded me to present a cocktail party in Paris in 2001 to celebrate Baudin's expedition to Australia. He went on to become a good friend and asked me to cook the Australia Day Dinner in London in January 2006 for 300 guests. Maurice and I had talked of the possibility several times over the years, and as it was to be his last year as chairman of that event, I jumped at the opportunity, on the understanding that I'd have a team to work with. A lot of planning was involved in choosing the dishes that would represent a truly Australian meal, sourcing the finest quality ingredients, and ensuring each dish would be simple enough to prepare in advance, particularly given the limitation of not having access to a kitchen at Australia House.

A preliminary trip to London set my mind at rest when I was introduced to Jackson Gilmour, the catering company who would be cooking my recipes. We sat around a table, tasted my recipes and dissected the menu, then talked logistics. I'm happy to say it turned out to be a wonderful occasion and one I was proud to be involved with.

I felt the main course for this meal had to be beef, and it had to be luscious and slow-cooked so we could prepare it in advance. My choice was wagyu beef cheeks braised in Barossa shiraz. It was beautifully unctuous and tender, and in my menu I simply called it 'Australian Wagyu braised in Barossa Shiraz', leaving out the fact that we used the cheeks.

2 kg beef cheeks

½ cup (125 ml) extra virgin olive oil,
    plus extra for drizzling

6 cloves garlic, roughly chopped

2 tablespoons juniper berries, crushed

2 star anise

3 sprigs rosemary

10 small fresh bay leaves

sea salt flakes and freshly ground
    black pepper

½ cup (125 ml) vino cotto (see Glossary)

2 cups (500 ml) good red wine,
    such as a Barossa shiraz

2 large onions, roughly chopped

2 stalks celery, roughly chopped

2 cups (500 ml) reduced veal stock

rind of 1 orange, peeled in strips

The day before cooking, toss the beef cheeks in a little olive oil and marinade with garlic cloves and all the spices and herbs.

Preheat the oven to 120°C. Drizzle the beef cheeks with 60 ml olive oil and season with salt and pepper. Heat a frying pan over medium heat, then brown the cheeks on each side and place in a heavy-based casserole. Deglaze the frying pan with vino cotto and red wine then reduce by half and add to the casserole. Wipe out the frying pan and add the remaining olive oil, then add the onions and celery and brown. Season with salt and pepper and transfer to the casserole.

Add the stock and place the covered casserole in the oven. Turn the beef frequently. Check after 3 hours – depending on their size and the breed of cattle, they may take up to 6 hours to become tender. Remove the lid for the final 2 hours of cooking.

FILLET OF BEEF IN BALSAMIC VINEGAR OR VINO COTTO   *Serves 4*

While I give instructions for roasting in this recipe, the marinated fillet can also be grilled in one piece on a barbecue for 8 minutes per side. After grilling, put the hood down, turn the barbecue off and allow the meat to rest.

For a simpler dish, pan-fry seasoned thick slices of a beef cut of your choice in a heavy-based frying pan. Begin at a high temperature to seal the meat on one side, then turn it down until you're ready to flip the steak onto the other side. Seal that side at a high temperature, then turn it down again. Deglaze the pan with vino cotto, remove from the heat and leave to rest, then serve with the pan juices.

1 × 650 g fillet of beef

1 lemon (meyer, if available)

3 sprigs rosemary

1 sprig oregano

100 ml extra virgin olive oil

¼ cup (60 ml) balsamic vinegar *or*
vino cotto (see Glossary)

sea salt flakes and freshly ground
black pepper

Trim the meat of all sinew, then tie the thin end back on itself with kitchen string (this ensures even cooking). Dry the fillet well with kitchen paper. Remove the rind from the lemon with a potato peeler, in one piece if possible. Make a marinade of the remaining ingredients, except the salt, then add the lemon rind and the meat and marinate for several hours, turning the meat to flavour all sides.

Preheat the oven to 250°C. Season the meat, then brush with the marinade and roast in a shallow roasting pan for 10 minutes. Turn the meat over and cook for another 10 minutes. Meanwhile, warm the marinade in a pan over medium heat. Remove the meat from the oven, then pour the warmed marinade over it and leave to rest for 20 minutes before serving.

OXTAIL WITH ORANGE, OLIVES AND WALNUTS *Serves 12*

3 large onions, roughly chopped

2 sticks celery, roughly chopped

½ cup (125 ml) extra virgin olive oil

115 g shelled walnuts

4 kg oxtail, trimmed and cut into 5 cm pieces

plain flour, for dusting

sea salt flakes and freshly ground
black pepper

100 g butter, chopped

2 cups (500 ml) red wine

4 cloves garlic, finely chopped

10 stalks flat-leaf parsley

2 sprigs thyme

2 fresh bay leaves

500 g fresh *or* canned tomatoes,
peeled and seeded

2 litres veal stock

4 strips orange rind

40 black olives

½ cup (125 ml) red-wine vinegar

⅓ cup (75 g) sugar

Preheat the oven to 220°C. Toss the onion and celery with a little of the olive oil in a roasting pan, then roast for 20 minutes or until caramelised. Dry-roast the walnuts on a baking tray in the oven for 6 minutes, then rub their skins off with a clean tea towel and set aside.

Toss the meat in flour seasoned with salt and pepper, shaking off the excess. In a heavy-based frying pan, brown the oxtail in batches in the remaining olive oil and the butter over high heat. Transfer each batch to a large heavy-based casserole. Deglaze the frying pan with the wine, scraping to release all the caramelised bits from the browning. Add the garlic, onions, celery, herbs and tomatoes to the frying pan and reduce the wine a little over high heat, then tip the lot into the casserole. Add the veal stock, making sure that everything is immersed, and simmer over low heat, covered, until tender – this could take 3–4 hours. Add the orange rind and olives in the last 20 minutes of cooking.

Strain the cooking juices from the meat and skim as much fat as possible from the top. Set the meat aside in a warm place. In a stainless steel or enamelled saucepan, combine the red-wine vinegar and sugar and boil until the vinegar has evaporated and the sugar has caramelised. Reduce the cooking juices to a syrupy consistency, then add the caramel mixture to taste. Toss the cooked oxtail with the walnuts and pour the sauce back over the oxtail. Serve with mashed potato, creamy polenta or pasta.

SLOW-ROASTED OYSTER BLADE WITH ONION CREAM
AND BRAISED CAVOLO NERO
Serves 10–12

1 × 2 kg piece oyster blade, for roasting
½ cup (125 ml) verjuice
½ cup (125 ml) extra virgin olive oil
1 sprig rosemary
2 fresh bay leaves
finely chopped rind of 1 lemon
finely chopped rind of 1 orange
sea salt flakes and freshly ground
    black pepper
Braised Cavolo Nero (see page 183),
    to serve

ONION CREAM
2 large onions, roughly chopped
¼ cup (60 ml) extra virgin olive oil
2 cloves garlic, chopped
¼ cup (60 ml) verjuice
½ cup (125 ml) cream
sea salt flakes and freshly ground
    black pepper

Marinate the beef overnight in the verjuice, olive oil, rosemary, bay leaves and citrus rinds.

Preheat the oven to 100°C. Season the meat with salt and pepper, then transfer it to a roasting pan with the marinade and cook for approximately 4½ hours. Remove from the oven and take the meat out of the pan, reserving the pan juices.

In a large frying pan, seal the beef on each side to caramelise, then rest for 30 minutes. Meanwhile, skim any fat from the surface of the pan juices and reduce over high heat to a sauce consistency.

For the onion cream, sauté the onions in a saucepan over low heat with the olive oil until soft, adding the garlic after the first 5 minutes; do not let the onions brown. When the onions are soft, deglaze the pan with the verjuice. Cook for another 5 minutes and then add the cream. Cook until the cream evaporates – about 10 minutes over low heat – stirring often so that no colour develops. Remove from the heat and season to taste. Pass the onion mixture through a mouli or pulse in a food processor just enough to combine the ingredients. Set aside.

Place a bed of the onion cream on a serving platter. Slice the roast beef and place it on top of the onion cream, drizzling it with the pan juices, then serve with the braised cavolo nero.

CARPETBAG STEAK

The oysters my father used when making carpetbag steak in the 1960s were not sold on the shell as we would buy them today; instead they were Hawkesbury River oysters bottled daily in large glass jars. As our wonderful South Australian oysters are at their prime between May and September (particularly those from Smoky Bay) and this dish is both simple and spectacularly special, I commend it to you for every even slightly celebratory occasion at that time of the year.

1 × 1 kg fillet of beef *or* piece of rump, trimmed of all sinew	2 tablespoons extra virgin olive oil
freshly ground black pepper	sea salt flakes
18 fresh oysters	50 g butter
	2 sprigs rosemary

Preheat the oven to 230°C. With a sharp knife, cut a pocket down the length of the meat deep enough to hold all the oysters (do not cut right through the meat!). Grind pepper over the oysters and use them to fill the pocket, making sure the oysters aren't too near the edge. Using kitchen string, tie up the beef like a parcel. (If using a fillet, determine the thickness of the final slices by using string to define where you will cut each serving.) Rub the outside of the beef with the olive oil and season with salt and pepper.

Heat the butter to nut-brown with the rosemary in a heavy-based roasting pan. Brown the beef on all sides, then transfer the pan to the oven for 15 minutes. Remove the beef from the oven, then turn it over and leave it to rest for 15 minutes. Slice the beef thickly and serve with salt, pepper and the juices from the roasting pan.

CRABAPPLES

CRABAPPLES ARE NOT SOMETHING YOU SEE FOR SALE IN THE
greengrocer as a rule. My first introduction to them was in 1983 on a visit to
the beautiful garden of my friend, Lady Mary Downer, near Williamstown.
Our main purpose for the visit was to collect some pheasant breeders, having
lost all our birds that year in the Nuriootpa flood. (These breeders were the progeny of
birds we had sold years earlier; this and other kind offers from all over Australia helped us
re-establish our pheasant line and continue farming.) While the pheasants were our main
focus, I couldn't help but be distracted by a crabapple tree in the garden.

I had never seen such a luxuriant tree so laden with fruit, and didn't need a second offer
to take up the bounty. We picked the tree clean and, once home, I proceeded to look for as
many uses as possible for the crabapples. The search was not particularly rewarding, and
I had visions of these wonderfully decorative – and potentially productive – trees all
around the countryside with their fruit left to drop and rot for lack of advice.

I am now a passionate advocate of the crabapple, and in my home orchard of some
thirty trees I have three different varieties – the Wandin Pride, John Downie and Maypole.
I have been told that crabapples can tolerate almost any neglect. I've proved that to be
true – when I planted our first at the Pheasant Farm the ground was fairly inhospitable
and we only had bore water, which tended to be very salty in the summer when the garden
required extra attention. Only the hardiest plants survived, so the crabapples were a joy.

When buying fruit and nut trees I prefer to deal directly with experts as the amount of
information on nursery tags is minimal by nature. Experts can give advice on especially
interesting trees and will find varieties you might have read about in obscure magazines.
Here in South Australia I deal with Perry's Nursery of McLaren Flat, which specialises in
fruit and nut trees and deals interstate.

Crabapples are a great addition to any garden, even if you are not initially interested in
harvesting the fruit (although I hope you won't be able to resist trying some of the ideas

here). If they're of the weeping kind, the trees tend to be sparse and willowy, each branch hanging heavy with beautiful blossom in the spring. Of the varieties that are easily available, the weeping Wandin Pride has a large apple that is sweeter than others. It is actually like a medium-sized Jonathan, mostly green with a red blush. A particular favourite in my orchard is the Downie. It has fairly large reddish-orange fruit that can be eaten off the tree, but the flavour is sharper than that of the Wandin Pride. Echtermeyer, another weeping crabapple, has smaller, sour purple fruit suitable for jelly. The productive Maypole has a sharp, deep-purple small apple that also makes a great jelly. A variety I don't have but that is the most readily seen in South Australia is the heavy-cropping Gorgeous – its long, slim bright-crimson fruit hang on the tree until late autumn.

The larger crabapples are more likely to be eaten straight from the tree – they are tart but a good accompaniment to a rich and creamy cheese. The smaller ones, which are very high in pectin, are best made into a jelly, pickle or syrup. If you are looking for a breakfast treat, I can thoroughly recommend a really nutty piece of wholemeal toast spread with lashings of unsalted butter and crabapple jelly.

Roast pheasant served with Spiced Crabapples (see opposite) was a favourite dish of the day in our restaurant. I took some of the crabapple preserving syrup and added it to the reduced pheasant jus to give a wonderfully sharp lift to the dish; the crabapples themselves were added to the sauce in the last few minutes of cooking. I tended to use fresh rosemary in the roasting – rosemary and crabapples seem to be a natural pairing. This combination also teams well with rare roasted kangaroo or grilled quail.

Verjuice and crabapples work in harmony, too. Remove the cores from 500 g large crabapples and cut them into eighths. Heat 60 g unsalted butter until nut-brown, sauté the crabapples until cooked through and just beginning to caramelise then deglaze the pan with 80 ml verjuice. Add a little freshly crushed cinnamon and some honey, if you like, and serve over hot pancakes with crème fraîche.

I've heard that when visiting people in Iran one is offered a sweet drink or sherbet made from sour fruit. A homemade fruit syrup based on crabapples, quinces, lemons, sour cherries or pomegranates is diluted with water and ice is added. I make this with less sugar than is traditional and pour it over ice cream. A vanilla bean in the syrup makes a wonderful addition, especially if you make your own vanilla ice cream to accompany it.

SPICED CRABAPPLES

Makes 5 cups

2 kg crabapples (preferably with stems on to enhance presentation)	3 cloves
	10 allspice berries
1 lemon	10 coriander seeds
brown sugar	½ cinnamon stick
white-wine vinegar	

Discard any bruised crabapples and wash the remainder. Put the crabapples into a large preserving pan and just cover with water. Remove the rind from the lemon in one piece using a potato peeler and add to the pan, then simmer over low heat for 15–20 minutes or until the crabapples are just tender. Using a slotted spoon, take out the crabapples and set them aside in a bowl.

Strain and measure the cooking water. For each 500 ml add 300 g brown sugar and 150 ml white-wine vinegar, then add the spices. Boil this spice syrup in the rinsed-out pan over high heat for about 10 minutes or until reduced to a light caramel consistency, then return the crabapples to the pan and cook for another 20 minutes or until the apples are almost transparent but still holding their shape. Transfer the crabapples and their syrup to a sterilised (see Glossary) wide-necked jar and seal. Leave the crabapples for 10 days before use – they keep indefinitely.

KATHY HOWARD'S WILD CRABAPPLE
AND SAGE JELLY

Makes about 3 litres

Kathy Howard, the mother of my friend Jacqui Howard, no longer produces her wonderful crabapple and sage jelly commercially, sadly, but through her generosity in sharing this recipe we can all make it now. She has told me how her family used to collect masses of wild crabapples along the roads in Victoria's Kiewa Valley on their way back from Falls Creek each year. They gathered these little 'cannonballs' in January when they were inedible raw but full of pectin – perfect for jelly. A swim in the Bright waterhole was 'payment' for the kids, including Jacqui.

Kathy smears a chicken with this jelly before roasting it with a spoonful or two of water in the pan to stop the juices burning, then deglazes the roasting pan with verjuice to create a delicious sauce. I love the jelly on barbecued short-loin lamb chops or a fillet of pork, where it melts deliciously. Wonderful with game, this jelly is also good spread over a leg of lamb ready for the oven with slivers of garlic tucked into the meat.

This jelly can be made without the sage (resulting in a straightforward crabapple jelly), or rosemary can be added instead. Pan-fry fresh rosemary leaves in a little nut-brown butter, then leave them to drain on kitchen paper before adding them to the jelly.

½ cup fresh *or* 3–4 tablespoons home-dried
    sage leaves
4 kg crabapples, washed and roughly
    chopped (including stems, peel and cores)

white-wine vinegar
sugar

To dry the sage leaves, spread them out on a tray and place in the direct sun for 3–4 hours, then finely chop them. Put the chopped crabapples into a large preserving pan. Barely cover with water and simmer gently over low heat for about 45 minutes or until crabapples are soft, then leave them to sit in the cooking liquid for a few hours. Put the crabapples and the liquid into a jelly bag or a muslin-lined sieve (even a clean Chux will do) and allow to drain over a bowl or bucket overnight.

Next day, measure the collected juice (do not press down on the crabapples or the jelly will be cloudy rather than sparkling clear) and discard the solids. For every 1 litre of juice, add 250 ml white-wine vinegar and 800 g sugar, then gradually bring the mixture to the boil, stirring to dissolve the sugar. Maintain a rolling boil for 10 minutes or until setting point is reached. (Test by placing a spoonful of jelly on a saucer in the fridge for a few minutes. If it wrinkles when you push it with your finger, it is set.) As the mixture boils, skim the froth from the surface very carefully. When setting point is reached, remove the pan from the heat, pour the jelly into sterilised jars (see Glossary) and leave to cool. When the jelly has started to firm up, add the sage so it sits on top. Seal once completely cool.

CRABAPPLE JELLY

Jellies are made with the juice of the fruit rather than the pulp. When we make quince paste we drain the pulp overnight first to acquire juice to make jelly. You can do the same with any fruit – try damson plums or apples, for example. Try adding flavourings or herbs as well, as in the recipe opposite.

2.5 kg crabapples, roughly chopped

castor sugar

4 tablespoons lemon juice

Boil the crabapples in just enough water to cover for about 30 minutes or until very soft, then strain the pulp overnight through a jelly bag or a muslin-lined sieve (even a clean Chux will do) into a bucket or large bowl. Don't press down on the fruit to extract more juice the next morning as you'll lose the clarity of the jelly.

Measure the collected juice into a large, heavy-based preserving pan, and for every 500 ml of juice add 500 g castor sugar. Add the lemon juice to the pan and stir over medium heat until the sugar has dissolved, then boil rapidly over high heat for about 20 minutes or until the jelly sets. Test this by placing a spoonful of jelly on a saucer in the fridge for a few minutes. If it wrinkles when you push it with your finger, it is set. Pour the jelly into warm, sterilised jars (see Glossary) and seal.

FENNEL

FENNEL IS AN ANCIENT VEGETABLE WELL WORTH BECOMING acquainted with. A member of the parsley family, this aniseedy bulb, also called Florence fennel, grows wild in the Mediterranean. I'm so partial to bulb fennel I become impatient waiting until autumn for it; although these days baby fennel bulbs are available throughout summer, the large plump bulb in all its glory is worth the wait.

We in the Barossa would be lost without fennel seeds, which come from the bulbless common fennel plant. They are added to cooking pots of yabbies, bread dough and dill pickles, among countless other preparations. Try making a caramel of verjuice and sugar and mix in fennel seeds, sliced dried figs, roasted almonds and fresh bay leaves – serve it sliced with coffee. Rustic bread flavoured with fennel seeds teams well with cheese and dried figs. And if you've developed a love of these seeds, look out for Italian pork sausages flavoured with them (Steve Flamsteed, a very special former employee who is still very much a part of our lives, uses fennel-seed sausages in a wonderful dish in which he incorporates grape must).

If you've enjoyed the seed you must try the bulb. For those of you who have seen the whitish-green fennel bulb in the greengrocer's, with its feathery fronds of vivid green, and not known what to do with it, try peeling back the outer layer of skin to reveal the edible part. If the bulb is fresh from your garden, you don't need to do this – in transit the outer skin is handled and becomes marked, and it can be tough if it is an old specimen. When choosing your bulb, the tighter it is the fresher and sweeter it will be. If it is round and bulbous, it will be female; if longer and thinner, it will be male. Taste and see if you think there is a difference. It is usually so with birds and animals (the female is usually sweeter!), so why not plants? And if you buy fennel, chop off the fronds (but don't discard them) to minimise deterioration.

Fennel marries well with fish, chicken, anchovies, pancetta, garlic, olives, Parmigiano Reggiano, flat-leaf parsley and oranges. It can be eaten raw, cut thinly or grated into autumn and winter salads, or just quartered and placed on the table at the end of the meal as a *digestif*. Steamed, boiled, deep-fried or poached in extra virgin olive oil or chicken stock, fennel is transformed into a wonderful cooked vegetable – it is sweet, yet its distinctive mild aniseed flavour refreshes.

To serve fennel fresh from the garden in a salad, cut off the fronds only if they look tired and dull, and discard the stalks only if fibrous (even then they can be used to add a delicate flavour and fragrance to chicken or fish stock). Trim the root end and outside skin, if necessary, then, with a very sharp knife and a steady hand, cut the fennel into paper-thin vertical slices. Arrange half the slices on a large flat dish, then season them with a little sea salt and add a layer of shaved best-quality Parmigiano Reggiano (use a potato peeler for this – I prefer the black wide-handled peeler I use for quinces). Generously sprinkle the dish with roughly chopped flat-leaf parsley, drizzle it with a fruity extra virgin olive oil, then add another layer of fennel, and so on. Grind black pepper over the lot, add the smallest amount of red-wine vinegar or lemon juice, and serve immediately. Just wonderful for an autumn lunch, sitting behind our huge stone wall, with one end of the table in the shade of the old willow for my husband Colin and the rest of us lapping up the last of the sun.

One of my favourite ways to cook fennel is to gently poach it in extra virgin olive oil and verjuice at a simmer. First toss a couple of trimmed bulbs, cut in half lengthways or quartered if large, in verjuice to stop oxidisation, then place in a stainless steel pan just large enough to hold them snugly in one layer. Add enough quantities of three parts extra virgin olive oil and one part verjuice to half cover the fennel. Lay on top a piece of baking paper cut to a similar size as the pan to act as a cartouche (see Glossary) during cooking. Simmer gently for about 20 minutes on low–medium heat, then turn the fennel over and cook for another 10–15 minutes until cooked through but not falling apart. I like to serve the fennel warm with such accompaniments as a roasted head of garlic, olive bread croutons crisped in the oven just before serving, or chunks of just-melted goat's cheese.

Whether cooked like this or sliced and grilled on the barbecue, fennel has a great affinity with seafood, from shellfish to almost any fish from the sea, but particularly fish with a high oil content such as tommy ruffs or sardines. It is also a great balance for the sweetness of riverfish. The late Catherine Brandel, a delightful American who was with Alice Waters' Chez Panisse restaurant for many years, made a salsa at a conference I attended once in Hawaii. It was a great combination of flavours: finely chopped fennel, diced green olives and tiny segments of thinly sliced meyer lemon all held together with extra virgin olive oil

Fennel with goat's curd

and lots of flat-leaf parsley. I can't remember what it was served with then, but I can highly recommend it with quickly seared tuna or swordfish.

Fennel oil is useful to have on hand, particularly if you cook fish regularly. Simply chop up a few trimmed bulbs and cover them generously with a good extra virgin olive oil in a stainless steel saucepan. (If the oil you start with is not good, the oil you finish with will not be either.) You can add some fennel seeds, too, but this shouldn't be necessary if the fennel you are using is truly fresh. Bring the pan to a simmer very, very slowly and leave it to cook long and slowly (for about an hour or so) at a low temperature until the fennel has almost melted into the oil. Allow the fennel to cool in the oil, so that the flavours are well infused. Strain the oil into a sterilised jar and seal. Fennel oil can also be tossed through pasta and brushed onto pizzas and bruschetta.

Caramelised fennel can become a bed for grilled fresh sardines with a squeeze of lemon juice, a little extra virgin olive oil, tiny capers and flat-leaf parsley. Halve the fennel lengthways, then cut each piece into quarters and liberally brush with extra virgin olive oil. Roast the fennel with sprigs of fresh thyme in a shallow roasting pan at 250°C for about 10 minutes or until the underside is caramelised. Turn the fennel over and cook for another 10 minutes until it has cooked through and the second side has caramelised.

FENNEL WITH GOAT'S CURD

Serves 4 as an accompaniment or 2 as a light meal

40 g unsalted butter

⅓ cup (80 ml) extra virgin olive oil

1 large, plump fennel bulb, trimmed and quartered, fronds reserved

4 fresh bay leaves

1 meyer lemon (optional), cut into 6 wedges

sea salt flakes and freshly ground black pepper

½ cup (125 ml) verjuice *or* fruity white wine

80 g goat's curd

baby purple basil *or* freshly chopped flat-leaf parsley, to serve

Melt the butter over low heat in a heavy-based frying pan until nut-brown, then add a splash of the olive oil and gently seal the fennel quarters on both sides. Add fennel fronds, bay leaves and lemon, if using, then season with salt and pepper.

Add the verjuice or white wine and remaining olive oil, then cover and simmer for about 20 minutes or until cooked through. Remove the lid, then increase the heat to high and cook for another 5 minutes, or until fennel is coloured and pan juices are reduced to a syrup.

Remove the fennel, season to taste and serve as a warm salad, topped with spoonfuls of goat's curd and baby purple basil or chopped parsley.

PASTA WITH CARAMELISED FENNEL, PRESERVED LEMON AND GARLIC

Serves 6

You could use my Duck Egg Pasta (see page 179) for this dish.

3 fennel bulbs, fronds and stalks trimmed, then sliced

18 cloves garlic, peeled

extra virgin olive oil, for cooking

3 quarters preserved lemon, flesh removed, rind rinsed and thinly sliced

sea salt flakes

500 g good-quality dried *or* fresh pappardelle

½ cup flat-leaf parsley, roughly chopped

freshly ground black pepper

freshly shaved Parmigiano Reggiano, to serve

Steam the fennel for 3–5 minutes until almost cooked, then set aside.

Place the garlic cloves into a small heavy-based saucepan and cover them with olive oil. Cook very gently over low heat for about 20 minutes or until the garlic is golden, then remove the garlic from the oil and set it aside, reserving the oil.

Preheat the oven to 250°C. Brush the fennel with the reserved olive oil and roast in a shallow roasting pan with the preserved lemon for about 10 minutes or until caramelised (this can also be done over high heat on the stove).

To cook the pasta, bring 4 litres water to the boil in a large saucepan, then add 2 tablespoons salt. Slide the pasta gently into the pot as the water returns to the boil, then partially cover with a lid to bring it to a rapid boil. Cook the pasta according to the manufacturer's instructions, stirring to keep it well separated (a tablespoon of olive oil in the water can help this too). If using fresh pasta, it only needs to cook for 3 or so minutes. Drain the pasta – this is easiest if you have a colander for this purpose that fits inside your pot – and reserve a little of the cooking water in case you want to moisten the completed dish. Do not run the pasta under water as you'll lose the precious starch that helps the sauce or oil adhere.

Toss the hot pasta with the caramelised fennel, garlic cloves and preserved lemon, then add a drizzle of extra virgin olive oil, the parsley and a grind of pepper. You may not need salt, depending on the saltiness of the preserved lemons. Serve immediately with lots of freshly shaved Parmigiano Reggiano. Anchovies would be a great addition to this dish too.

TEA-SMOKED OCEAN TROUT WITH FENNEL

Serves 6

You need a barbecue with a hood or lid for this dish. The cooking time depends on how close the fish is to the heat source. Slower (further away from the heat source) is actually better – the slower the cooking, the smokier the flavour. You only need to cook the fish until the flesh has just set.

If serving off the bone worries you, ask your fishmonger to take the spine out of the fish, leaving it whole.

125 g green tea *or* orange pekoe tea

250 g brown sugar

250 g castor sugar

2 small fennel bulbs, very thinly sliced
(including the fronds)

extra virgin olive oil, for cooking

1 × 1.75 kg ocean trout *or* Atlantic salmon,
cleaned and scaled

1 orange, sliced

1 lemon, sliced

sea salt flakes and freshly ground
black pepper

capers and lemon slices, to serve

Make 3 rectangular 'boxes' for the smoking mixture using several layers of foil (I make the packages 15 × 12 cm to fit under the griller of my barbecue). Combine the tea and sugars and divide the mixture between the foil containers, then set them aside. Heat the barbecue to medium–high.

Sauté the fennel with a little olive oil in a frying pan over medium heat for about 5 minutes, then stuff it into the cavity of the fish with the orange and lemon. Season the fish generously and moisten it with olive oil. Skewer the opening shut with small metal or bamboo skewers to keep the stuffing in. If using bamboo skewers, soak them in water first so they won't burn.

Oil the racks of the barbecue and make sure they are absolutely clean. Put the foil containers on the coals and wait for the aroma – there will be a strong smell from the sugar caramelising but it will dissipate quickly. Turn the barbecue down to low. Put the fish onto the grill, shut the lid of the barbecue and cook for 4 minutes. Heat builds up quickly in these barbecues and the thermometer may climb as high as 150°C. If this happens, turn the fish over and turn the heat off. Cook the fish for another 4 minutes. If it is not cooked enough for your taste, or your barbecue hasn't reached 150°C, leave the fish for another 4 minutes with the heat off.

Serve the fish immediately, cut into thick slices, with capers, lemon slices, sea salt flakes and a drizzle of extra virgin olive oil.

FIGS

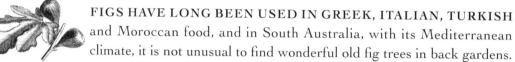

FIGS HAVE LONG BEEN USED IN GREEK, ITALIAN, TURKISH and Moroccan food, and in South Australia, with its Mediterranean climate, it is not unusual to find wonderful old fig trees in back gardens. If you have a tree you will know how fleeting figs are. As with so many other fruits, it is a race to see who gets them first, you or the birds! Particularly vulnerable are the large black figs I know as Black Genoa. As with all figs, they are only perfect when left on the tree until they are really ripe and turn such a deep, deep red. This variety, and the large green fig, the Smyrna, are the two most commonly available at your greengrocer, packed in trays of moulded plastic to protect the fragile fruit as much as possible. The Brown Turkey or sugar fig used to be more widely available and is wonderful for jam. Sadly, most newer fig plantings are of the varieties that are better eaten fresh, so I often struggle to find enough Brown Turkey figs for my burnt fig jam and burnt fig ice cream.

Fig farmers or orchardists deserve every cent of the price they receive, as figs must be picked ripe to reach their potential (even though that is true of most fruits, it is particularly so for the fig). Yet when they are so beautifully ripe and luscious, they are also incredibly fragile and last only days at their peak; so much so that the farmer has to go through each tree on his orchard at least every second day, picking the next batch of fruit to ripen. There is none of this picking the whole tree at a time, as there is with other fruits – and all of this presuming that the farmer has found a way to keep the birds away from the fruit.

The only way I have found to keep birds at bay is to hang silver-painted plastic snakes (from a toy shop) on the trees. They even frighten me if I am walking through the orchard distracted by other things, so I can see quite clearly how they affect the birds. Not that I am suggesting a commercial orchardist would resort to such child's play, but I am passing the tip on to those frustrated backyard fig growers, if they have anywhere near the same problems I've had with birds.

If buying figs, go to a really top-class greengrocer and select your figs with the utmost care. If you are fortunate enough to have your own source, you will find they are the most obliging of fruit, as the trees have two flushes if the season is good, the first of which comes before Christmas. Their next flush then kicks in from late January through to April. Each year they will deliver, day by day, just enough to keep you going on your own private fig-fest.

Even though we have two wild fig trees on our farm, in the creek bed of our original vineyard, that bear like crazy, the fig trees I planted at home took over ten years to be productive. There was obviously something missing in our soil, or perhaps because it is such deep sandy loam the water the trees need isn't retained.

Of all the old wild fig trees I've seen, nothing can touch the one my friend Belinda Hannaford has on Kangaroo Island – her fig tree is the size of a house block. The tree is so old and gnarled that she has been able to make steps in the branches so you can actually walk through the tree and sit under the canopy for lunch on a summer's day. There is space for at least twenty people. One just reaches for a fresh fig to accompany the cheese platter.

A plate of figs, deep purple or vivid green and bulging with ripeness, is a feast for the eye. Cut them in half and that inner rosy glow, so shiny and jewel-like, is like opening a chest in Aladdin's cave. Bite into them and their soft ripeness yields. When sucking the flesh away from the skin, it almost melts in the mouth – truly, the most sensuous fruit!

Whilst there are fabulous fig growers, it's only when you have your own tree that you will get figs so richly red and ripe they are almost molten – with no need to do anything but eat them, absolutely unadorned.

Perhaps I haven't revered enough the small, greeny-brown fig, duller inside but sweeter for eating fresh. When I take the time to make jam, I follow my mother's tradition of burning it (or at least, 'catching' it), which stops it being super-sweet – something that happened without her intending it, she said. The result, burnt fig jam, is always a sensation. Ironically, our fig growers, with whom we necessarily share a very close relationship, dislike my burnt fig jam and wish I would make a normal one, but the caramelisation that happens when catching the pan on the bottom is the only way for me; it is certainly my point of difference and an absolute sentimental favourite.

So often you'll buy figs that will look great but, because of the problems of transporting them, they will have been picked before they are fully ripe. If you find this, I'd halve the figs, brush them with some extra virgin olive oil and grill them to get the maximum flavour out of them. Or they could be quickly baked with some fresh ricotta or goat's curd and tossed into a salad.

When you have the perfect ripe fig, either from your own tree or a farmers' market, try the classic of fresh figs with prosciutto: the sweetness of the fig and the saltiness of the prosciutto are a perfect match. This time-honoured combination had a delightful twist when Janni Kyritsis served figs as an entrée at his former restaurant, MG Garage, in Sydney; they came with very ripe, diced rockmelon and crème fraîche and were divine. I then ordered figs again for dessert, and this time they arrived in a tart, latticed with fine pastry and accompanied by more fresh, hot grilled figs and a walnut cream.

For a simple, complete meal, set out a really chewy piece of ciabatta with fresh, ripe figs, the prosciutto again and some goat's curd; all it needs is a little green extra virgin olive oil. Or, for dessert, cut fresh figs in half and drizzle with chestnut honey. If the figs aren't as ripe as you'd hoped, halve and bake them drizzled with chestnut honey and serve with crème fraîche when cooled. Fresh figs can also be served with a plate of ripe creamy Gippsland blue cheese instead of dessert.

For another simple dessert, take whole figs that are very ripe and wash carefully. While the figs are still damp, dip them into dark brown sugar and pack tightly in a baking dish. Bake for about 10 minutes in a very hot (240°C) oven, being careful they don't burn. When they are cooked, the sugar turns into caramel in the bottom of the dish. Cool and serve with a big pot of mascarpone moistened with the pan juices.

If you prefer to peel the figs, try marinating them in a little almond or walnut liqueur for about an hour after you've peeled them. Take a roasted walnut, squeeze it into the centre of each fig and coat with a batter of self-raising flour and water, then deep-fry in extra virgin olive oil in the smallest saucepan you can find so it is not too extravagant. Dusted with icing sugar and served hot, these are incredibly more-ish.

To make fig ice cream, simply purée some ripe figs and add a little lemon juice or even some finely sliced glacé ginger. Stir into some homemade vanilla ice cream and freeze. Serve with almond biscuits.

Don't forget the leaves of the fig: they can be used in so many ways to serve food. I found this wonderfully evocative quote in *Honey from a Weed* by Patience Gray: 'I recall only the "fig bread" served as a dessert in the shape of a little domed loaf unwrapped from its fig leaves, made of pressed dried figs flavoured with aniseed and bay leaves.'

Dried figs are an important part of culinary life and can be called upon in many a cooking emergency. Try stuffing them with roasted almonds and baking them in the oven for a sweetmeat to finish dinner. Then there are those wonderful dried figs of chef Cheong Liew's, poached in port and chocolate (see page 42) – a great finish to a meal.

Because figs have a natural affinity with lamb, try roasting a shoulder of lamb, boned and stuffed with fresh figs, garlic and chopped lemon rind. The same stuffing would go well with kid and quail. Don't prepare any of these in advance though, as figs have an enzymatic reaction with meat or poultry that starts to break them down. Pot-roast the lamb very slowly in some extra virgin olive oil, add seasoning and moisten with stock if it begins to dry out or the figs are causing it to burn. The meat will give off a syrupy glaze that should be served with the lamb.

Figs can also be added to pizza. First 'cure' the pizza base in the oven, by cooking it three-quarters through. Then take it out, drizzle with extra virgin olive oil, top with thick slices of fresh fig and goat's curd, return to the oven and finish cooking. Alternatively, use a combination of fresh figs and caramelised onions as a pizza topping. Add dobs of goat's cheese or ricotta and a final flourish of extra virgin olive oil and chopped flat-leaf parsley.

Who needs a recipe for figs when the best way to eat them is as they are? Here, however, are a few ideas for those times when you have a glut on your hands.

✦ Wrap figs with prosciutto and stand them in a shallow terracotta dish or a roasting pan. Drizzle with extra virgin olive oil and add a sprig or two of thyme. Bake at 240°C for 10 minutes and serve immediately. You could also either stuff the figs with blue cheese or dot goat's cheese or blue cheese over the figs for a fabulous lunch.

✦ Grill halved ripe figs topped with a tiny knob of butter under a preheated, really hot grill until caramelised, then serve hot with cream or mascarpone.

✦ Drizzle honey and squeeze lemon juice over peeled figs, then bake them at 240°C for 10 minutes.

✦ Semi-dry halved figs in a home dehydrator. Toss roasted almonds and toasted fennel seeds with a little extra virgin olive oil and the grated rind of a lemon. While they are still warm from the dehydrator, make a sandwich of the figs with the almond mixture inside. Or serve cooled figs with a ripe soft cheese.

FRESH FIG AND PROSCIUTTO SALAD   *Serves 4*

8 ripe figs (the figs will be at their best
   if not refrigerated)
1 bunch rocket, trimmed, washed and dried
extra virgin olive oil, to taste
balsamic vinegar *or* vino cotto
   (see Glossary), to taste

squeeze of lemon juice
8 slices prosciutto
freshly shaved Parmigiano Reggiano,
   to serve

Cut the figs in half, then toss with the rocket in a bowl. Dress with a vinaigrette of 3–4 parts olive oil to 1 part balsamic vinegar or vino cotto (the specific quantities depend on the quality of the ingredients). Add lemon juice to taste. Divide evenly among 4 plates, then drape over two slices of prosciutto. Top with shaved Parmigiano Reggiano and serve immediately.

FIG AND PRESERVED LEMON SALAD WITH WALNUTS AND GOAT'S CURD

Serves 6

3 quarters preserved lemon, flesh removed,
    rind rinsed and thinly sliced
verjuice, for soaking
1 cup walnuts
12–18 ripe figs, depending on size, halved
¼ cup (60 ml) vino cotto (see Glossary)

½ cup (125 ml) extra virgin olive oil
sea salt flakes and freshly ground
    black pepper
lemon juice, to taste (optional)
1 bunch rocket, washed and dried
½ cup goat's curd

Soak the preserved lemons in enough verjuice to cover for 1 hour. Preheat the oven to 200°C, then place the walnuts on a baking tray and lightly roast for 10 minutes or until golden. Rub skins off with a clean tea towel, then leave to cool.

Brush the figs with a little vino cotto, then grill under a hot griller until lightly caramelised. Place in a bowl, then drizzle with the remaining vino cotto and leave for 30 minutes.

Drain the preserved lemons, discarding the verjuice, then gently strain the vino cotto from the figs, reserving the vino cotto. Combine the vino cotto with the olive oil, whisk to emulsify, then season to taste with salt and pepper. Balance the dressing with lemon juice if required. Combine all the ingredients, except the goat's curd, then gently toss together with the dressing. Dollop the goat's curd onto the salad immediately before serving.

DRIED FIG TAPENADE

Makes 2 cups

This fig tapenade keeps well, covered with olive oil in the refrigerator, and can be pulled out to turn barbecued lamb chops or quail into something a little more special.

3 sprigs rosemary
1 cup (250 ml) extra virgin olive oil
¾ cup reconstituted dried figs, topped and
    tailed, then finely chopped
1 cup (150 g) kalamata olives, pitted

2 tablespoons capers
10 anchovy fillets
80–100 ml lemon juice
sea salt flakes and freshly ground
    black pepper

Pan-fry the rosemary sprigs in a little of the oil, then remove the rosemary and set it aside, reserving the oil. Cool the rosemary-infused oil and then add it to the balance of the oil. Process the figs, olives, fried rosemary, capers and anchovies to a purée in a food processor. Season with lemon juice, salt and pepper. With the motor running, pour in the olive oil slowly as if making a mayonnaise.

PICKLED FIGS, FARM FOLLIES STYLE

Makes 10 medium-sized jars

A bottle of pickled figs in the pantry can be used to complement poultry for a last-minute meal, and is especially good with duck or quail. Roast or pan-fry the poultry with fresh rosemary and deglaze the pan with a little of the pickling liquid. Add a little chicken stock to the sauce and then toss in some sliced pickled figs, rosemary and slices of lemon.

225 g salt
3 kg figs

PICKLING MIXTURE

1 tablespoon mixed spice
2 cloves per fig
1 litre white-wine vinegar
2 kg sugar

Add the salt to 2 litres of water to make a brine. Soak the figs in the brine for 12 hours.

To make the pickling mixture, boil the mixed spice, cloves, vinegar and 1.5 kg of the sugar for 15 minutes. Cook the fruit slowly in this syrup for 1 hour. Leave to stand overnight.

The next day, bring the figs and syrup to the boil, then drain them, reserving the syrup, and place in sterilised jars (see Glossary). Add the remaining sugar to the syrup and boil for 30 minutes. Cover the figs with the syrup and seal the jars.

FIG AND GORGONZOLA TART

Serves 8

If the figs aren't as sweet as they could be, then roast some walnuts, rub off their skins, toss them in your best honey and dot them on top of the tart.

1 × quantity Sour-cream Pastry
(see page 177)
250 g gorgonzola piccante (see Glossary)
or other sharp blue cheese, crumbled
250 g mascarpone

4 free-range eggs, beaten
sea salt flakes and freshly ground
black pepper
12 ripe figs
1 tablespoon unsalted butter

Make and chill pastry following instructions. Roll out the pastry and use it to line a deep 16 cm tart tin with a removable base, then chill for 20 minutes. Preheat the oven to 200°C. Line the pastry case with foil and pastry weights, and blind bake for 10 minutes, then remove foil and weights and bake for another 6–8 minutes or until the pastry is cooked. Reset the oven to 180°C.

Mix the blue cheese with the mascarpone. Beat the eggs into the cheeses by hand, and season to taste; don't be tempted to leave out salt thinking that the blue cheese is salty enough.

Pour mixture into the hot tart shells, then bake for 12–20 minutes (depending on the depth of the tart mould) or until filling is almost set.

Meanwhile, cut the figs in half, place on a grill tray and dot with a little butter, then grill under a hot griller for approximately 10 minutes, or until the figs are caramelised.

Just as the tart is setting, lay the figs on top of the gorgonzola custard and return it to the oven for a few minutes. Leave to cool for 20 minutes before serving with a salad of rocket, witlof (both red and white) and roasted walnuts.

FIGS IN PUFF PASTRY WITH CRÈME ANGLAISE   *Serves 8*

This dessert can be made as one large pastry, or 8 individual ones, cut to whatever shape you wish.

1 × quantity **Rough Puff Pastry**
(see page 179)

1 egg, lightly beaten

16 figs

butter, for frying

lemon juice *or* verjuice, to taste

pure icing sugar (optional), to serve

CRÈME ANGLAISE

2 cups (500 ml) milk

2 cups (500 ml) rich double cream

1 vanilla bean, halved lengthways

8 egg yolks

120 g sugar

Make and chill pastry as instructed. Preheat the oven to 220°C. Roll out the pastry and rest it in the refrigerator for 30 minutes before cutting it to your desired shape (I like to cut 8 rectangles) and brushing it with beaten egg – make sure you don't brush the egg right to the edges as this will inhibit the rising of the pastry layers. Cook for about 10–15 minutes or until golden brown and cooked through. Cut each piece in half and pull out any uncooked bits of pastry if necessary.

For the crème anglaise, bring the milk and cream to the boil in a heavy-based saucepan, then remove from the heat. Scrape the vanilla seeds into this mixture, then add the vanilla bean and leave to infuse. Whisk the egg yolks and sugar until thick and pale. Carefully stir the heated milk mixture into the egg mixture. Return the crème to the pan and heat over low heat, stirring gently and constantly with a wooden spoon until the mixture begins to thicken. Take the mixture off the heat from time to time if it looks like getting too hot. Have a large bowl of iced water standing by in case you take the crème too far and need to place the saucepan in iced water to cool it down quickly. The crème should be thick enough to coat a wooden spoon and leave a trail when you draw your finger across it. Remove the vanilla bean.

Cut the figs into thick slices and fry them quickly in a little butter in a large frying pan over high heat. Don't put too many in the pan at a time – this may cause them to sweat instead of caramelise. Add a squeeze of lemon juice or verjuice.

Assemble by placing one piece of pastry on a serving plate, piling it up with figs and topping with another piece of pastry, sprinkling with a little icing sugar if you wish. Pour the crème anglaise around the pastry and serve. (If you pour crème anglaise on the plate first and then place pastry on top, your pastry will get soggy.)

CHOCOLATE CAKE WITH A FIG CENTRE AND GANACHE   *Serves 8–10*

This is an amazingly luscious cake that is best made with figs picked ripe from the tree. The base recipe is in fact Simone Beck's Very Rich Chocolate Cake with Cherries from *Simca's Cuisine*, an old favourite; the page in my copy is very fingered and chocolate-splattered! This cake is rich rather than sweet, so is perfect for my taste.

450 g bitter chocolate, chopped

1 tablespoon best-quality instant
   coffee granules

½ cup (125 ml) brandy *or* fruit liqueur

4 free-range eggs, separated

150 g unsalted butter, chopped

⅓ cup (50 g) plain flour

pinch salt

⅓ cup (75 g) castor sugar

8 plump, ripe figs, peeled and chopped

GANACHE

225 g bitter chocolate, chopped

150 ml cream

2 teaspoons best-quality instant
   coffee granules

Preheat the oven to 190°C. Grease and line a 26 cm springform cake tin. Melt the chocolate with the instant coffee granules and brandy in a heavy-based enamelled or stainless steel saucepan over low heat until smooth, then remove from the heat. Mix one egg yolk at a time into the chocolate mixture. Return the pan to the heat just to warm the yolks and thicken the mixture. Remove from the heat again and add the butter, a knob at a time, stirring until it is all incorporated. Sift the flour and stir it into the chocolate mixture.

Beat the egg whites with the salt until they form soft peaks, then add the castor sugar and beat until stiff. Fold the warm chocolate mixture carefully into the egg whites and turn the batter into the prepared tin. Bake for 20–25 minutes and remove from the oven (it is important not to overcook the cake). It will puff like a soufflé in the centre and must be left to cool in the tin for 45 minutes before it is turned out onto a wire rack. The cake will shrink and crack as it cools.

Cut a 12 cm-wide circle in the middle of the cooled cake and scrape out the cake with a dessertspoon, leaving a 2.5 cm border and the base intact. The cake you extract will be so moist and rich you could roll it into balls like truffles – instead, mix it with the figs and pile it back into the hollowed-out cake.

For the ganache, melt the chocolate with the cream and instant coffee granules in a heavy-based enamelled or stainless steel saucepan over low heat until smooth and shiny. Cool the ganache, then cover the cake generously with it. Put the cake in a cool place until required – don't refrigerate it or the ganache will lose its sheen.

FIG AND WALNUT TART

Serves 8

One of my most requested desserts, which is almost embarrassingly simple, is a fig and walnut tart. It is really just a meringue made with dark-brown sugar. This tart is meant to be sticky, soft and rustic-looking. As it is so rich, I prefer it cut in thin slices to have with coffee.

180 g walnuts	250 g soft dark-brown sugar
330 g plump dried figs, stems removed and fruit finely chopped	crème fraîche *or* sour cream, to serve
6 free-range egg whites	slices of candied *or* fresh lime (optional), to serve

Preheat the oven to 220°C. Roast the walnuts on a baking tray for about 5 minutes, shaking the tray to stop the nuts burning. Rub them in a clean tea towel to remove their bitter skins, then sieve away the skins. Allow to cool. Reduce the oven temperature to 180°C.

Line and grease a 24 cm springform cake tin with baking paper. Toss the walnuts and figs together in a bowl.

In the bowl of an electric mixer, whisk the egg whites until soft peaks form, then slowly add the sugar in heaped tablespoons until incorporated, and the resultant meringue is thick and stiff. Take a spoonful of the meringue and mix it through the figs and walnuts, then tip this mixture into the meringue and fold through. Spoon the meringue mixture into the prepared cake tin and bake in the oven for 45–50 minutes or until the meringue pulls away from the sides of the pan and the top feels 'set'. Leave to cool.

I serve this with crème fraîche or sour cream spread over the top. Candied or even fresh lime is a wonderful accompaniment to this tart – decorate the edge with a ring of very thin lime slices.

CHEONG'S FIGS
Makes 12 figs

My friend Cheong Liew, one of Australia's most important chefs and an amazingly generous and knowledgeable man, used to serve a wonderful sweetmeat in the days when he ran Adelaide's famous Neddy's restaurant. It was a Portuguese speciality based on figs stuffed with a mixture of ground almonds and grated chocolate. Cheong then poached the figs in chocolate and port. He says he used to have them sitting in a glass jar of port ready to serve after coffee. They make a stunning dessert served with crème fraîche.

¾ cup (120 g) almonds, roasted and ground
120 g dark chocolate, grated, plus 120 g
    for poaching
250 g (about 12) dried figs

1½ cups (375 ml) port (I often use
    white port *or* 12-year-old St Hallett's
    Pedro Ximenez)

Mix the almonds and grated chocolate together. Loosen each fig at the bottom and create a hole, then stuff with the almond and chocolate mixture. Place the figs in a heavy-based saucepan with the port. Simmer, but do not boil, over low–medium heat for 10 minutes. Add extra grated chocolate to taste and simmer for another 5 minutes. Take the figs out and put them in a jar. Reduce the poaching liquid until it forms a glaze and pour into the jar.

BURNT FIG JAM SLICE
Serves 8

½ × quantity Sour-cream Pastry
    (see page 177)
300 g jar Maggie Beer Burnt Fig Jam

½ cup (125 ml) crème fraîche, mascarpone
    or sour cream

Preheat the oven to 220°C. Prepare and chill the pastry as instructed. Roll out the pastry to 5 mm thick, then place it on a flat scone tray and bake until golden (about 15 minutes). While the pastry is still warm from the oven, spread generously with the jam. Cut into 4 pieces and serve with crème fraîche, mascarpone or sour cream.

GRAPES

BY FEBRUARY EACH YEAR THE BAROSSA VALLEY VINTAGE IS IN full swing. Over the 40 years I have now lived here, there has been a gradual eroding of the harvesting traditions and there are now fewer hand-picking gangs. For economic reasons machine picking has become a fact of life, and with it some of the colour of the Valley has gone. The women of the Barossa were the core of the picking gangs, helped by hundreds of itinerant workers who would descend on the Valley looking for work. They were often young people on working holidays, and so over the years we had lawyers, teachers, nurses and chefs picking for us. The traditional grape pickers' party in late April at the end of the vintage was often a very spirited affair. After all the hard work of picking there was an atmosphere of camaraderie and satisfaction in the air at seeing the crop in. For years we still handpicked the grapes that were to go into our Home Block Shiraz and Beer Bros Old Vine Shiraz, our top wine, but these days mostly the grapes are machine picked.

The biennial Barossa Vintage Festival, the celebration to mark the end of vintage, is a very special time in the Valley and picnics have always been a highlight. Several festivals ago, our then Farmshop manager, Jane Renner, made the setting picture perfect. Under the gum trees by the side of the dam at the Pheasant Farm Restaurant, trestle tables were covered in bright cloths and laden with bowls of grapes, figs and pomegranates. Seating consisted of a mixture of wooden folding chairs, hay bales or blankets. A big box of timber, piles of vine stumps and cuttings for fuel, and two drum spits for cooking completed the scene.

My idea was to celebrate the grape in every course, and I had planned the picnic months in advance so that it could be included in the festival program. But plans made so long beforehand easily go awry. The yabbies that were to feature in the first dish of the day were suddenly unavailable due to the long Easter break, so the menu required a late change. A few phone calls to Kangaroo Island and marron was ordered – in the end much more than a mere replacement.

Each picnicker received a plate with a marron, a terrine and a jelly as a starter; all including grapes or their by-products in one way or another. The blanched and halved marron were painted with extra virgin olive oil and verjuice before being finished in the oven. Each individual Barossa Chook terrine had been lined with both a vine leaf cooked in verjuice and the skin of the chicken, and the leg meat was simply diced and tossed with basil, roasted garlic, salt and freshly ground black pepper before the terrines were cooked in a bain-marie – the little round terrines looked beautiful turned out, vine leaf uppermost. Finally, alongside sat a scoop of grape and verjuice jelly – bearing in mind that jellies always melt at picnics, I had added some extra virgin olive oil, along with some fresh chervil, so that as it melted the jelly made its own vinaigrette.

The main course was boned, milk-fed lamb that had been stuffed with sautéed figs, walnuts, pancetta, onion, breadcrumbs and lots of rosemary and thyme. I made two bundles of lamb wrapped in caul fat with fresh bay leaves and cooked them gently over the open fire fuelled by vine cuttings. When I found myself faced with the slowly sautéed golden shallots I had meant to serve with the marron, I tossed these with boiled kipfler potatoes (cut in half and sprinkled with sea salt and freshly ground black pepper) and chopped flat-leaf parsley, to serve with the lamb bundles. Fennel pot-roasted in olive oil and deglazed with verjuice completed the dish.

My friend Sheri Schubert had cooked a huge amount of her very ripe shiraz grapes a few weeks previously and put them through a food mill before freezing the pulpy juice. The day before the picnic, Sheri used these to make two huge pots of her Rotegrütze (see page 50), the traditional Barossa dessert of grape and sago. I was keen to serve it in two large bowls from my own kitchen from which we could spoon out portions, so the sago was measured out extra carefully to get the 'set' just right. We made almond and lemon friands to serve with the rotegrütze, and thick-as-thick churned cream collected that morning from the Kernich dairy at Greenock really finished it off.

Continuing the grape theme, the bread we served with lunch was made by Tanunda's Apex Bakery using the ferment from Orlando shiraz grapes. And to finish off the picnic, we had my grape Schiacciata (see page 48), made with some very ripe grenache grapes picked at Grant Burge's vineyard the day before, which we served with Laurie Jensen's Shadows of Blue cheese from Tarago River, Victoria. The juxtaposition of the sweetness of the bread and the saltiness of the creamy blue cheese was a pretty good way to end the day, and for me a true celebration of vintage.

Only having grown wine grapes, I hadn't realised that table grapes were trellised and grown quite differently until my friend Stefano de Pieri asked me to help out at a Slow Food Dinner, to be held under the vines at the Garreffa family's property near Mildura in Victoria. I was asked to make verjuice custards for the 120 guests. A dinner in a vineyard for that number of people isn't the easiest logistical exercise, but the Garreffas had a large shed which Stefano had set up as a camp kitchen. A visiting chef from the United States had volunteered to help and the Garreffa family and friends were all happy to be involved in the food preparation.

We arrived at the vineyard in the early evening, when there was still some fierceness in the sun. We mingled with the crowd, having a glass of local wine and eating the deep-fried pastries that were being cooked over an open fire. The difference in grape growing was remarkable – the table grapes are grown on a trellis system that seems almost like hedgerows; the vigorous vines are then canopied over 2 metres high. A long table had been placed down the row between the vines, and covered in generously draped white tablecloths – a beautiful sight. The roof of vines between the rows was hung with lanterns, giving a magical feel to the evening. On my return I looked for the right position to create something similar at home. Several years have passed now and nothing has yet transpired, but I promise myself – one day!

The Garreffas are not only very serious table grape growers, they also produce sultanas, currants, raisins and muscatels under their brand Tabletop Grapes, which are of such a high quality they bring a whole new dimension to dried grapes.

While wine grapes aren't the norm for eating, they are wonderful to cook with at the end of the season, when they're sweet and intense in colour. Not everyone has access to wine grapes, as I do, however just about every fruit shop stocks sultana grapes, that versatile and seedless grape first planted for drying and then used for bulk wine-making in years of excess. Nowadays, mint-green sultanas for the table are more to my taste than those left to ripen until golden and sweet. Today the fruit is protected by the vine canopy, making it less sweet, which suits my palate.

I can't bear to waste the grapes not captured by the mechanical pickers at the end of each season, so if we're having a party in the autumn and lighting up our wood-fired oven I pick buckets of these leftovers. We cook either really good pork sausages, beef shin or lamb shanks in huge but relatively shallow terracotta dishes. The meat, first gently sealed in nut-brown butter with a dash of oil, sits on a bed of soffrito (sweated onion and garlic) with chopped rosemary, some bay leaves and citrus rind. This mixture is then topped with the grapes and cooked until they reduce and become a thick syrupy mass. Remember that wine grapes have pips, and more sensitive souls may find this a problem. (Do we? Of course not!)

When you tire of eating bunches of fresh grapes, there are many other ways to use them. I love grapes tossed through a green salad, with a dressing of walnut oil and a little red-wine vinegar (keeping it in the grape family). I enjoy the explosion of grape juice when I come across whole grapes among the salad leaves, particularly if they are icy cold.

I've never gone as far as peeling grapes for a dish. I do, however, halve large red globe grapes and at times remove the pips before tossing them in a salad or marinade. It's not that the pips trouble me; rather, it's that the cut surface takes up the vinaigrette so much better than if the grape is left whole to slip around in the dressing protected by its skin.

Pickled grapes are the perfect accompaniment to pâtés and terrines, and also tongue, either smoked or in brine. To pickle grapes, place them in sterilised jars (I like to leave the grapes in bunches, if possible) and pour in a spiced vinegar that has been brought to the boil – you can make your own or use a commercial one. Be sure to seal immediately whilst the vinegar is over 80°C. Leave the grapes in the jar for 6 weeks to mature; they will last for up to 12 months. I prefer a large black grape for this, such as Black Prince. I also like to preserve grapes using verjuice, rather than water. This gives me not only lovely sweet–sour grapes, but every bit of the verjuice can be used in sauces or pot-roasting.

Grapes team well with offal such as duck livers or hearts, or even sweetbreads, as the freshness of the grapes cuts through the richness of the offal. Just cook the livers, hearts or sweetbreads as normal and, 30 seconds before serving, throw a handful of grapes picked from the stem into the pan. If you want to go to a little more trouble, you could present the grapes in a little pastry tart. I love to toss grapes in at the last moment when making a sauce for chicken, pigeon, quail, pheasant or guinea fowl. Or try grapes in a stuffing – add them to the traditional breadcrumbs with onions, fresh tarragon and an egg to bind. Pour verjuice over the skin of the chicken three-quarters of the way through the cooking (¼ cup for a large bird).

At vintage, I always try to use the grape in every way I can. We now even make our own non-alcoholic 'bubbles' – based on verjuice. It began life as Desert Pearls but is now called Sparkling Ruby Cabernet and has a wonderfully fruity nose, with the mouthfeel of wine and a dry finish, for those times when you don't want to drink wine. And as much as I am proud of my quince, cabernet, fig and blood plum pastes to go with cheese, during vintage I'd rather serve a bunch of fresh grapes alongside.

At this time of year I also make a simple butter cake that includes fresh sultana grapes, which keep the cake so moist it lasts a week. For another sure-fire hit, coat fresh sultana grapes with a little honey and a squeeze of lemon juice and put them under the grill until caramelised. Serve with cream or mascarpone for an instant dessert.

SCHIACCIATA

Makes 2 loaves

One of the treats for me at this time of year is to add wine grapes to cakes, desserts and festive breads. The Italians are fond of this combination too: the famous Tuscan bread *schiacciata con l'uova* sees a little sugar and olive oil added to a yeast dough studded with the region's sangiovese grapes. The bread is cooked until the edges are just burnt, so that it isn't oversweet and its surface appears dimpled.

20 g fresh yeast *or* 2 teaspoons dried yeast

180 ml warm water

25 g castor sugar

150 ml extra virgin olive oil

2 tablespoons finely chopped rosemary,
    plus small sprigs to scatter

2⅔ cups (400 g) strong flour
    (see Glossary)

pinch salt

1 kg ripe black grapes, washed
    and stems removed

Combine the yeast, warm water and 1 teaspoon castor sugar in a small bowl and set aside for 5–10 minutes until frothy. Gently warm the olive oil and chopped rosemary in a saucepan over low heat for 5 minutes, then leave to cool.

Place the flour and salt in a bowl, then make a well and add the yeast mixture and half of the rosemary-infused oil. Add 400 g of the grapes and mix vigorously, then turn the dough out onto a well-floured bench. Knead the grapes into the dough for 5 minutes (don't try using a dough hook as it will smash the grapes) – it will be very soft and sticky.

Return the dough to the cleaned and lightly oiled bowl and brush it with a little rosemary oil. Cover the bowl with plastic film and allow the dough to rise slowly in a draught-free place for 1½–2 hours, or until doubled in volume.

Turn out the dough and divide it into two portions (there is no need to knock it back). Generously brush 2 ovenproof frying pans or 24 cm springform cake tins with rosemary oil and, using your hands, flatten the dough over the base of each. Push the remaining grapes into the surface of the dough. Generously brush the dough with the remaining rosemary oil, then sprinkle over the rosemary sprigs and 1 tablespoon castor sugar. Leave to rise in a draught-free spot for about 30 minutes. Meanwhile, preheat the oven to 220°C.

Place the loaves on a baking tray, as the juices from the grapes will bubble up and may overflow. Bake for 20 minutes, then reduce the temperature to 180°C and bake for another 10 minutes. Slide out onto a wire rack and serve warm or at room temperature.

ALMOND AND GARLIC SOUP WITH GRAPES

Serves 4

At harvest time, as it would so often still be very hot, I loved to make this cold soup with seedless grapes for lunch. I first saw this recipe in the *Time Life Fruit Book,* but it is a well-known tradition of the Mediterranean. It is made a little like a mayonnaise, and if it is too thick it calls for iced water to be stirred in just before serving; I substitute chilled verjuice instead. It should be just like a gazpacho in thickness. The grapes are added at the last moment and they sink to the bottom very quickly – try to serve the soup straightaway, as the bobbing grapes add so much to the dish.

250 g bread, cut from a baguette

milk, for soaking

2 large cloves garlic, peeled

150 g almonds, roasted for flavour
   (I use skins and all)

2 tablespoons white-wine vinegar

½ cup (125 ml) extra virgin olive oil

sea salt flakes (optional)

iced water *or* ice blocks made of verjuice

200 g sultana grapes (I prefer them green; if they have turned yellow, they will be over-ripe for this dish)

Soak the bread in milk for 20 minutes. Gently squeeze the milk out of the bread, then put the bread in the blender with the garlic, almonds and vinegar. With the motor running, add the oil slowly until well blended. Add salt if required, then refrigerate. Just before serving, pour in iced water or add ice blocks of verjuice to suit desired taste and consistency. Add the grapes to the soup immediately prior to serving.

GRAPE GROWER'S CHICKEN   *Serves 4*

The cooking of poultry with grapes is well documented in French and Italian cookbooks. In particular, game birds such as pheasant, guinea fowl or partridge go with grapes or their juice in classic combinations: the fruit is either cooked with the bird (added at the last minute just to warm through) or a bunch of grapes is squeezed into the pan in the final moments of cooking. If you grow your own grapes, freeze some to use this way later in the year. Verjuice gives the same flavour and adds a desirable piquancy. If you wish to make this dish when grapes are out of season, take ½ cup raisins and soak them overnight in some verjuice. Add these to the sauce in the last 5 minutes of cooking. This recipe can also be made with pheasant.

180 ml verjuice *or* 1 kg unripe sultana grapes, to yield 180 ml verjuice

walnut oil, for cooking

1 tablespoon butter

sea salt flakes and freshly ground black pepper

4 large chicken marylands, thighs and drumsticks separated

¾ cup (180 ml) reduced Golden Chicken Stock (see page 181)

100 g unsalted butter, cubed and chilled (optional)

1 cup sultana grapes, to add to the sauce

If making your own verjuice, pick the green grapes off the stem, discarding any that are spoiled, and blend and strain the grapes to yield 180 ml juice. Heat enough walnut oil and butter to just cover the bottom of a heavy-based saucepan, season the chicken pieces and gently seal them over low–medium heat until golden brown. Add the verjuice and stock and gently braise the chicken, covered, over low heat. Be careful not to let the skin stick or the verjuice caramelise – if this starts to happen, add a touch more stock or water. Cook for about 20 minutes, or until tender and cooked through, and then remove the chicken pieces from the pan and set aside on a separate dish to rest, covered, for about 10 minutes.

Reduce the juices over high heat. Whisk in the chilled butter to 'velvet' the sauce while it is boiling rapidly (the butter is optional in these health-conscious days). Throw in the grapes in the last few seconds and serve the chicken with the sauce, along with a salad and boiled waxy potatoes in their jackets.

SHERI'S ROTEGRÜTZE *Serves 4*

Rotegrütze is a local Barossa dessert made with leftover mataro or shiraz grapes at the end of vintage. It is such a simple dessert, using only the cooked grape, which is puréed and then simmered with sago. It's taken so seriously that there is a rotegrütze competition at the Tanunda Show each year. This dish is particularly significant because the Silesian immigrants brought the tradition of rotegrütze with them, but rather than making it with the berries traditionally used in their homeland, they adapted the dish to use the grapes they grew. A base of 550 ml grape juice and 2 tablespoons sago will serve 4.

very ripe black grapes (preferably shiraz)   **sago**

To extract the juice from the grapes, either use the finest setting on a food mill or purée the grapes in a food processor, and then strain through a sieve, pushing down on the solids to extract as much juice as possible. If a large amount of juice is required, gently heat whole bunches of grapes in a large saucepan until the grapes are soft enough that their stems can be pulled away easily. This mixture can then be strained and the skins and seeds discarded. This juice will be thicker than the juice made using a food mill.

Measure the juice into a stainless steel saucepan and bring it gently to a simmer over low heat. For every 550 ml juice gradually stir in 2 tablespoons sago. Simmer gently, stirring occasionally, for 45–50 minutes or until the sago is clear.

Pour the rotegrütze into a serving dish and leave it to cool, then chill in the refrigerator and leave it to set slightly. Serve with rich, runny cream.

GUINEA FOWL

GUINEA FOWL MAKE GREAT WATCHDOGS. I DEFY ANYONE TO sneak into a property that has guinea fowl in the yard. I'm sure some country people choose to have them for just this reason, and the bonus is that they are delicious to eat, and a nice change from mutton or chook.

In my experience, the French prefer guinea fowl to pheasant, and although this was a debate I once preferred to stay out of given that my restaurant was called the Pheasant Farm, we often bred our own guinea fowl for the menu. It wasn't until I spent time in both France and Italy – where my husband Colin and I enjoyed many holidays with friends, and we would cook the local guinea fowl, which was so plump and luscious – that I understood why it is so revered in these countries. We would rent a villa so that we could experience the joy of shopping at the local markets and cooking; we did this so enthusiastically we had to draw up a roster for who would have the privilege of cooking each day.

The guinea fowl we found in these markets, even though exactly the same genus as those found at home, were vastly superior, as the Australian stocks have had no new bloodlines introduced. This is for good reason, though – our authorities have tried to protect Australia from Newcastle's disease (a highly contagious virus that affects poultry and game) by not allowing the importation of poultry, with a blanket ban that lasted over 50 years. Although some poultry importation is now allowed, only the large poultry industries can afford the huge costs involved. This means that guinea fowl, pheasants and other game birds are not likely ever to be as good here as their counterparts in Europe. Having said that, they still have a wonderful flavour and I'd compare them to wild rabbit, in that they are both delicious but are trickier to cook than guinea fowl from Europe, which, along with farmed rabbit, are luscious enough even when overcooked, as can often unwittingly happen in the hands of the less experienced cook.

When cooked with care, guinea fowl is sweet, moist and delicious and marries particularly well with orange, lemon, thyme, rosemary or bay leaves, walnuts, liver and pancetta or bacon. It can be pot-roasted or baked, but not grilled as it doesn't have enough fat to remain moist.

It is easy to confuse raw guinea fowl and pheasant as their skin colour and leg meat are similar. Guinea fowl can be identified by the dark black spots on the skin of the upper breast and under the wings. Its breast is whiter, and the meat more delicate in taste, texture and structure than the pheasant's.

When buying guinea fowl, it is very important that you are aware of its age. At 12 to 14 weeks it is perfect to oven roast – any older and it will require pot-roasting. Farmers who keep only a few birds often let their flocks run together, which makes the birds' ages hard to gauge. It is also unusually difficult to determine the sex of guinea fowl, as males and females are identical to the untrained eye (and even to some very experienced eyes). This makes keeping breeding stock rather haphazard. Recently though I saw a program on British TV, *The View From River Cottage* (Channel 4), where a farmer was shown holding a young chicken, whose sex at that stage was unknown. The farmer placed a piece of white paper under the neck feathers in much the same way as a hairdresser would select one section of hair at a time and, when just a layer of feathers was accented by the paper, the rounded feathers showed the chicken was a hen (as pointy feathers would show it was a cockerel). I suspect this might well be the case with all poultry.

In Australia, a guinea fowl usually weighs 600 g to 1 kg. You really need a bird of at least 750 g to feed two people. Although some farms breed 450 g birds for single serves, I personally wouldn't bother, as these immature birds lack flavour. Incidentally, it is best to steer clear of frozen guinea fowl: although many types of game freeze fairly well, the guinea fowl has much less meat on its bones than, say, a pheasant or a duck, and so does not freeze successfully. Don't forget guinea fowl eggs – scrambled or pickled, they are a great treat. They are larger than quail eggs, yet smaller than chook eggs, and very creamy.

Very few cookbooks contain recipes for guinea fowl. Most chicken or pheasant recipes can be interchanged with guinea fowl, but as they have less flesh and little fat, guinea fowl will need a shorter cooking time or a lower temperature. Brush with a marinade of extra virgin olive oil and orange juice, lemon juice or verjuice and salt. This is both for flavour and to caramelise the skin. If you wish, marinate the bird first and add herbs or spices of your choice. My favourite additions are rosemary, thyme and citrus rind.

LIVER CROSTINI   *Serves 4*

200 g guinea fowl *or* chicken livers,
    cleaned and cut into quarters
8 sage leaves, finely chopped
150 g butter
1 tablespoon red-wine vinegar

1 tablespoon capers, drained
2 anchovy fillets, finely chopped
1 tablespoon flat-leaf parsley, chopped
4 slices of baguette

Preheat the oven to 220°C. Melt 75 g of the butter and brush one side of each bread slice with melted butter, then bake on a baking tray until golden.

Fry the livers and sage in a frying pan over high heat in the remaining butter until just pink (a bit over a minute on each side), then set aside to rest for 3–4 minutes. Add the vinegar, capers, anchovies and parsley. Serve on top of the baked croutons.

GUINEA FOWL IN ONION, GARLIC AND PROSCIUTTO SOFREGIT   *Serves 4*

Here I have borrowed the principle of a sofregit (usually based on olive oil, onion and tomato) from Colman Andrews' *Catalan Cuisine* and adapted it to cooking with game birds.

2 × 900 g guinea fowl
extra virgin olive oil, for cooking
6 sprigs thyme, leaves picked
1 lemon, thinly sliced
4 onions, finely chopped
3 heads garlic, separated into cloves
    and peeled
juice of ½ lemon

1 cup (250 ml) verjuice
1½ cups (375 ml) Golden Chicken Stock
    (see page 181)
4 fresh bay leaves
100 g prosciutto, cut into 5 cm-long strips
sea salt flakes and freshly ground
    black pepper
freshly chopped flat-leaf parsley, to serve

Rub the guinea fowl with olive oil, thyme leaves and sliced lemon, then cover and set aside in the fridge for 2 hours.

Pour about 1 cm olive oil into the base of a heavy-based cast-iron or enamelled casserole, then sweat onion and garlic cloves gently over low heat until softened and golden brown. Remove and set aside.

Cook the guinea fowl over low–medium heat in the casserole for 8–10 minutes, or until browned all over, adding olive oil as needed. Add the lemon juice, verjuice and stock to the pan and reduce by half over high heat, then add the bay leaves, a quarter of the prosciutto, and the onion and garlic mixture. Season with salt and pepper if needed. Simmer, covered, over low heat for about 10 minutes. Turn the guinea fowl over and simmer for another 10 minutes, then check for 'doneness' – they are cooked when the thighs pull away from the breast easily, and the thickest part of the breast feels springy to the touch. If the guinea fowl

Guinea fowl in onion, garlic and prosciutto sofregit

are not cooked, turn them back over to the other side and cook for another 5 minutes. Remove guinea fowl and set aside, covered. Reduce the sauce over high heat for 10 minutes or until it reaches a sticky consistency. Add the remaining prosciutto and check seasoning.

Cut the guinea fowl in half, then carve the breasts and legs off the frames and serve with the reduced sauce and lots of chopped flat-leaf parsley.

STUFFED GUINEA FOWL WITH RED-WINE SAUCE *Serves 4*

The very first guinea fowl we ever sold in the early days of our farm was to some French customers who were kind enough to pass on their method of cooking it. They made a stuffing of onions, walnuts, juniper berries and the livers of the guinea fowl. This is a dish I have reproduced many times and I love the combination of flavours. Using such a stuffing, I might then serve the bird with a red-wine sauce.

If you prefer not to stuff the bird you could serve a Liver Crostini (see page 54) with the bird and the sauce.

2 × 900 g guinea fowl

STUFFING
1 large onion, finely chopped
1 sprig rosemary
butter, for cooking
200 g guinea fowl livers *or* chicken livers,
    cleaned and roughly chopped
3 juniper berries, crushed
sea salt flakes and freshly ground
    black pepper
½ cup (50 g) walnuts, roasted and
    skins rubbed off
100 g coarse, roasted breadcrumbs

SAUCE
200 ml red wine
50 ml port
1 tablespoon redcurrant jelly
1 tablespoon Dijon mustard
juice of ½ lemon
1 cup (250 ml) well-reduced game stock
butter (optional), for cooking

Preheat the oven to 180°C. For the stuffing, sauté the onion and rosemary in a frying pan in a generous amount of butter. Quickly toss in the livers for about 30 seconds on each side to seal, then set aside to rest. Add the crushed juniper berries, salt and pepper, then add the walnuts and breadcrumbs. Stuff the guinea fowl and sprinkle with salt.

Roast the birds in a roasting pan on one side first for 10 minutes, then turn onto the other side and roast for another 10 minutes. Sit the birds breast-side up and cook for another 6–10 minutes. They are cooked when the thighs pull away from the breast easily and the thickest part of the breast feels springy to the touch. At the end of the cooking period I like to turn the birds upside-down in the roasting pan, covered loosely with foil, and leave them for about 20 minutes before carving them.

To make the sauce, reduce the red wine and port by three-quarters in a saucepan over high heat, then whisk in the redcurrant jelly, mustard, lemon juice and stock. Bring to a rapid boil and reduce a little more. If you wish to 'velvet' the sauce, whisk in some butter.

GUINEA FOWL WITH CÈPE BUTTER AND
GOLDEN SHALLOTS
Serves 6

finely chopped rind and juice of 2 oranges

2 tablespoons extra virgin olive oil

6 fresh bay leaves

12 sprigs thyme

2 teaspoons crushed juniper berries

3 × 800 g *or* 2 × 1.3 kg guinea fowl

1 kg golden shallots, peeled

sea salt flakes and freshly ground
   black pepper

1 litre reduced Golden Chicken Stock
   (see page 181)

½ cup (125 ml) verjuice, plus extra
   for deglazing

CÈPE BUTTER

50 g dried cèpes

verjuice, for soaking

200 g softened unsalted butter, chopped

2 tablespoons extra virgin olive oil

sea salt flakes and freshly ground
   black pepper

3 sprigs thyme, leaves picked

For the cèpe butter, cover the dried cèpes with verjuice and leave overnight to reconstitute.

Put the orange rind, orange juice, olive oil, bay leaves, thyme sprigs and juniper berries in a bowl and stir to combine. Place the birds in a glass or ceramic dish and pour over the marinade, then leave to marinate for at least 2 hours.

To make the cèpe butter, strain the cèpes, reserving the verjuice, then roughly chop. Sauté the cèpes in a frying pan in a little of the butter and the olive oil over medium heat, season with salt and pepper then deglaze the pan with the reserved verjuice. Cook for another 2 minutes or until the verjuice becomes syrupy. Place the cèpes (including any pan juices) and butter in a food processor and blend, then add the thyme leaves and blend again.

Remove the guinea fowl from the marinade and loosen the skin from the breasts and thighs. Ease the cèpe butter carefully under the skin of each breast and finish with a final rub all over the outside of the skin. Place the guinea fowl in a roasting pan and return to the refrigerator for 1 hour to let the butter firm.

Preheat the oven to 180°C. Add the shallots to the roasting pan. Season the birds and roast them on one side first for 10 minutes, then turn onto the other side and roast for another 10 minutes. Sit the birds breast-side up and roast for a further 6–10 minutes. They are cooked when the thighs pull away from the breast easily and the thickest part of the breast feels springy to the touch. »

Transfer the birds and shallots from the roasting pan to another dish, placing the birds breast-side down. Pour in ¼ cup of the stock (warmed) and ¼ cup verjuice, cover loosely with foil and rest for 20 minutes. To make the sauce, heat the roasting pan over high heat, deglaze with remaining ¼ cup verjuice, add the balance of the stock and reduce by half, then add the resting juices. Carve the birds by separating the legs from the breasts, then the thighs from the drumsticks. Carve the breasts from the frames and serve with thigh meat, sauce, shallots and vino cotto-glazed radicchio.

If not serving immediately, you can leave the guinea fowl to cool completely. Carve off the bone, leaving the guinea fowl breasts cut-side down in a little of the jus in the base of the pan. Save the bones to make stock. Before serving, place in a 180°C oven to warm with just a little of the sauce for a few minutes, then serve with the remaining reduced sauce.

HARE

'VIGNERON'S REVENGE' IS AN INTERNATIONALLY RECOGNISED tradition in the wine industry. At the 1996 Melbourne Food and Wine Festival, Italian winemaker Paolo di Marchi from the Isole e Olena winery in Chianti talked of the satisfaction he got from eating wild boar, which regularly decimate his vines. James Halliday talks of wine-maker Bailey Carrodus traditionally serving an end-of-vintage pie full of the starlings and blackbirds that plague his crop in the Yarra Valley. For us in the Barossa, the hare is our curse. Hares and, of course, rabbits, nibble the young vines and over the years have caused us a great number of setbacks. I love eating hare – but not only because of its love of tender new shoots.

When we had the Pheasant Farm Restaurant I put the word out that I would buy any hare (usually only shot for dog meat) brought to the kitchen door. The parameters were clear: only head shots were paid the premium price and no pellet shot was allowed. I always became very tense when deliveries would arrive at the restaurant during the busy lunch service, but the one exception I made was for a vigneron with a hare. Mind you, the many requests for a wine-makers' dinner of saddle of hare always left me anxious to the last that I would have enough. These days one can order wild hare (in small quantities only) through a game supplier or top-class butcher.

I prefer to hang hare skin on and with guts intact for a week in cool-room conditions. In the restaurant I gave enthusiastic would-be cooks something of a test by asking them to stand by my side while I gutted a hare: if they were not squeamish, I felt they deserved a chance (remember, mine was a game restaurant!). Many of the locals who ate hare at home at the time soaked it first in milk or vinegar and water to make the meat paler and rid it of strong game flavours. Not me – I think the flavour of a rare-roasted saddle of hare, where the meat is ruby-red, is one of the greatest game experiences of one's life.

Renowned chef Cheong Liew has been a great source of inspiration over the years and his depth of knowledge never ceases to amaze me. During a class on game I conducted with him years ago when he taught at Regency Park College of TAFE in Adelaide, he told me about the Chinese tradition of curing hare, skin intact but gutted, hanging between hams as they smoked. I sent my very next hare delivered in the skin to Schulz's, the Barossa's wonderful butcher and smallgoods manufacturer. I didn't put it in brine first and merely had it cold-smoked for three days. The resulting meat from the saddle had the most amazing texture – almost like butter. Not everyone shared my enthusiasm for it, finding it over-rich, but I'm not sure those words were in my vocabulary then, although they are now. I can still taste the hare as I sit here writing and can imagine it being served with a spiced plum sauce.

Jugged hare, that speciality of the English, is jointed hare marinated (jugged) in wine and herbs before being cooked very slowly with vegetables. However, recipes often omit the main ingredient required for authenticity: the blood of the hare. If the hare has already been gutted – or paunched, as they say in more polite circles – then it must be quite fresh if any blood is to be collected from behind the 'lights' (lungs). Once the blood has been drained, half a teaspoon of vinegar is added to keep it fresh while the hare is hanging.

The first time I served jugged hare was at the request of a graduating class of commercial cooks, inspired by Trish Vietch, a member of the class and an outstanding student who had worked with both Phillip Searle and Cheong Liew. How I wish every class would ask for such a menu: it was entirely local, in season, balanced and adventurous. Beginning with salsify (a type of root vegetable) teamed with South Australian oysters and oyster mushrooms, it moved on to jugged hare with noodles and baby beetroot and was followed by game consommé as a palate cleanser. Pears poached in sherry with ginger finished the meal.

In many books hare and rabbit are used interchangeably. Although they have much the same body configuration, and are both at their best when the legs are cooked separately from the body (or saddle), there is actually a huge difference in flavour. Rabbit is pale, sweet and moist, whereas hare is dark, robust and gamy, and has a dense texture.

A very young (and therefore small) hare is quite wonderful baked whole. However, as young hare is not always available, I find the best method is to separate the legs from the saddle, and cook the front legs together as a confit, and the back legs long and slowly in a crockpot. Alternatively, if you wish to take the trouble to separate the muscles from each back leg and remove the sinew, you can then slice the meat and pan-fry it. This works best with hare that has been hung for a while. The saddle, as mentioned earlier, can be roasted rare.

If cooking the saddle of hare on the bone, it is essential that you first remove the sinew that protects the meat. This can be quite tricky but gets easier with practice, and is not unlike taking the sinew off a fillet of beef or skinning a fish. It is best undertaken with a long, thin, flexible knife – ideally either a fish or boning knife. There are two layers of sinew, and the trick is to get the knife under both layers and strip them off together. The meat should then be moistened with extra virgin olive oil and black pepper or bruised juniper berries and left to sit a while before roasting; it can, in fact, be left in the refrigerator for anything from a few hours to a few days. The fillets can be taken off the bone of the saddle (they are often referred to as backstraps). Once stripped of their sinew, hare fillets only take minutes to pan-fry in nut-brown butter. However, cooking the saddle whole then carving it off the bone after resting is the ultimate way to go.

Hare marries well with strong flavours such as port, red wine, sherry, balsamic or red-wine vinegar, bacon and mustard. Try cooking sliced golden shallots slowly in a little extra virgin olive oil and butter until almost caramelised. Scatter the sinew-free hare fillets with some chopped herbs, then season and seal them in the pan with the shallots over high heat. Turn the heat down to medium and turn the fillets over – depending on the thickness of the fillets, the cooking will only take 4–6 minutes in total. Remove the meat from the pan and leave it to rest for the same length of time it took to cook, then deglaze the pan with a good sherry or balsamic vinegar. Serve the hare fillets and the pan juices with fresh noodles.

Dare I write about the Hare Pies (see page 64) I made that didn't work? I was cooking a baroque banquet in the Octavius cellar at Yalumba, for 120 guests who were to see Purcell's opera *Indian Queen* as part of the 1995 Barossa Music Festival. And it was meant to be my last-ever big function (that still hasn't quite happened!). There were no kitchen facilities other than a barbecue, so the hare pies and sides of saltbush mutton had to be ferried from various ovens several kilometres away. We couldn't even tip any water down the drains for fear of interrupting the normal workings of the winery, so had to transport the dirty dishes back to the main Yalumba kitchen.

I planned to use Stephanie Alexander's wonderful lard pastry to encase sweet–sour hare and its incredibly rich stock. But I had forgotten to check whether the pastry could be made with a food processor: it tasted sublime but it fell apart! Not quite the ornately decorated pies I'd envisaged: we had to spoon the hare onto plates and balance the delicious but crumbling pastry on top. I felt every bit as bad as the pastry looked.

The real highlight of the night for me was the pure theatre going on 'behind the scenes' in the cellar, as the opera proceeded in the adjoining room. All the guests had to walk through the Octavius cellar on their way to the opera, and as only half of them had booked for the banquet, I wanted them all to experience the grandeur of the room (built in 1895, it has a soaring roof and rows of barrels lining each side, leaving only a narrow central aisle), whilst still keeping an element of surprise for those who were coming to dinner. As the guests walked through, candelabras stood sentinel along the length of the room, and the slow carriage of these people walking through, two or three abreast and filling the length of the room, with the heady aroma of maturing wine in the air, was a spectacle in itself.

Once the opera had begun, all our work 'backstage' in the cellar had to be undertaken in silence. We only had an hour and a quarter to transform the empty walkway into one long table draped with white linen and set for a banquet. The tables, handmade by Yalumba carpenters to fit exactly between the pillars that run down the central aisle, had to be installed using muffled wooden mallets. The staff, led by Colin, all garbed in academic gowns and jabots (the closest thing to period costume we could devise) noiselessly recovered the cutlery, glasses and linen from behind the barrels where they'd been hidden from view and put them all in place without a word spoken and with lots of pointing. Everyone hurried silently in the dim light of the candles. The dirt floor was dampened regularly so that no dust would be seen on the glasses, and noisier tasks such as putting bottles into ice barrels were timed to coincide with the crescendos of the orchestra. Suffice to say we were keyed up to fever pitch by the time the opera finished. Hare pies aside, it was a night to remember and would have been a wonderful way to bow out.

HARE COOKED IN DUCK FAT   *Serves 8*

This very rich meat is good with pasta, gnocchi, spätzle or polenta. Any leftover meat can be steeped in the duck fat and kept refrigerated for up to several months.

2 × 2 kg hares

extra virgin olive oil, for cooking

freshly ground black pepper

2 litres duck fat

1 clove garlic, crushed

2 teaspoons bruised juniper berries

2 small sprigs rosemary

sea salt flakes

2 cups (500 ml) reduced Golden Chicken
   Stock (see page 181)

10 pickled walnuts in brine, including
   a little pickling liquid (see page 161)

Joint the hares, separating the front and back legs from each saddle. Trim the sinew from the saddle, then rub the meat with olive oil and pepper and set it aside to be cooked separately. Melt the duck fat in an enamelled casserole, camp oven or crockpot on the stove. Add the garlic to the duck fat with the front and back hare legs, juniper berries and rosemary, then season. Cook for 2–4 hours over low heat until the hare almost comes off the bone. (As wild game is of an indeterminate age it is only by feel that you will know when each leg is tender.)

When ready to serve, preheat the oven to 230°C. Make sure the saddles are well oiled, then seal them in a heavy-based roasting pan on the stove. Transfer the dish to the oven and roast the saddles for 5 minutes. Remove the dish from the oven – if the meat is still not 'set' (it should be firm to the touch), turn the saddles over and return them to the oven for another 3 minutes. Rest the meat for 10 minutes before serving.

While the saddles are resting, reduce the oven temperature to 200°C. Warm the hare legs in the oven for about 5 minutes only, on an enamelled plate or similar to allow any excess duck fat to melt away. Reduce the stock with just a little of the walnut pickling liquid by half over high heat. Pull the muscles of the legs apart and reject any that are sinewy (the larger muscle is always so). Put the legs and saddles on a serving dish and pour over the reduced stock. Garnish with sliced pickled walnuts to taste and serve with mashed potato, parsnip or celeriac and a salad of bitter greens.

HARE WITH PINE NUTS, LEMON AND SULTANAS

Serves 4

This is one of my favourite dishes using hare and is the result of combining two recipes – one from Elizabeth David's *Italian Food* (I have borrowed the title of her recipe) and the other from Ada Boni's *Italian Regional Cooking* (hare in sweet-and-sour sauce). The addition of chocolate will give another dimension of flavour to the dish rather than make it taste of chocolate.

1 × 2 kg hare (including heart,
    lungs and liver)
extra virgin olive oil, for cooking
1½ tablespoons sugar
½ cup (125 ml) red-wine vinegar
2 tablespoons pine nuts
2 tablespoons sultanas
30 g bitter chocolate
freshly ground black pepper

MARINADE FOR HARE
2 onions, roughly chopped
3 sticks celery, roughly chopped
3 sprigs rosemary
3 stalks flat-leaf parsley
600 ml red wine

MARINADE FOR OFFAL
rind of 1 lemon, chopped
150 ml red wine
1 tablespoon pine nuts
1 tablespoon sultanas
½ teaspoon sugar
pinch ground cinnamon
4 cloves

Joint the hare, separating the front and back legs from the saddle. Trim the sinew from the saddle. To make the marinade for the hare, combine the onion, celery, rosemary, parsley and red wine with the hare. To make the marinade for the offal, combine the marinade ingredients. Dice the heart, lungs and liver (if no gall bladder is attached) and add to this marinade. Marinate both the hare and the offal in the refrigerator overnight.

Drain and dry the hare, reserving the marinade. In a large enamelled heavy-based casserole, gently brown the hare legs in 125 ml olive oil over low–medium heat, then turn up the heat, add the vegetables from the marinade and cook at a high temperature until burnished, then add the marinade. Add the offal and its marinade and cook very, very slowly on the stove top over the lowest heat possible (use a simmer pad if you have one), turning the hare several times, for 2–4 hours. (As wild game is of an indeterminate age it is only by feel that you will know when each leg is tender.) »

Preheat the oven to 250°C. In a small enamelled or stainless steel saucepan, slowly dissolve the sugar in the vinegar over low heat, then add the pine nuts and sultanas. Strain the liquid from the cooked hare legs into another saucepan and bring it to a rolling boil over high heat to reduce it if necessary – it should be thick enough to coat the meat. (Alternatively, the vegetables and cooking liquid can be put through a food mill and returned to the pan to warm through.) Stir the vinegar syrup into the cooking juices, then check for balance and add the chocolate.

Rub olive oil, salt and pepper into the saddle, then seal it over high heat in a heavy-based roasting pan on the stove. Transfer the dish to the oven and roast the saddle for 5 minutes. Remove the dish from the oven – if the meat is still 'unset' (it should be firm to the touch), turn the saddle over and return it to the oven for another 3 minutes. Rest the meat for 10 minutes before serving. Carve the saddle and add it to the leg meat, then pour over the sauce. This dish is great served with parsnips.

HARE PIE

Serves 4

The famous hare pie. Stephanie Alexander's pastry is like a traditional one from the north of England: it has a flaky tender crust and is somewhat biscuit-like. Don't, whatever you do, repeat my mistake of trying to make it in a food processor – by hand only!

1 × 2 kg hare

extra virgin olive oil, for cooking

250 g large flat mushrooms

2 sprigs thyme, leaves picked and chopped

sea salt flakes and freshly ground
    black pepper

125 g sugar-cured bacon, rind removed
    and meat cut into 2.5 cm cubes

12 golden shallots, peeled

1 tablespoon redcurrant jelly

butter, for cooking

1 tablespoon plain flour

1 egg, beaten with a little milk

SAUCE

1 large onion, roughly chopped

1 large carrot, roughly chopped

1 stick celery, roughly chopped

4 juniper berries, bruised

extra virgin olive oil, for cooking

150 ml red wine

50 ml port

2 cups (500 ml) reduced veal stock

STEPHANIE'S LARD PASTRY

200 g plain flour

200 g self-raising flour

pinch salt

200 g lard, at room temperature

180 ml cold water

To make the pastry, sift the flours together with the salt onto a work surface, then quickly rub in the lard. Make a well in the centre and work in the cold water, then knead the mixture for 2–3 minutes until you have a fairly soft, springy and elastic dough. Form the dough into a ball, then wrap it in plastic film and chill for 20 minutes before rolling.

Joint the hare, separating the front and back legs from the saddle. Using a sharp knife, follow the contours of the backbone and take the fillet off the saddle in a single piece, then remove the two layers of sinew. Smother the fillet with a little olive oil to keep it moist and set it aside. Dissect the back legs into their three main muscles. Trim away the sinew, then slice the meat across the grain, drizzle it with olive oil and put aside with the fillet. Chop the saddle, front legs and bones from the back legs into 5 cm pieces.

Preheat the oven to 220°C. To make the sauce, combine the onion, carrot, celery, bruised juniper berries and chopped hare bones in a roasting pan and drizzle with olive oil. Roast for 30–40 minutes until well caramelised. Deglaze the pan with the wine and port and reduce over high heat to a syrup. Add the reduced veal stock to the pan and boil vigorously until thick and luscious, then strain the sauce and leave it to cool.

Toss the mushrooms with the thyme and season. Render the bacon in a dry frying pan over high heat, then set aside the bacon and caramelise the shallots in the fat. Stir in the redcurrant jelly and leave it to melt, then set aside.

Thickly slice the hare fillet and seal it in a little olive oil and butter in another frying pan. Put the fillet aside, then seal the leg meat and set it aside too. Sprinkle the flour into the hot pan, then add the bacon, the shallot mixture and the mushrooms. Immediately remove the pan from the heat and stir in the strained sauce. Let the mixture cool, then carefully combine it with the meat and transfer it to an ovenproof pie dish.

Preheat the oven to 200°C. Roll out the chilled pastry and cut a lid to fit the pie dish. Brush the edge of the dish with the egg wash made by beating the egg with a little milk, then carefully place the pastry lid over the pie dish. Press the edges firmly and brush the surface with the egg wash. Bake the pie for 15 minutes, then lower the temperature to 180°C and bake for another 15 minutes. The filling needs only to be heated up in this process, so as soon as the pastry is cooked the pie is ready to eat.

MUSHROOMS

WILD FOOD – FORAGING FOR IT AND THEN COOKING THE BOUNTY – is one of my great loves. I remember well our first local mushroom sortie. It was a long weekend in the Barossa, and streams of people were walking through the trails of the forest yet, to my surprise, we were the only ones gathering mushrooms. What a different experience it was from walking in the woods of Umbria, on our first holiday there in 1995, where the hunt was intense. On a seemingly deserted mountainside the silence would suddenly be broken by the put-putting of small motorised bikes with baskets on the back to carry the spoils. Some gatherers were so secretive that, as we walked past, they stopped searching and pretended to be just contemplating the sky. Others proudly displayed their finds and pointed out where they had come from.

While autumn is generally believed to be the optimum season for mushrooms, all that is needed for a new flush of heads to peek provocatively from the ground is the right amount of rain and a burst of warmish sunshine.

I think foraging for food is an undervalued activity. So much goes to waste in the forest and it seems a great shame. We always go mushrooming on a weekday and we are often the only people around. It is wonderfully eerie to walk into the woods through the long straight rows of trees. The pine needles are so thick on the ground that they cushion your feet and it is so silent that you feel you are walking on air, as if you are floating. The pine trees are so tall they tend to block out the sun but every now and then powerful shafts of sunlight push through and add to the ethereal atmosphere.

You will definitely need some advice about what to pick and what to leave behind and it is important that you either gather scientific information from a book and study it carefully, or find a friend who already has the mushrooming bug and has become what English gastronome and opera critic Paul Levy calls a 'fungi bore'.

For over 30 years, my mushroom adviser has been my great friend Peter Wall, now retired from Yalumba. He has, all his Barossa life at least, been a gourmet of note, and an

Smoked mushrooms with rosemary and thyme (see page 71)

avid cook with an encyclopaedic mind and a passion for mushrooms, so what better person to learn from? When our families went mushrooming I felt very safe. Times are changing, though, and if foraging for mushrooms appeals to you, you should first find out what sprays are being used in the pine forests where you usually find mushrooms. Some of the spots where we used to mushroom are now sprayed by light aircraft and I wouldn't be eating the mushrooms until I'd had them tested.

Years ago now, when I was already, I thought, a confident forager, I couldn't resist a class being offered at the Melbourne Hyatt by George Biron, then of Sunnybrae Restaurant in Victoria. I was stunned by the breadth of his knowledge and for the first time realised there were many varieties of the familiar field mushroom that were just as dangerous as some of the poisonous exotics. A sobering thought. Not only did George show us specimens he'd been hunting for days, both edible and poisonous, he cooked a selection and tantalised us with some bread he'd baked to accompany them, brushed with truffle oil as it came from the oven – its perfume so overpowering. Like all foods found in the wild, mushrooms can be over-harvested, so make sure you leave some of the spore-generating bodies intact, simply by leaving behind some of the less-perfect specimens.

FIRSTLY, WHAT NOT TO PICK

Amanita verna Commonly called Destroying Angel. This is a pure white, stately, often large species. The best way to describe these fungi is that they grow out of a cup which becomes visible when you brush away the grass from the stem. This egg-shaped cup, called the 'volva', holds the mushroom in place. Other *Amanita* species (all of which are poisonous), including the beautiful Fly Agaric (*A. muscaria*) with its large, bright-red cap with white spots, can also be found in Australia, so caution is necessary.

Puffballs Some are edible, some are not. Without an expert in tow, it is best to leave these alone.

WHAT YOU CAN PICK

What you can pick and enjoy includes far more than the common field mushroom.

Suillus (or Boletus) granulatas This mushroom grows in pine forests and has a reddish-brown cap with a yellow stalk and spores. The upper part of the stalk is distinguished by granules. Its texture is quite chewy or rubbery. It is great sliced into salads or pickled.

Suillus (or Boletus) luteus Commonly known as slippery jack. The cap is slimy and pine needles easily stick to it. It is a dark, dull, reddish-brown when young. The tubes are yellow and there is a ring of a purplish-brown colour on the stalk. Wipe the slime from the cap and remove the tubes before cooking. These slippery treasures are the cousin of the famous cèpe of France or porcini of Italy, and in their fresh state are considered the poor side of the family and rejected by many, yet I love the delicate earthy flavour they have when the small firm heads are picked.

As my cooking is driven by what is available locally, it is the slippery jack that has become a staple. As delicious as they are fried and tossed with freshly cooked pasta and extra virgin olive oil, used in soups and risotto, or brushed with a mixture of walnut oil and verjuice and then barbecued, they also have an amazing affinity with yabbies, marron or Murray cod. Larger mushrooms, if not too wet and spongy, are great for drying. You can be creative by either stringing them up to dry naturally – scrub out an incubator if you happen to have one or invest in an electric dehydrator that sits on the kitchen bench through the season – or simply resort to the oven and dry them overnight with the pilot light on.

Coprinus comartus Known as the ink cap mushroom, this is one of the best-flavoured mushrooms and is also the one most commonly left behind. It is often thought to be a toadstool, since it looks like a parasol with a shaggy white coat. As it grows older, the cap dissolves into an inky mass. This mushroom must be picked really young. It is so prevalent in the Barossa that I find specimens in the most unlikely places, such as in the grass around the export kitchen and at home, where they are so strong that they actually push up some of the large terrace tiles (which measure about 12 × 12 cm, so that's no mean feat). Sadly, by the time I see the tiles raised, the mushrooms are too mature to eat. When picked young, before they become truly inky, they have a great flavour.

Agaricus campestris and ***Agaricus robinsonii*** These are the common or garden, wonderfully tasty, field mushrooms that poke through the ground from as early as April, when the soil is still warm and the first rains occur. These are still most people's favourites as they are easy to recognise and don't require specialist knowledge in order to identify them. *A. campestris* has a white cap, and *A. robinsonii* a brownish cap, and is not as intensely flavoured. Peter Wall cooks these with butter, a fresh bay leaf and a splash of champagne. **A word of caution**: There is a robust mushroom (Yellow Stainer: *A. xanthoderma*) often seen in urban lawns, which, although a white-capped, pink-gilled *Agaricus*, can cause severe gastro-intestinal reactions in some people. This mushroom has squarish immature caps, and cut or bruised surfaces stain bright yellow. It should *not* be eaten.

There are also many native fungi but they are a mystery to all but traditional Aboriginal wisdom, plus botanists and scientists. I'd love to think that we might have something as special as the flavour of the *Boletus edulis*, which is commonly known by its French name, cèpe, or Italian name, porcini. There are also native morels (*Morchella* species), but although technically edible, they are disappointingly bland compared to their European relative, the Yellow Morel (*Morchella esculenta*).

I've often delighted in cooking my local *Boletus granulatas* or *Boletus luteus* picked in selected pine forests, and have dried bucket after bucket of the more mature specimens to great effect. I suspect these are even better than most imported dried cèpes/porcinis, which vary greatly in quality. In Australia I've rarely tasted dried cèpes/porcinis of the quality I've experienced in Europe. I have such a lingering 'flavour memory' of walking down a steep cobbled street – was it in southwest France or in Tuscany? My memory of the place eludes me but it was a market town at breakfast time, and in one of the ancient buildings someone was pan-frying these mushrooms in nut-brown butter; the smell of them cooking on the street as we passed

was the most beautiful mushroom smell I've ever experienced. I can smell it now as I write – quite wonderful.

And then there are those wild mushrooms I'm unable to name. During Tasting Australia in 1995 we had a riotous night in the Valley when Antonio Carluccio, the well-known television presenter and mushroom expert, came to stay. It happened to be a Wednesday night, which is the night of my singing group. So before we ate, singing took place and Antonio good-naturedly joined in, and then sat whittling a walking stick for me out of one of the saplings by the dam. There was so much activity that night and, as I had to prepare dinner for twelve after the singing was finished, there wasn't much talk of mushrooms until the next morning. Antonio had been out walking and came back with samples of tiny mushrooms that he said were very edible, which grow in what we've always called 'fairy circles'. One was quite dried out and full of aroma and the others still quite young, so after each rain now I'll wait until they have come into full circle and pick them. For inspiration in cooking wild mushrooms I can rec-ommend Antonio's book *A Passion for Mushrooms*. In his London shop he sells the perfect tool for mushrooming fanatics – it is a knife at one end and a brush at the other, to dust away any debris.

I really must emphasise, though: *always* check with an expert before you eat a wild mushroom, and if remotely unsure it's better not to experiment.

Mushrooms have so much flavour that they can be cooked very simply. A special break-fast can be made by simply pan-frying mushrooms in butter with freshly ground black pepper and serving them on toast. Elizabeth David suggests that if in spring or summer you yearn for field mushrooms, you can bake cultivated mushrooms in vine leaves and olive oil to give a wonderful earthy flavour. It really works!

To make sautéed wild mushrooms on toast, wipe or peel (depending on the condition of the skin) the tops of a basket of boletus mushrooms. Slice them about 8 mm thick. Preheat the oven to 220°C. Cut thick slices of bread such as a baguette, then brush with extra virgin olive oil and rub with garlic. Toast the sliced bread on a baking tray in the oven until golden on both sides. Using a light frying pan, so that heat penetrates quickly (a non-stick one works well), add 2 tablespoons butter and heat until nut-brown, adding a dash of olive oil to stop it from burning. Working in batches, toss the mushrooms through quickly, just sealing each side and adding only enough at one time so the mushrooms are seared to golden brown. Liberally season each batch with salt and freshly ground black pepper and set aside. Take the juices that accumulate in the pan, reduce over high heat and add to the mushrooms with some roughly chopped flat-leaf parsley. Pile atop the croutons and serve.

Smoked mushrooms have a wonderfully intense flavour, and are delicious served as a light appetiser with rosemary and thyme. An easy way to smoke your own mushrooms is using a large wok lined with foil. Soak a few handfuls of vine cuttings or bought wood chips in water for half an hour, then place them in the bottom of the wok, and position a small 'cooling' rack over them. Heat the wok over high heat on the stove until the cuttings or chips begin to smoke (this should take about 10 minutes), then place your mushrooms on the rack, cover the wok with a lid and smoke for about 2 minutes (the mushrooms won't be cooked all the way through).

TRUFFLES

There are certainly indigenous Australian truffles but, as far as I know, no native versions with the scent and flavour of the imported ones. However, there is now a whole industry of truffle growing, which started in Tasmania and has grown to include south west Western Australia, Canberra and Victoria and, I suspect, next in South Australia too. While still in its infancy, it certainly has great potential if the flavour of the truffles matches those of France and Italy.

Just being able to grow truffles, however, is not enough. While in France in 2005 and cooking at La Combe, a beautifully restored farmhouse run by my colleagues Wendeley Harvey and Robert Cave-Rogers, I heard stories at the local markets from the truffle farmers about how beautifully formed Chinese truffles are being imported into France. They have so little aroma, which in truffles equates to flavour, that the importers take out the centres of the Chinese truffles and replace them with wonderfully perfumed French truffle. As truffle permeates everything around it, the French truffle scents the Chinese one; the unsuspecting buyer, sniffing the truffle, will be delighted – at the time of purchase, at least. When they get home and find that the pervasive aroma of the French truffle has faded, they will undoubtedly be most disappointed and, I suspect, very angry.

GERARD MADANI'S MUSHROOM SOUP *Serves 6*

This recipe comes from Gerard Madani, an exciting chef I worked with at the Hotel Intercontinental in Sydney when I was a guest chef there eons ago. Gerard uses button mushrooms, which can be obtained all year round, for this tasty soup.

1 small onion, chopped
1 kg cultivated button mushrooms,
    roughly sliced
30 g butter
300 ml white wine
bouquet garni (2 stalks flat-leaf parsley,
    2 sprigs thyme, 1 bay leaf,
    ¼ stick celery, ¼ leek)

200 ml veal stock
200 ml Golden Chicken Stock (see page 181)
1 litre cream
6 teaspoons gewürztraminer wine

Sweat the onion and mushrooms in butter, without browning them, in a large saucepan over low heat. Add the white wine and bouquet garni, then increase the heat to high and reduce the liquid by two-thirds. Add the veal and chicken stock and bring to the boil. Add the cream and bring back to the boil, then simmer over low heat for 2 hours. Pass the soup through a fine strainer and season. Pour some of the strained mushroom soup into each warmed soup bowl, along with a teaspoon of the wine, then serve immediately.

PIGEON AND FIELD MUSHROOM PIE *Serves 6*

6 pigeons
12 golden shallots, peeled
butter, for cooking
350 g field mushrooms, thickly sliced
200 g sugar-cured bacon, cut into strips
½ cup (125 ml) red wine
fresh herbs (whatever is available – I like to
    use thyme, marjoram or oregano)

1 litre reduced Golden Chicken Stock
    (see page 181)
1 × quantity Rough Puff Pastry
    (see page 179)
1 egg, beaten with a little milk
salt

In a frying pan, salt and gently brown the pigeons with the shallots in a little butter over low–medium heat and transfer to a heavy-based cast-iron casserole or saucepan, or use a pressure cooker and follow the manufacturer's instructions (the cooking time will vary enormously, depending on the method of cooking). You could also use a crockpot, an electric casserole-style appliance that cooks very slowly and can be left on low for long periods.

In the same frying pan, quickly toss the mushrooms in a little butter over high heat and transfer to the casserole, then brown the bacon and add to the casserole. Deglaze the frying pan with the red wine, reduce quickly over high heat and add the wine to the casserole, then cover the pigeons with fresh herbs and stock. The six birds may each have different cooking times as most pigeons we buy are wild and of varying ages.

If you are using a pressure cooker, cook using the lowest pressure possible and check every 30 minutes. If there is a lot of liquid remaining at the end of cooking, reduce to the desired consistency, either over high heat on the stove or in the pressure cooker with the lid off. A crockpot could safely be left on low overnight. A pot-roast on top of the stove would have to be checked during the cooking period and perhaps more stock added to the pan; the cooking time could vary from 30 minutes to 3 hours. The pigeons are cooked when the meat easily comes away from the bone in large pieces. Remove from the heat and leave to cool.

Make and chill the pastry as instructed, then preheat the oven to 220°C. When the pigeons have cooled, take the meat off the bones and place in the bottom of a pie dish and spoon over the mushrooms, bacon and juices. Roll out the puff pastry, then cut into a circle slightly larger than the diameter of the pie dish and let it rest in the refrigerator for 20 minutes before putting it over the pie dish and brushing with an egg wash. Bake for about 20 minutes or until the pastry is golden.

RISOTTO WITH MUSHROOMS   *Serves 4*

Years ago now, I greatly enjoyed *Risotto*, by Constance del Nero – a book devoted entirely to this subject. Now that making risottos is so much a part of daily life, many variations are possible.

1.5 litres Golden Chicken Stock (see page 181) *or* vegetable stock	2 cups (400 g) Arborio rice (see Glossary)
12 large mushrooms, stalks removed and reserved, caps sliced	190 ml dry white wine
160 g butter, chopped	60 g freshly grated Parmigiano Reggiano
1 onion, finely chopped	2 tablespoons freshly chopped flat-leaf parsley

Place the stock and mushroom stalks in a large heavy-based saucepan and bring to the boil over high heat, then simmer over low heat for 30 minutes. Keep the stock hot over low heat while making the risotto.

Melt 120 g of the butter in a large cast-iron or enamelled saucepan over low heat. Add the onion and cook gently, stirring, until translucent. Increase the heat to medium, add the rice and stir well to coat with the butter. When the rice glistens, pour in the wine. When the alcohol has evaporated, stir in a ladleful of the hot stock, stirring until it is absorbed. Continue to add ladlefuls of hot stock, one by one and stirring until each has been absorbed, for another 10 minutes. Fold the sliced mushrooms into the risotto. Continue adding stock and stirring for another 10 minutes. The rice should be al dente and there should still be a little liquid left. Remove the pan from the heat and stir in the cheese, parsley and remaining butter.

Serve with a green salad and a dry white wine.

OLIVES

OF THE FEW BOOKS THAT SURVIVED MY FAMILY'S UPHEAVAL WHEN I was a teenager and my parents lost their business were works by Aldous Huxley and Rudyard Kipling. Every now and then I dip into them, glad to have something of my father's that survived. I love the lines in Aldous Huxley's *The Olive Tree*: 'If I could paint and had the necessary time, I should devote myself for a few years to making pictures only of olive trees. What a wealth of variations upon a single theme.'

It is much more accepted these days to be as passionate as I am about olives and, of course, extra virgin olive oil. I love everything about the olive, from the tree to the fruit to the oil, but it took me many years to convince my husband, Colin, of the beauty of the trees. He agreed to plant an olive grove for practical agricultural reasons but, as much as I wanted to have our own olive oil, I would have planted them just for the wonderful landscape they provide. We now have two groves of about 1000 trees for our oil, as well as 40 kalamata trees just for pickling; as it happens, they also make a good oil, but as good pickled olives are quite hard to find I prefer to use them for that.

As a cook and a grower, my greatest passion is reserved for extra virgin olive oil, but I would never want to be without olives for the table. Groves of olives are now a common sight in many areas of Australia and, while wild olive trees remain, they have been declared a noxious weed. Some council areas take this very seriously, while others are happy to leave them in the landscape. Whether used for oil or pickling, the small wild olives have amazing flavour, since most of these trees have the advantage of age, which seems to add flavour, just as an aged vine does to wine. There is certainly much competition in the Greek and Italian communities in Adelaide for these olives, including those from the trees in the Adelaide parklands.

For those lucky enough to have wild olive trees nearby, I urge you to give the fruit a try – no matter how small the olives, you'll find their flavour headily intense. It's a help, too, to get in before the birds start spreading the stones. In South Australia, there was

Baked olives (see page 79)

a very real danger of wild olive trees overtaking our native bush in some areas, and so we watched sadly while councils cut them down, as no one was prepared to accept the responsibility of pruning and picking these trees – I had even tried (unsuccessfully) to gather a group to look after some solitary roadside specimens that bore particularly well. The sad thing was not only to see age-old trees cut down, but to witness the beautiful wood turned into chips or burnt.

If foraging for food is not your style, then a trip to your local market between May and July should yield boxes of fresh olives of many different varieties for pickling. I've never actually seen them for sale with their varieties named, though kalamatas, which grow particularly well in South Australia, are a great pickling olive and are easily identified by their pointy end. There are lots of olives that I can assure you aren't worth pickling, so it's a good idea to get to know your varieties. All olives start out 'olive green' and turn to green tinged with violet, then purple, then black as they ripen. Each stage has a different taste: the green olive is bitter and tart, with firmer flesh than the riper black olive.

You wouldn't think pickling olives would be difficult – it has been going on for centuries after all. However, the ancient process of pickling with just salt, or salt and water, introduces more pitfalls than you could imagine. It is essential that you use basic but thorough hygiene, sterilise your jars and throw away any olives that develop mould or blisters on them at any stage of the pickling process.

I've been pickling olives on and off for over twenty years now and have had good years and bad. In the early days of the restaurant we'd have quiet times mid-week, so we'd close the doors early afternoon in winter and all go out picking wild olives. This meant I then had buckets and buckets to pickle, so we'd set up the 'service yard' of the restaurant to tackle the forty-day process Stephanie Alexander first talked about in her book *Menus for Food Lovers*.

It was a laborious and messy job but worth it for the result, though I learnt that some olives take a lot longer to pickle than others. The difference in time needed lies in the level of ripeness when you pick the olives – many wild olive trees might have one side full of really black but unripe fruit and super-ripe fruit on the other side (if the tree is not in full sun, the fruit will not be nearly as ripe). Some olives take months to lose their bitterness, so just keep trying them – don't be reckless and throw away all your good work just because some of the olives are bitter.

Having wondered in the past why one bucket might spoil and others not, I was anxious before starting on this year's olives to find out as much as I could, but little has been written about the process. One occasional problem I have had has been the formation of a gas pocket, apparently the most common defect of table olives. Nothing can be done, and you must throw them out. If you were producing on a semi-commercial scale, this would certainly be cause for concern as it is an indication of bacteria being present.

None of this should stop you from following your neighbours' favourite recipe, particularly if they are Italian or Greek, but it's worth trying to pickle a small batch first. If luck is with you, the olives will be delicious and you'll eat them so quickly that 'keeping qualities' won't be an issue.

For several years I've used the dry-salt method of pickling for wild olives, layering 10-litre cream buckets, with holes in the bottom, alternately with olives first, then salt, until the bucket is about two-thirds full. The olives then need to be weighted down and the buckets covered and left for at least a month. This method leaves the olives very crinkled and dry and very salty, but their flavour intensifies amazingly – though I still don't have the secret for getting it right every time.

In 2000 we picked our own kalamatas for the first time; 40 trees gave us 80 kg, not a huge quantity but enough to trial salt-curing. They were sweeter and nuttier than any other olives I have tasted. I'm sure the success was due to a combination of variety, climate and terroir (soil), but perhaps most of all because we picked and cured the olives immediately.

If you're considering a semi-commercial operation, I urge you to get a copy of a fairly new paper, 'Processing Technology of the Table Olive', by Suzanne Colmagro, Graham Collins and Margaret Sedgley from the University of Adelaide. Suzanne chased every lead she had, researching and talking to everyone she could find with practical experience of pickling olives. The paper has an academic tone, as you would expect, and it gives more information on what not to do rather than including the perfect recipe but, as there is such potential in this burgeoning olive industry of ours, it's important to spread the word of any research that assists in maximising both flavour and quality.

With thousands of olive trees being planted across Australia, another essential read for olive lovers is Patrice Newell's *The Olive Grove*. This wonderful book gives a great account of the practicalities of starting out. It may take the romance out of the idea of growing olives for some, but this is farming after all.

The commercial pickling process uses a lye solution (potassium hydroxide), instead of water and salt. This, for me, has huge disadvantages: the olives lose flavour and texture, the lye masks the natural colour and then the lye has to be disposed of after processing, which can cause environmental problems. Lye-treated olives can be readily identified, as they are uniformly deep black.

Commercially prepared olives also differ in quality, depending on how they are pickled. Kalamatas are the most consistently high-quality black olive, though be wary of cheaper imports. Treating olives with water and salt is a longer and more expensive process, but the flavour is far more 'olivey', with a desirable edge of bitterness and some loss of colour.

Only a tiny proportion of the kalamatas consumed in Australia is grown here. Look out for the superb Coriole Kalamatas from South Australia, sold in cryovac packs. Kalamatas picked ripe go well with orange, thyme and rosemary or oregano; or orange, garlic and bay leaves; or thyme leaves, chopped flat-leaf parsley and tiny dice of preserved lemon; or honey and quince; or even toasted cumin seeds and tiny dice of raw fennel, finely chopped chilli and garlic and a fresh bay leaf.

Olives are best of all when bought from local groves, where they are sold in cryovac packs without any additives or extra flavourings. Some small producers, both local and international, present their olives in wine vinegar and olive oil, and these are worth seeking out too. Avoid those pre-sliced black olives often used in commercial pasta dishes and pizzas – they taste like rubber. I also abhor the olives that are sold in supermarkets with stale dried herbs or chillies and poor-quality oil.

To marinate your own, start with good olives as a base and toss in your best extra virgin olive oil with some rosemary or thyme and, particularly if using kalamatas, some orange rind. In some gourmet shops you'll find Ligurian or Taggiasche olives from Italy. These are tiny wild olives with a large stone and not a great deal of flesh but an incredible intensity of flavour.

I keep an earthenware crock on the kitchen bench filled with olives immersed in brine or a mix of olive oil and wine vinegar. A harmless mould may form on the surface and can be removed – not with your fingers, which will introduce bacteria, but with an olive spoon (a wooden ladle with holes). There is no need to refrigerate them unless you've added

flavourings that may perish, such as citrus or garlic cloves. If you do so, bring them to room temperature before use.

To cook with olives, bear in mind that they taste better when cooked with the stones in (but warn your guests) and that heating makes the flavour more intense. To bake olives, just cover the base of a baking dish with olives, olive oil, fresh chillies (if so inclined), cloves of garlic and rosemary, and bake in a 180°C oven until the olives are wrinkly and the garlic is cooked through. Add to pizzas, breads or polenta or toss through pasta with a roasted tomato sauce. Or add olives to pot-roasting lamb, kid, duck or veal, but only during the last part of the cooking or the dish will be too salty. Make a sauce from puréed pitted olives, fresh oregano, some chicken stock and a touch of cream to serve with poultry or rabbit.

You can make dips with olives; better still, make a classic tapenade where they are minced with extra virgin olive oil, capers and anchovies; try adding a splash of Cognac to the batch, and then serve with freshly toasted bread. You can also add olives to salads (not the pre-pitted pitch-black ones though), such as a classic Niçoise.

I've come to love green olives but finding really good ones is difficult. Large green olives are too large to pit with an olive or cherry pipping tool, but you can buy good-quality pitted green olives called Conserviera. Plump and fleshy, they are good for stuffing, especially with an anchovy. Or try deep-frying olives filled with meat or cheese.

I've given up trying to pickle green olives myself – I suspect they require quite different varieties to those we grow. One day I'll put together the cracked green olives with orange blossom tossed in extra virgin olive oil that I've heard so much about but never tried.

BAKED OLIVES
Serves 6–8

2 cups pickled olives

2 cloves garlic, finely chopped

rind of 1 orange, thinly sliced

4 bay leaves

⅓ cup (80 ml) extra virgin olive oil

2 tablespoons verjuice *or* lemon juice

2 teaspoons chopped rosemary

Preheat the oven to 180°C. Toss the olives with garlic, orange rind, bay leaves, olive oil and verjuice or lemon juice. Place in a baking dish and bake for 5–10 minutes. Leave to cool just a little before serving. If all the moisture is absorbed, add extra olive oil and verjuice or lemon juice along with the chopped rosemary, then serve with drinks.

GREEN OLIVE GNOCCHI WITH GREEN OLIVE SAUCE
Serves 4

This is one of my family's favourite comfort foods. My younger daughter Elli in particular will always ask for green olive gnocchi – and don't forget the sauce, Mum!

750 g desiree potatoes

125 g plain flour

freshly grated nutmeg, to taste

sea salt flakes and freshly ground
    black pepper

20 large green olives, pitted and
    finely chopped

2 egg yolks

butter, for pan-frying

SAUCE

3 cloves garlic, finely chopped

1 large onion, finely chopped

1 tablespoon extra virgin olive oil

100 ml Golden Chicken Stock
    (see page 181)

100 ml cream

200 g green olives, pitted and chopped

lemon juice, to taste

Steam the potatoes until cooked right through and mash while still warm. Allow to cool a little and then add flour, nutmeg, salt, pepper and chopped olives. Mix in the egg yolks to make a fairly firm dough. Knead it gently for a few minutes, then divide it into quarters and leave to rest on the bench for 20 minutes.

Bring a large saucepan of salted water to the boil. Roll each dough quarter into logs, 1 cm in diameter. Cut logs into 1 cm lengths and cover with a damp tea towel while you wait for the water to boil. Gently place the gnocchi into boiling water, and as they come to the surface, cook them for 1 minute. Remove with a slotted spoon and set aside.

To make the sauce, sweat the garlic and onion in olive oil in a saucepan over medium heat until softened. Add the chicken stock and cream and bring to the boil. Add the olives and adjust the flavour with lemon juice if necessary. Leave to cool a little before puréeing in a blender, and then return to the clean pan to gently reheat.

Just before serving, pan-fry the gnocchi in a frying pan in some nut-brown butter for a minute or two until they are golden brown. Serve with the warmed sauce.

AILEEN'S OLIVE BREAD

Makes 2 loaves

Aileen Proudfoot, such an important member of our restaurant and pâté-making team for so many years, was incredibly talented at everything she put her hand to, whether it was making fabulous bread, arranging flowers, or creating wonderful gardens from scratch.

2 tablespoons rosemary, finely chopped	15 g dried yeast
2 tablespoons extra virgin olive oil	⅔ cup pitted black *or* green olives
5⅓ cups (850 g) strong flour (see Glossary), plus extra for flouring	about 2 cups (500 ml) warm water (the exact amount used varies every time, depending
large pinch salt	on the weather, humidity and flour)

Fry the rosemary in the olive oil in a small frying pan until fragrant, then set aside. In a large bowl, mix the flour, salt, yeast and the rosemary oil mixture. Make a well in the centre, then add the pitted olives and begin to pour in the warm water to make the dough.

When the mixture reaches the desired consistency of a soft dough, remove to a floured bench and knead until smooth and satiny to the touch – this will take at least 15 minutes by hand. Smear the bowl with a little olive oil and return the dough to the bowl, then leave covered with a wet tea towel or plastic film for 1½ hours or until the dough doubles in size. Knock back the dough and shape it into rolls or loaves as required. Put on trays or in 2 greased loaf tins and leave to rise again for another 20 minutes, covered with a damp tea towel. Meanwhile, preheat the oven to 220°C.

Bake bread for 15–20 minutes, then turn upside-down and bake for another 5 minutes. Turn out onto a wire rack to cool. Eat with unsalted butter.

PARTRIDGE

PARTRIDGE ARE LITTLE KNOWN IN AUSTRALIA, BUT WHEN WE had them on our menu at the Pheasant Farm Restaurant their delicate flavour was always commented on, and for many customers it reawakened wonderful memories of eating partridge in Europe, particularly England.

Rather than the grey and red-legged partridge known in Europe, the chukhar breed is farmed in Australia (the French are now crossing the chukhar and red-legged partridge, although the latter breed still dominates there). The meat of the chukhar is not as dark as that of the grey and red-legged partridge, but once you have mastered the cooking technique it is full of flavour. The birds range in size from 350 to 500 g, making them a perfect main course for one person.

Farming partridge commercially is frustrating, as my husband Colin and I know only too well. It is almost impossible to sex the birds, which is problematic since the hen is tenderer than the cockerel. All partridge, young or old, look identical and don't become scrawny with age as a pheasant does. As there is such a difference in how a young and an old bird of any species should be cooked, mistaking old for young and vice versa can be disastrous for the cook. A gate left open between runs caused much confusion in our first breeding season. Another year, my daughter Saskia came running in to say she had found a partridge walking down the track to the farm (the whole breeding stock, it transpired, had wandered off through an open gate).

In 1993 we finally had our first real season's breeding, of just a few hundred birds. It coincided with a huge dinner that Marjorie Coates, of Vintners Restaurant, and I put on at Seppeltsfield for the Barossa Vintage Festival. We based the main course on a 'partridge in a pear tree' theme, and I roasted the birds at home and then ferried them up the road to Seppeltsfield while the meat was resting. Working on low trestle tables in a makeshift kitchen set up in a huge tent, we cooked pears and caramelised garlic and pancetta while the birds were carved. As that dinner took almost the whole year's supply, I only had a few partridges with which to experiment before the restaurant closed later that year. After all those years of trying and almost giving up on the breeding, I now find it sad not to have more opportunities to cook and serve this bird.

The demand for our partridges fluctuated almost as much as the number we were able to successfully produce each year. One year we'd breed a large number, and nobody would be interested, then the next we'd have a bad hatching and only produce a few birds, and

demand would be sky-high. Colin had all but decided to give it up, when one year both Stephanie Alexander and Sydney chef Kylie Kwong decided they loved the birds. Stephanie and I cooked her delicious partridge pies together for special dinners at her Richmond Hill Cafe and Larder. After a weekend retreat in the Barossa with us, Kylie came up with a wonderful recipe for partridges using Chinese master stock, so very different to the way either Stephanie or I had cooked them before. However, this flutter of popularity would be short-lived, and again partridges would be off the menu. While Colin no longer breeds partridges in any great numbers, there are a few other small producers, and Game Farm in New South Wales.

If you can get your hands on partridge they make a very special dinner, but be warned, the legs and breast need different cooking methods, unless you use a recipe like Stephanie's Partridge Pies (see page 87). I can tell you that the lard pastry, which encases these pies, is truly magnificent – perfectly flaky and tender.

The breast of the partridge is the prime part of the bird. No matter how hard you try, if you cook the bird whole, the legs will always be on the chewy side. Even though I think we are a little too fixated on everything needing to melt in the mouth (I would much prefer to have flavour than melt-in-the-mouth blandness), the trick to avoiding chewy legs is to separate the breast from the legs, keeping the breast on the frame and both legs connected in one piece. The only time I deviate from this is if I am grilling partridge. In this case, I 'spatchcock' the bird by cutting it down the spine and, with the cut-side down on the bench, squash it as flat as I can with the palm of my hand.

When cooking spatchcocked partridge, you must be sure you have a young bird with a certain amount of fat. I make a marinade of walnut oil, verjuice, fresh thyme and freshly ground black pepper and turn the bird in this mixture for several hours. The marinated, salted partridge can be cooked on a chargrill plate, where it should be turned frequently to prevent it charring too much, or it can be brushed with the marinade and roasted at 250°C. Either way, the bird will take 10–15 minutes to cook, with about 10 minutes resting time away from the heat. If you've roasted the partridge, deglaze the roasting pan with a good dash of verjuice and a few tablespoons of reduced chicken stock to make a delicious jus. Surprisingly, a warm Anchovy Vinaigrette (see page 157) is a wonderful accompaniment, too.

Partridges, grapes and vine leaves or pancetta are a heady combination and, while cooking poultry on the bone always produces more flavour, there are times when it is handy to do the boning in advance. To stuff boned partridges, sweat a finely chopped onion and a couple of garlic cloves in extra virgin olive oil until softened, then combine with breadcrumbs made from day-old bread, sage leaves crisped in butter and seedless green grapes. Pack the stuffing into the boned partridges so that the birds regain their shape, then wrap them in either pancetta or fresh vine leaves poached in verjuice and brush them with walnut oil and more verjuice. Grill the birds if you have a good griller, otherwise roast them at 230°C for 10–15 minutes in a shallow roasting pan turning over halfway through the cooking (so that they get a good blast of heat all over), with 10 minutes resting time. To caramelise the skin, seal the salted birds first in nut-brown butter on the stove. Serve the partridge with a vinaigrette of 125 ml walnut oil, 2 tablespoons verjuice, ½ teaspoon champagne vinegar (or a good squeeze of lemon juice), a small handful of seedless green grapes and 30 g roasted and skinned walnuts.

If you need further inspiration for using partridge, you will find it in Spanish cookbooks. I love roasted or grilled partridge with pomegranate sauce. More of a vinaigrette than a sauce, almond oil is combined with pomegranate juice, then pomegranate seeds are added at the last moment before the lot is poured over the cooked bird. Wonderful! The classic Catalan paste of ground almonds, garlic and sherry that I use with pheasant (see page 7) is equally good with partridge.

Escabeche, the Spanish technique of steeping cooked fish or poultry in a hot marinade and then leaving it to cool for 24 hours, is great when partridge breast meat and legs, herbs and garlic are used. It was acclaimed Australian chef Cheong Liew who first taught me how to do this, years ago when we were exploring ways of using every possible part of the pheasant. When I first tried it I cooked the birds three-quarters of the way through, knowing that the hot marinade would continue the cooking. However, I also know that dealing with partially cooked poultry is like playing with fire, so I now recommend simmering spatchcocked birds for about 25 minutes in 2 parts red-wine vinegar to 1 part mild extra virgin olive oil and 1 part water, with lots of peeled garlic cloves, fresh bay leaves, black peppercorns and sprigs of thyme – make sure the birds are completely covered. After cooking, remove the pan from the stove and leave to cool to room temperature. The birds can be refrigerated in their cooking juices for 24 hours. Escabeche is served at room temperature, making it perfect for eating outdoors in our glorious autumn weather.

PARTRIDGE 'PUDDINGS' WITH SULTANAS AND VERJUICE   *Serves 4*

In 1994, Peter and Margaret Lehmann, winemakers and friends of ours, asked me to do a series of dinners in Melbourne and Sydney to launch their Stonewall shiraz. As our restaurant was no longer running by then, this seemed the perfect opportunity to showcase these birds, in a dish that was the essence of the Barossa. The Grand Hyatt in Melbourne and the Regent in Sydney allowed me to cook with their teams on the night, and we put on a true Barossa show in the big smoke.

1½ tablespoons sultanas	1 stick celery, roughly chopped
verjuice, for soaking	1 onion, roughly chopped
2 partridge	extra virgin olive oil, for cooking
¼ cup (60 ml) walnut oil	¼ cup (60 ml) white wine
2 tablespoons verjuice	butter, for greasing
2 sprigs thyme, leaves picked	6 rashers very thinly cut streaky bacon,
freshly ground black pepper	rind removed
1 carrot, roughly chopped	

Soak the sultanas overnight in enough verjuice to just cover them.

Next day, remove the breast meat from each partridge. Gently flatten each breast between sheets of baking paper with a wooden mallet until even, then cut into 2 cm pieces. In a bowl, mix the walnut oil, 2 tablespoons verjuice, thyme leaves and pepper and marinate the breast meat in this while you make the stock.

Preheat the oven to 220°C. Toss the carrot, celery, onion, partridge carcasses and legs in a roasting pan with a little olive oil and roast for 30–40 minutes or until caramelised. Over high heat on the stove, deglaze the pan with the wine and tip the contents into a stockpot. Barely cover the vegetables and bones with water, then simmer over low heat for 2 hours to make a flavoursome stock. Remove the stockpot from the heat, strain the stock into a bowl, then chill it and remove any excess fat when cold.

Pour 250 ml of the stock into a clean saucepan with 125 ml verjuice and reduce by two-thirds over medium heat, then remove from the heat. As it cools, the stock will become quite jellied.

Preheat the oven to 180°C. Smear the base and sides of 4 soufflé dishes or dariole moulds with butter and then line them with the bacon, reserving enough to cover the dishes later on. Remove the soaked sultanas and discard the verjuice. Layer the marinated meat, sultanas and jellied stock in the bacon-lined dishes until each has been filled. Top with the remaining bacon and cover with baking paper.

Stand the dishes in a roasting pan filled with boiling water, making sure the water comes two-thirds of the way up the sides of the dishes, then bake for 20 minutes. Carefully remove the pan from the oven, then the dishes from the pan. Leave them to cool a little before gently inverting them onto serving plates. Heat the leftover jellied stock and spoon it over the warm 'puddings' before serving with lamb's lettuce (mâche) or other delicate green salad.

PARTRIDGE WITH SAVOY CABBAGE, PANCETTA, WALNUTS AND VERJUICE

Serves 4

Partridge with cabbage has to be the most traditional of combinations and was the one I rejected for the longest. I'm now sorry I did, as Savoy cabbage, properly cooked, is the perfect foil to the richness and density of partridge breast. If you don't have a really large casserole it may be better to split the following ingredients between two dishes.

24 shelled walnuts

8 thin slices pancetta

4 partridge

juice of 1 lemon

sea salt flakes and freshly ground
    black pepper

¼ cup duck fat

1 large sprig rosemary, leaves picked
    and chopped

1 Savoy cabbage, trimmed, cored
    and shredded

1 cup (250 ml) verjuice

butter, for cooking

Preheat the oven to 220°C. Dry-roast the walnuts on a baking tray for 6 minutes, then rub off the skins with a clean tea towel and put the nuts aside. At the same time, place the pancetta on a baking tray and crisp in the oven, then put on kitchen paper to drain.

Separate the legs from the breast of each partridge, keeping both legs attached and in one piece and the breast on the frame. Squeeze lemon juice into the cavity of each bird and season. Melt the duck fat with half the rosemary over low–medium heat in a large heavy-based enamelled casserole dish with a tight-fitting lid. Brown the partridge pieces very slowly on all sides over low heat until almost cooked through. Don't crowd the pan or the skin will poach rather than caramelise – do it in batches if necessary. Remove the partridge from the casserole and set aside, reserving the duck fat in the pan.

Toss the cabbage in the reserved duck fat in the casserole over medium heat and season it very well, then return the partridge to the pan. Pour in the verjuice and cover with the lid. Increase the heat to high so that the verjuice reduces, the cabbage cooks in about 3–5 minutes and the cooking of the partridge is complete. The breasts may be ready before the legs. If the breasts feel firm, take them out and keep them warm and covered (the legs may only need a few more minutes – check by piercing a leg at its thickest point to see if the juices run clear).

In a frying pan, heat a knob of butter with the remaining rosemary until nut-brown, then toss in the walnuts. Discard the rosemary and tip the walnuts and butter into the cabbage, along with the crisp pancetta. Serve immediately.

KYLIE KWONG'S CHINESE-STYLE PARTRIDGE WITH POMEGRANATE-CARAMEL SAUCE

Serves 6

3 partridge

CHINESE MASTER STOCK

3 litres cold water

1½ cups (375 ml) Shao Hsing rice wine
    or dry sherry

1 cup (250 ml) dark soy sauce

½ cup (125 ml) light soy sauce

1 cup (220 g) brown sugar

6 cloves garlic, crushed with back of knife

½ cup unpeeled ginger slices

4 spring onions, trimmed and
    halved lengthways

½ teaspoon sesame oil

5 star anise

2 cinnamon sticks

3 strips orange rind

POMEGRANATE-CARAMEL SAUCE

¼ cup (55 g) brown sugar

2½ tablespoons fish sauce

2 tablespoons lime juice

2 pomegranates, seeds removed
    and juice reserved

SICHUAN SALT AND PEPPER
(OPTIONAL)

1 tablespoon Sichuan pepper

¼ cup sea salt flakes

For the Chinese master stock, place all the ingredients in a large stockpot and bring to the boil over high heat. Reduce heat to low and simmer gently for 40 minutes to allow the flavours to infuse. Meanwhile, rinse the partridge under cold water. Trim away any excess fat from inside and outside the cavities, but keep the necks, parson's noses and winglets intact.

Lower partridges, breast-side down, into the simmering stock, ensuring they are fully submerged. Poach birds over low heat for exactly 9 minutes. There should be no more than an occasional ripple breaking the surface; adjust the temperature, if necessary, to ensure that stock does not reach simmering point again. Remove stockpot immediately from the stove and allow birds to steep in the stock for 2 hours at room temperature to complete the cooking process.

Using tongs, gently remove birds from the stock, being careful not to tear the breast skin. Place them on a tray or a plate and leave to cool.

For the sauce, melt sugar and fish sauce in a heavy-based saucepan over medium heat, stirring until sugar dissolves to create a caramel. Add lime juice and pomegranate seeds and juice. The texture should be thick, runny and caramel-like, and the flavour should be intense – salty, sour and sweet all at once. Remove from heat and set aside.

For the Sichuan salt and pepper, dry-roast pepper and salt in a heavy-based saucepan over medium–high heat. When the pepper begins to 'pop' and become aromatic, remove from the heat. Leave to cool, then grind using a spice grinder or a mortar and pestle.

Carve partridge as required and smother them in the sauce before serving. Sprinkle with Sichuan pepper and salt, if using.

STEPHANIE'S PARTRIDGE PIES

Makes 8 muffin-sized pies

Stephanie Alexander has been a part of my food life ever since we met at the first Symposium of Gastronomy in Adelaide over twenty years ago. Through the intervening years we've travelled together many times and I'm always in awe of her knowledge of any food matter that we're presented with. Ever since our holiday in Italy in the early 1990s, which led to the Tuscan cooking school we held, we've had so many food adventures together, along with my husband Colin and a group of close friends, across many countries. We are always armed with Stephanie's research about not-to-be-missed food experiences, and we have a lot of fun together. Here is Stephanie's melt-in-the-mouth partridge pie recipe, utilising Colin's partridges.

1 × quantity Stephanie's Lard Pastry (see page 64)
120 g fat pork belly
120 g partridge leg meat, plus heart and liver
1 clove garlic, chopped
120 g minced chicken
20 g foie gras *or* rich liver pâté, finely chopped

salt
pinch Quatre-Épices (see page 172)
2 teaspoons Armagnac
1 egg
dash milk

Make and chill the pastry following the instructions.

Preheat the oven to 200°C. Mince the pork in a food processor, then add the partridge and garlic and mince again. Mix well with the minced chicken, then add the foie gras and combine. Season with salt and quatre-épices, then add the Armagnac.

Roll out pastry to 5 mm thick, then cut out 16 pastry rounds slightly larger than the diameter of the holes of a 12-hole muffin tin. Line 8 of the holes with pastry rounds and spoon in the filling. Cover with remaining pastry rounds and seal well. Beat the egg with a dash of milk and brush the pastry with this egg wash, then bake for 5 minutes. Lower oven temperature to 180°C and cook for another 30 minutes or until golden.

PEARS

WHEN WE FIRST BOUGHT OUR PROPERTY IN 1987, THERE WERE three pear trees in the garden that were each more than a hundred years old. They still bore prolifically, but over the years we lost two to white ants and wind damage (though we rescued the pear wood from one of the trees and it's still 'curing', ready to be made into furniture). The remaining tree at the bottom of the garden is by the side of the dam with the well at its feet.

Every year this wonderful pear tree blossoms on the first weekend in October, which used to coincide with our Barossa Music Festival. In the years when it also coincides with the dam being full, it is the most beautiful place on earth to us. After a couple of weeks in full bloom the petals start to fall at the first strong wind. That's when I love to be home, having friends for a drink under the pear tree with the blossoms falling gently upon us.

The year before last we had our biggest winter rains in ten years and the pears were better than ever. Contrast that with this year, our worst drought ever, and the pears are dropping before maturity from lack of water. Considering how old our tree is, except in times of drought it crops amazingly well, and each year my husband Colin and our friend Peter Wall talk about making pear wine. They have it all worked out, but somehow neither of them ever has the time – there is always next year! In the meantime the fruit is not wasted, as we stack green pears into wooden boxes and store them in the cellar to use in the winter, the perfume lingering long after the last one has been eaten.

Living in the Barossa has given me such a sentimental attachment to pear trees. It is said that the Silesian settlers planted pear trees here even before building their houses, to make the well water sweet. Many grand old specimens are still standing, but as I look down from my attic window, our magnificent pear tree, older and taller than the cottage itself, is to me the most beautiful of all those I've seen.

Sentimentality aside, I do have a practical streak too. As soon as we realised we would lose two of the original three trees, we resolved to carry on the tradition, and planted five

Glazed pears (see page 96)

of the best eating varieties available to us. Those beautiful old trees were so tall that you could almost touch the blossom from the attic windows – the new trees won't reach such heights in our lifetime, but planting trees for our grandchildren and their grandchildren to enjoy is what we do.

Our first choice was the doyenné du comice, as I'd read so much about this being the *crème de la crème* of pears. They fruited for the first time this year; I picked the pears green and firm and ripened them in darkness (as you should with all pears to achieve maximum flavour), but 4 weeks have passed and I'm still waiting to see the telltale yellow flesh that indicates ripeness. My pear expert from the Barossa Farmers' Market, Margaret Ellis, tells me I should have put them in a brown paper bag to hasten the ripening (along with a banana, the ethylene in which speeds the process up even more). Over the years I've had lots of experience of leaving pears on the tree too long so that they become brown around

the core, so perhaps I moved a little too early this time, even though they came off the tree into my hand easily, which is one of the signs to look for. Maybe next time I will wait until the blush of pink on the skins is a little more intense.

We planted two trees that bear the tiny bella face pears, which are the perfect size for pickling whole. They grow particularly upright in stance, which makes them wonderfully easy trees to pick from and great to espalier against a wall.

Then we planted a Bartlett, also known as Williams or Duchess, which, contrary to widely held opinion, produces fabulous eating pears. When they are perfectly ripe and the skin has turned from green to pale yellow, and as long as they are not bruised, the pears are so juicy and delectable that every bit can be eaten, even the core, which seems to almost disappear into the flesh.

The last tree we planted was the brown beurre bosc, with its elegantly shaped fruit; so good to eat raw and wonderful to cook with. Sadly, this year the tree produced just one pear, with almost none of its usual russet colour (Margaret Ellis says this is because of the drought). I love beurre boscs peeled and poached in red wine with a stick of cinnamon, a vanilla bean or a piece of fresh ginger, or roasted or grilled to serve in a salad or as an accompaniment to game.

Whilst there are other varieties I'd like to plant or graft onto existing trees, like the winter cole and of course the corella (that beautifully rosy pear that began its life here in the Barossa), I'm not so tempted to grow the Packham triumph, a larger, knobbly pear that's probably the most widely available, as one of my guiding principles is to grow lesser-known varieties of fruit and vegetables that have great flavour.

As you'll rarely find pears in the greengrocer's in perfect condition for eating (if they were truly ripe they would be instantly bruised), buy your pears green and ripen them at home in a brown paper bag with a banana inside (don't keep them in the fridge).

Other than eating a ripe pear and experiencing the joy of having the juice dribble down your arm, what else can you do with this fruit? Eat pears dried or pickled, or make wine or liqueur with them. Pears and cheese are a traditional coupling: a firm, but not unripe, green pear, a slab of Parmigiano Reggiano and some new season's extra virgin olive oil is top of my list. A pear that is to be served with a blue cheese should be riper, as should a pear that is to be sliced and served on a bed of bitter greens with chunks of goat's cheese or blue cheese, roasted walnuts and a vinaigrette of walnut oil and lemon juice.

I love using pears in salad, either raw with rocket and Parmigiano Reggiano, or grilled or pan-fried in butter and then, whilst still warm, tossed together with fennel, watercress, prosciutto and a few dollops of gorgonzola. Such a simple combination, but what great flavours it produces.

I like a soup so intense that you need nothing else but a salad of bitter greens and crusty bread to complete the meal. Stilton soup, a rich number, is taken to another dimension if a pear purée is spooned on top just before serving. Roasted and ground walnuts cooked with a good reduced chicken stock then puréed can be finished with the same pear purée and served with a watercress salad.

Pears are an all-time dessert favourite. Perhaps my favourite way of preparing them is to make a compote of pears with quince and a vanilla bean and serve it with a vanilla Crème Anglaise (see page 39). Or sprinkle pears with a little sugar, dot them with knobs of butter and squeeze over a little lemon juice, then bake at 180°C for about 20 minutes before turning the oven up to 230°C or so for another 10 minutes to caramelise them – these are fantastic served with mascarpone or vanilla ice cream. Either fresh or dried pears can be poached in sugar syrup with verjuice or lemon juice added to give bite, then topped with a large dollop of cream. The combination of pear and chocolate works every time, especially when it comes to hot baked pears served with a richer-than-rich chocolate custard and super-cold slices of pear (skin on), or pear crumble with chocolate buttons mixed through the crumble mix.

SUN-DRIED PEARS, FARM FOLLIES STYLE

Peel and core firm, ripe pears. Place them in salted water as you go, then leave them for 15 minutes. This stops them going brown and also aids the drying. Lay the pears on wire racks in the hot sun, turning them as they dry. The exterior should form a skin, leaving the flesh moist inside. Store the dried pears in sealed airtight jars with sachets of silica gel (available from chemists).

Pan-fried pears with fennel, prosciutto, watercress and gorgonzola (see page 91)

DRIED PEARS POACHED IN VERJUICE
Serves 4

This is a savoury dish which can be used to make a perfect cool-weather salad, with rocket and radicchio, if in season, and slices of prosciutto. Add walnuts that have been roasted then rubbed of their skins, then toss the salad with a little extra virgin olive oil and slivers of blue cheese, bocconcini or goat's curd.

200 g dried pears	2 fresh bay leaves
1½ cups (375 ml) verjuice	6 black peppercorns
rind of 1 lemon	

Place all the ingredients in a heavy-based saucepan. Slowly bring to the boil over medium heat, then immediately reduce the heat to low and simmer for 8 minutes or until the dried pears are soft. Set aside, leaving pears to cool in the poaching liquid.

When the pears are cool, take out of the liquid and pat dry; this liquid can be used again for poaching or in the next vinaigrette you make.

POACHED PEARS ON FILO PASTRY WITH MASCARPONE
Serves 6

The same amount of dried peaches or nectarines could be used instead of pears.

1 cup (250 ml) verjuice	6 sheets filo pastry
½ cup (110 g) castor sugar	unsalted butter, melted, for brushing
200 g dried pears (about 12 pears)	200 ml mascarpone *or* thick double cream

To make the syrup, bring verjuice and sugar to the boil in a stainless steel saucepan over high heat, stirring until sugar has dissolved. Boil for 5 minutes or until syrupy. Add dried pears, then cover and poach gently over low heat for 20 minutes. Remove pears and set aside to cool. Increase heat to high and reduce syrup by half then set aside.

Preheat the oven to 200°C. Using a saucer as a template, cut 3 even circles into each sheet of filo pastry. Brush each circle with melted butter, then layer 3 filo circles on top of each other to make a total of 6 rounds. Place filo rounds on a baking tray lined with baking paper, then put the cooled dried pears atop the filo rounds, brushing the pears with the reduced syrup.

Bake for 8 minutes or until filo is crisp. Serve drizzled with extra syrup and a good dollop of mascarpone or double cream.

A TRIFLE OF PEARS, PRUNES AND SAUTERNES CUSTARD
Serves 12

I was tremendously fortunate to have the staff I did at the Pheasant Farm Restaurant, particularly in our last year, when Alex Herbert joined us; a driven person with so much talent and dedication, she always strove for perfection. I was very lucky to have her, along with my talented apprentice Natalie Paull and the always wonderful Steve Flamsteed. These three were the core of a group that made the last four months of the restaurant's life seem like one huge, exhausting party. It was the most exciting cooking time of my life. I knew that all those who came to my restaurant in those last weeks truly trusted me and, for the first time ever, I was able to throw caution to the wind. Nat called it organised chaos. All the team did an amazing job but Alex, Nat and Steve live in the history books of our family.

Alex and her husband have since moved to Sydney, where they became partners in their own restaurant, Bird Cow Fish, originally in Balmain and now in Surry Hills. This dessert of Alex's is for a special occasion – it's extravagant but marvellous. When I make it, the verjuice, pears, walnuts, lemons and eggs all come from our farm. I have always meant to make my own prunes, and am a step closer now that I have my own d'Agen prune plum tree. I should also put Sauternes production on the must-do list, but that's more of a pipe-dream!

This trifle can be moulded in a bowl and turned out after 24 hours, or it can be served from a traditional glass trifle bowl just a few hours after it has been made. Although it seems complicated, if done in two stages over two days, it is quite simple.

75 g shelled walnuts

375 g prunes, pitted

1½ cups (375 ml) Sauternes

½ vanilla bean

1 stick cinnamon

rind of 1 lemon, in large strips

8 beurre bosc pears

1½ cups (375 ml) verjuice

¼ cup (55 g) castor sugar

8 good-quality Italian macaroons

SYLLABUB

finely grated rind and juice of 1 lemon

2 tablespoons brandy

2 tablespoons castor sugar

300 ml thick cream

freshly grated nutmeg, to taste

GÉNOISE SPONGE

6 free-range eggs, separated

200 g castor sugar

135 g plain flour

100 ml melted clarified butter

CUSTARD

3 cups (750 ml) Sauternes

16 egg yolks

250 g castor sugar

1 litre 35 per cent fat cream
   (see Glossary)

Make the syllabub a day in advance. Put the lemon rind and juice into a bowl with the brandy and let steep for 12 hours. Next day, strain the brandy and lemon mixture into a large, deep bowl, then add the castor sugar and stir until it has dissolved. Pour in the cream slowly, stirring all the time. Grate in a little nutmeg, then whisk the mixture until it thickens and holds a soft peak on the whisk. Refrigerate until needed.

For the génoise sponge, preheat the oven to 190°C. Grease and line a round 26 cm cake tin. Beat the egg whites until soft peaks form, then beat in the castor sugar a tablespoon at a time until the mixture is stiff and all the sugar has been absorbed. Spoon a quarter of the egg white mixture into the yolks, fold it in then pour the lot back over the remaining egg white mixture and fold through. Sift the flour on top and then carefully fold it in. Fold in the cooled clarified butter to make a batter.

Pour the batter into the prepared tin and bake for 25 minutes or until the cake begins to come away from the sides of the tin and feels springy. Cool on a wire rack.

For the custard, heat the Sauternes in a saucepan over high heat and reduce it by half (you need 375 ml). In a bowl, whisk the egg yolks, then beat in the castor sugar until it has dissolved. In a saucepan, heat the cream until almost at boiling point, then add the reduced Sauternes and bring back to almost a boil over high heat, then add this to the egg mixture, whisking thoroughly and continuously. Pour the custard into the top of a double boiler over simmering water and cook it slowly until it coats the back of a spoon, then quickly strain it through a sieve into a clean bowl standing in iced water. If you don't have a double boiler, use a heatproof bowl that fits snugly over a pan of boiling water.

Preheat the oven to 220°C. Dry-roast the walnuts on a baking tray for 6–8 minutes, then rub off their skins with a clean tea towel. Soak the prunes in the Sauternes with the vanilla bean, cinnamon stick and lemon rind for 30 minutes. Peel and core the pears, then cut them into eighths and poach them gently over low heat in a saucepan with the verjuice and castor sugar for about 8–10 minutes or until softened.

Cut away the bottom of the génoise and set it aside – this will become the 'lid' of the trifle – then cut away and reserve the outer crust. Cut widthways across the trimmed cake to achieve thin, wide slices. Choose a bowl about the same diameter as the cake and line it generously with plastic film if you plan to turn out the trifle. Line the sides and base of the bowl with the slices of cake, then brush the cake with the juice from the pears and prunes to moisten and flavour it. Crush the macaroons and moisten them with these juices as well, then mould the macaroon mixture over the cake to form an inner shell.

Thinly slice the pear, then overlap the slices over the macaroon mixture to create another layer. Follow this with a layer of prunes. The bowl will be filling up by now and you will have created a strong outer structure. Spoon Sauternes custard over the pudding to moisten it, but don't make it too wet. »

Chop the roasted walnuts and, using a food processor, reduce the reserved outer crust of the cake to crumbs, then mix both into the syllabub. Smooth the syllabub mixture into the centre of the trifle, then top with the reserved base of the cake. Cover the trifle with plastic film and place a weighted plate on top, then refrigerate overnight.

If you are turning out the trifle, simply hold a plate over the top and invert the bowl, then carefully remove the plastic film. Rather than spooning out the dessert, as you would if it were still in the bowl, cut slices of trifle to show off its wonderful layers.

GLAZED PEARS WITH MASCARPONE *Serves 4*

1 vanilla bean, halved lengthways
200 g unsalted butter, chopped
150 g castor sugar
rind of 1 lemon and 1 tablespoon juice
2 teaspoons verjuice
4 medium-sized pears, peeled
(be careful to leave the stalks intact)

MASCARPONE
finely chopped rind and juice of 1 lemon
160 g mascarpone

Scrape out the vanilla seeds from the bean and set aside. Melt the butter in a heavy-based frying pan over low heat and add the sugar, lemon juice and verjuice. When the sugar has dissolved add the peeled pears, lemon rind, vanilla bean and scraped seeds. Cook over low heat for approximately 1 hour or until the pears are an even golden colour. If you have chosen ripe ones, this will take less time, but be careful not to overcook them while colouring. The final colour is important, so it's best not to use overly ripe pears or they will fall apart by the time you get the colour on them.

Check that the pears are done by inserting a thin-bladed knife or skewer into the centre and if there is no resistance when you pull it out, then they are ready. The cooking liquid should be a light caramel colour and can be used to give the pears a wonderful 'glistening' appearance on serving.

Gently fold the lemon rind and juice into the mascarpone; do not beat it as the mascarpone will become too runny.

Place a pear on each serving plate and pour over some caramel. Serve a dollop of the mascarpone next to the pear; its acidic creaminess will blend perfectly with the fruity, vanilla aroma of the poached pear.

PERSIMMONS

 SOME TIME AGO, WHILE BEING INTERVIEWED ABOUT MY book *Maggie's Orchard*, I was asked to name the fruit I would most like to be (or was it that I was most like?). My immediate response was 'a persimmon'. 'Why?' asked the journalist. 'Because of its rounded shape and luscious colour, and because when it is ready to eat it is squashy and mushy and sensuous,' I replied. (I could also have said that if it is not ripe, it is as astringent as hell and full of tannin!)

As it is, I love not only the fruit but the entire tree, particularly when it grows tall against a building (a stone one, for the best effect), lightly espaliered and climbing the wall in search of the sun. Planted this way, the tree shoots straight up and then branches thickly from the top. Should there be another building nearby, the branches arch out towards it, particularly if the tree is of one of the weeping varieties.

The large leaves are very decorative and become beautifully tinted with rich autumn colours before they fall, exposing the glowing reddish-orange fruit that remains on the bare branches. At every stage this tree is a study in the perfection of nature – even when its fruit has been picked, the wood of the tree is lovely to look at. If the tree is of the older astringent variety, I've found the fruit is best when left to totally ripen on the tree.

The big decision for anyone with room in the garden is whether to plant the astringent or non-astringent variety of persimmon. For the most part, the persimmons you buy at the market are non-astringent and can be eaten firm, though they too can be left until soft before eating, and I have learnt to appreciate them more this way.

Commercially, the non-astringent persimmon makes a lot of sense: it travels well and can be displayed in markets much more easily; it can be sliced to reveal its very attractive cross-section of seeds; and it can be eaten when quite hard. Firm, non-astringent persimmons make a crisp addition to a rocket or watercress salad dressed with a fresh lemon vinaigrette and can partner a wide range of other salad ingredients, from goat's cheese to smoked tongue.

However, while I now have many persimmon trees – some the newer non-astringent variety – nothing is quite as special as the astringent ones. I have to say that their jelly-like, sweet, unctuous fruit, left on the tree until almost diaphanous, is like nothing else. Unless you net your trees, you have to pick daily to beat the birds, so I had to resort to picking them just before they reached this stage, which makes them one step short of perfect. This way we had just-ripe persimmons to finish off every meal for weeks on end. As the skin is so edible when the persimmons are ripe, amongst friends we would eat them as one luscious lump rather than serve them formally. For first-time eaters, though, I slice off the top and offer a spoon to scoop out the flesh, and serve them with a dish of clotted cream and cat's tongue biscuits alongside.

I now net my trees to protect them from the birds, and I can tell you it is worth it, as I can let my persimmons ripen on the tree. Remember, the fruit is never better than when totally ripe upon picking – the calyx is easily plucked out and you can eat the fruit just like that, skin and all. Persimmons are so much about texture – to describe them you could say they are a little like a very ripe apricot. When eating the firm, non-astringent variety, take advantage of that star-like pattern in the cross-section of the fruit, which looks so attractive in either salads or fruit salad or dessert.

If you have lots of persimmons, there are many different ways to cook them. When our friends Margaret and Peter Lehmann returned from a trip to the United States some years ago, they brought with them recipes for Persimmon Bread (see page 101) and puddings. My perennial favourite, a Sour-cream Pastry (see page 177) tart case thickly spread with mascarpone (while still a little warm from the oven) and topped with fruit, is wonderful made with ripe non-astringent persimmons still firm enough to cut widthways, skin, seeds and all. A dusting of castor sugar and a quick grill or blast with a kitchen blowtorch, if you have one, caramelises the flesh – the vibrant colour alone is worth the trouble.

A faded note in my file suggests drying persimmons and grinding them to make a powder. Then take a green mango, slice it and dust the flesh with the persimmon powder and salt; the resulting flavour is savoury, sweet and salty. At the time I had dried persimmons in the hydrator or the oven and found that those that were unripe dried without any chalkiness. A footnote reads: 'Next year, dry lots!' I'll just have to make sure that I'm not away next May.

Harold McGee, in his second book on food science and lore of the kitchen, *The Curious Cook*, has a chapter called 'Persimmons Unpuckered', which I recommend as serious reading for persimmon lovers and others interested in tannins; persimmons are astringent because of the huge amounts of tannin they contain. McGee tells us that an atmosphere rich in carbon dioxide can bring about a reduction in astringency long before the fruit softens, and gives examples of simple methods to achieve this. It certainly makes fascinating reading and explains the steps that led to this discovery, with tales of boys in Chinese villages burying persimmons in the ground, smothering them in covered earthenware jars along with a stick of incense, or sealing them in airtight, empty Japanese sake barrels, all in an attempt to deprive the persimmon of air. The astringency can be reduced by freezing the fruit but in large packed volumes this takes 10–90 days and the fruit is mushy as a result.

McGee also tells us that the Portuguese love to dry persimmons, the Chinese preserve them with sugar, and that the fruit is a member of the ebony family and its wood is much sought after for making golf clubs, shoe lasts and weavers' shuttles. The persimmon is grown widely in Japan, where they also make a traditional dessert from a persimmon paste which is teamed with yuzu, a citrus fruit.

Melbourne cook, writer and teacher Penny Smith once teamed some of my smoked kangaroo with persimmon for a special Australian dinner she served to some visiting African dignitaries. She told me it was a startling success.

To finish, here is a small piece out of a book I love, *Please to the Table: The Russian Cookbook* by Anya von Bremzen and John Welchman: 'To me one of the simplest and most delightful conclusions to a meal with a Mediterranean accent is a plate of lusciously ripe persimmons, peeled, sliced and garnished with mint sprigs.'

SEARED TUNA WITH PERSIMMON AND FENNEL SALAD   *Serves 4*

1 teaspoon fennel seeds

1 teaspoon coriander seeds

1 fennel bulb, trimmed and thinly sliced,
    fronds reserved

sea salt flakes and freshly ground
    black pepper

150 ml extra virgin olive oil

4 × 200 g bluefin *or* yellowfin tuna steaks

2 meyer lemons

2 non-astringent persimmons, thinly
    sliced widthways

¼ cup chopped mint

juice of 1 lemon

¼ cup (60 ml) walnut oil

Toast the fennel and coriander seeds in a dry frying pan, then cool and grind using a mortar and pestle. Chop the reserved fennel fronds finely and, in a small bowl, combine with the ground spices, then season with salt and pepper. Add about 100 ml of the olive oil and stir in, then rub this mixture on both sides of the tuna steaks. Set aside for 20–30 minutes.

Meanwhile, cut the lemons widthways into 4–6 slices, depending on their size. Drizzle with 1 tablespoon olive oil. Grill lemon slices under a hot griller until caramelised on both sides, then set aside.

Sear the tuna on a hot chargrill plate for 1½ minutes, then turn over and cook for another minute. Remove from the heat, transfer to a plate and top with the lemon slices, drizzle with the remaining olive oil and leave to rest for a few minutes.

Place the persimmon, fennel, mint, lemon juice and walnut oil in a bowl and toss together. Season to taste with a little salt and pepper, then serve with the seared tuna.

MARGARET'S PERSIMMON BREAD

Makes 2 loaves

This is Marg Lehmann's recipe for persimmon bread. I love to serve it with a ripe blue cheese, a fresh persimmon and walnuts.

2 free-range eggs

1 cup (220 g) sugar

2 tablespoons melted butter

2 cups (300 g) plain flour

2 teaspoons bicarbonate of soda

2 teaspoons ground cinnamon

1 teaspoon freshly grated nutmeg

1 teaspoon ground cloves

½ cup (125 ml) milk

1½ cups persimmon pulp
(about 4 persimmons)

1 teaspoon vanilla extract

1 cup (170 g) raisins

1 cup (140 g) walnuts *or* pecans

Preheat the oven to 180°C. Mix the eggs, sugar and melted butter in a large bowl. Sift the flour, soda and spices into the bowl, then stir in all the remaining ingredients. Divide the mixture between two greased loaf tins, then stand these in a roasting pan filled with warm water. The water should come about halfway up the sides of the loaf tins.

Bake for 1¼ hours, then turn the loaves out of their tins onto a wire rack to cool.

PERSIMMON AND AMARETTO

Serves 1

1 very ripe, non-astringent persimmon

1½ teaspoons Amaretto

50 g mascarpone

honey, to serve

Place the persimmon in the freezer for 24 hours, then remove it 2 hours before serving (it should be just soft to the touch). This gives the fruit a lovely sorbet-like consistency.

Cut the persimmon in half and drizzle ½ teaspoon Amaretto over each cut side. Fold the remaining Amaretto into the mascarpone.

Spoon the mascarpone over the persimmon, then spoon over a little honey and serve.

JANE'S PERSIMMON PUDDING   *Serves 6*

Marg Lehmann gave me this recipe from a friend of hers in the United States. Marg says it is a taste sensation and, as persimmon is in season at Christmas over there, it is often served flamed with brandy and surrounded by holly.

This recipe is a classic example of one that has been passed on to friends and added to and tweaked along the way – I love all the options given to turn it out successfully. Opinion is divided as to whether the addition of nuts and fruit overpower the persimmon – my version uses them, but you can omit them if you like.

½ cup (50 g) walnuts	1 cup persimmon pulp (about 3 persimmons)
1 cup (220 g) sugar, plus extra for dusting	2 teaspoons bicarbonate of soda dissolved
125 g butter, melted	in 2 tablespoons warm water
2 free-range eggs	dash brandy
1 cup (150 g) plain flour	1 teaspoon vanilla extract
¼ teaspoon salt	1 cup dried currants *or* chopped raisins
1 teaspoon ground cinnamon	

Preheat the oven to 220°C. Dry-roast the walnuts on a baking tray for 6–8 minutes, then rub off their skins with a clean tea towel.

Mix together the walnuts, sugar, butter and eggs. Stir in the flour, salt and cinnamon. Add the persimmon pulp, bicarbonate of soda and water mixture, brandy, vanilla extract and currants or raisins.

Take a 2-litre-capacity pudding mould with a lid and grease it thoroughly, then coat with the extra sugar. Fill two-thirds full with the batter. (Or substitute with a clean 1 kg coffee tin, using a doubled piece of aluminium foil as a lid.) Using a saucepan or stockpot large enough to hold the mould, create a rack on the bottom with jar lids. Place the covered mould on this rack and add water until it reaches halfway up the side of the mould, then cover the saucepan with a lid. Bring to the boil over high heat, then reduce heat to low and steam the pudding for 2½–3 hours (longer cooking won't harm it – the finished pudding should be dark, springy and may pull away slightly from the mould).

To unmould, turn the mould upside-down on a plate. If the pudding does not drop right out, shake and pound the sides of the mould vigorously, right-side up, then invert it again. The next alternative is to leave the pudding inverted on a plate to drop out once it is cool. The last resort is to loosen the pudding with a flat knife; if it breaks, it can usually be reassembled.

Serve the pudding warm with Crème Anglaise (see page 39), runny cream or ice cream.

SANDOR PALMAI'S PERSIMMON TARTS   *Serves 6*

This tart is etched in my memory. It was made by a gifted young Barossa chef, Sandor Palmai, when he and his then wife had a tiny restaurant in Bethany called Landhaus. The tart truly showcased this fruit, bringing out the best of both astringent and non-astringent varieties.

The thin slices of the firm fruit created a counterbalance to the squelchy old-fashioned pulp of the astringent variety, and the addition of the lime sorbet was such a refreshing finish after the richness of the persimmon. Sandor Palmai suggests serving a lime sorbet adapted from *Jane Grigson's Fruit Book* with this dish. I find my Sour-cream Pastry (see page 177) also works well for this.

1 × quantity Sour-cream Pastry (see page 177)	**SORBET**
½ cup (125 ml) crème fraîche	250 g sugar
2 very ripe astringent persimmons	3 limes, rind removed and very finely chopped
2 ripe non-astringent persimmons	

To make the sorbet, stir 1 litre of water and the sugar in a large saucepan over low heat until the sugar dissolves, then increase the heat to high and boil for 2–3 minutes. Place lime rind in a saucepan of cold water, then bring to the boil, strain in a sieve (reserving liquid) and cool under cold running water. Simmer the blanched rind in 150 ml of the reserved liquid for about 15 minutes or until tender, stirring occasionally; watch that it doesn't burn. Squeeze the limes, mix the juice with the remaining liquid, rind and cooking syrup, then taste and add extra sugar or lime juice if necessary. Churn in an ice cream machine following manufacturer's instructions.

Make and chill the pastry as instructed. Roll out to a 5 mm thickness, then cut into 6 circles and use to line six 12 cm individual tart tins with removable bases. Line pastry with foil pressed well into the edges and fill with pastry weights. Chill pastry for 20 minutes.

Meanwhile, preheat the oven to 200°C. Blind bake the pastry cases for 15 minutes, then remove the pastry weights and foil and bake for another 5 minutes. Cool to room temperature.

Add 1 tablespoon crème fraîche to each tart case. Remove the calyx from the astringent persimmons and spoon out the pulp, discarding the seeds, if any. Divide the pulp equally among the tarts. Remove the calyxes from the non-astringent variety and cut the fruit widthways into thin slices, then arrange these over the pulp in each tart case.

Serve the persimmon tarts with scoops of lime sorbet.

PHEASANT

IN THE LATE 1970s, WHEN WE OPENED THE PHEASANT FARM
Restaurant, one rarely saw pheasant on a restaurant menu, let alone in the
kitchen of a private house. Even now it is still not common. Yet pheasant is
much more interesting to eat than chicken – it is sweet, moist and delicious, and
not as strongly flavoured as duck or pigeon.

Is the pheasant fresh or hung? When someone asks this question it usually indicates
that they are from Europe. Most game in Europe is wild and therefore of indeterminate
age, and so it must be cooked with care to avoid the meat being tough. Hanging helps to
tenderise the meat and gives the bird its 'high' gamy flavour. Many Europeans consider
pheasant not worth eating unless it is hung until it is so high that it 'walks away' and the
skin is actually green.

I would have to say that a hung bird would always be my preference, though ideally
with someone else to cook it for me (as the pheasant is hung with its skin on and guts
intact, the strong smell tends to permeate the cook's clothing and skin).

Late autumn is the time for pheasant, and of course it can be hung outside at this time
in the northern hemisphere. In the United Kingdom it used to be illegal to serve pheasant
in a restaurant outside of a twelve-week period each year, starting from 1 October, to
ensure the birds were fresh. This is changing now, but there certainly were large fines for
flouting this law, and restaurants could not serve birds that were caught in the season and
frozen for later.

In Australia the general public finds the idea of hanging pheasant repugnant, due largely
to our weather. An Australian autumn can be like an Indian summer, and game would go
off very quickly in these conditions. So here we enjoy our birds fresh in season, and frozen
at other times of the year.

Ultimately, the success of the Pheasant Farm Restaurant was a result of the direct link
between farmer and cook. As the cook, I was able to tell my husband Colin how I wanted

the birds presented, at what age and size they were the most succulent, and even how I wanted them processed. In short, Colin raised our pheasants to suit my requirements for the restaurant. You could hardly have a more direct link than that!

Not that I would suggest every primary producer go that far, but what worked for us is that we were passionate about our product, and we learnt all we could about it by immersing ourselves in every bit of information available, as well as getting direct feedback from the public. Also, we loved to eat pheasant. I have heard many farmers say that they don't even like their product; how then can they truly believe in it, improve on and market it?

Pheasants are expensive – one reason for this is that they take a minimum of sixteen weeks to reach maturity. The birds are not given antibiotics to accelerate growth; they are free-ranged and given as much green feed as possible. Their vegetarian diet is of vital importance. Pheasants are particularly prone to misadventure, which, combined with low hatchability and a long growth period, sometimes made us wonder why we ever started breeding them.

Colin's dream of raising wild game dated back to his days in New Zealand when he took his commercial pilot's licence. He was based on the South Island, where game was plentiful, and it just seemed like a good idea to him as a country boy. In 1978 he was awarded a Churchill Fellowship to tour Europe and America to study the rearing of game birds, and on his return began breeding pheasants in earnest.

As much as I love pheasants, just sometimes I wondered how it would be to have called the restaurant 'The Guinea Fowl Farm' for a change of pace! In those days I cooked all sorts of game, but about 65 per cent of our customers insisted on pheasant. I was always seeking new ideas for using the birds that we raised and utilising every part, from the liver for pâté to the giblet and heart for confit and the head and feet for stock. I smoked the breeder birds and even had people collect feathers for fly fishing and jewellery.

Pheasant is very simple to cook when you know how to treat it. Cooking is all about enjoying yourself in the kitchen, so forget all you've read in European cookery books about larding (threading the fat through the meat with a larding needle) and barding (wrapping the meat in fat), or roasting the bird for anywhere from 40 minutes to 1½ hours. No wonder people think pheasant is dry!

The trick to cooking pheasant is to pot-roast it to a just-cooked state and then leave it to rest in its own juices. Alternatively you can roast it quickly in a very hot oven (although this can be tricky and may take some practice to get right). Easier for the home cook is to start it off at a high temperature to caramelise the skin, then cook it for longer at a lower temperature, or to gently seal the skin first in nut-brown butter before roasting.

The easiest way to prepare pheasant for roasting is to 'spatchcock' it. To do this, cut the spine out with kitchen scissors, making an incision either side of the vent, then flatten the bird with the heel of your hand. Brush generously with a marinade of olive oil, orange or lemon juice, fresh thyme and/or juniper berries, and leave it to sit in those juices in a dish in the refrigerator for several hours to allow all the flavours to penetrate.

If roasting at high temperature, say 220°C, brush the skin with orange juice and extra virgin olive oil and add salt just before cooking to aid caramelisation. Choose the shallowest roasting pan you have as the bird cooks for such a short time that the heat must penetrate the flesh with as few barriers as possible. Don't attempt to cook more than two birds at a time in a normal household oven, and position the shelves as far apart as possible. Make sure the oven has reached its peak heat before sliding the birds in; and be as quick as you can to minimise heat loss. Most ovens will need all the help they can get to obtain and sustain the heat required to caramelise the skin to perfection and ensure the fast cooking that produces moistness.

The cooking time depends on the size of the bird, the efficiency of the oven, and the thickness of the material from which the roasting pan is made. It will take anything from 12–20 minutes to cook a 900 g bird: it is ready when the thigh pulls away easily, the thickest part of the breast is springy to the touch, and the skin is golden brown. Remove the pan from the oven, then turn the bird upside-down and leave it to rest for another 20 minutes before carving it from the bone. Delicious.

MY WAY OF COOKING PHEASANT   *Serves 2*

In the restaurant days I always used the high-temperature method and always separated the legs from the breast, which I left on the frame. As so many people would order pheasant, I had to be able to cook it quickly so as to turn orders around in reasonable time. Since then, my experience has shown that a less fraught way for the home cook, given that ovens vary so much, is to cook it at a lower temperature than I used in the restaurant, as I've done here.

Renowned chef Cheong Liew gave me this recipe for his favourite marinade. It helps to give the skin a wonderful caramelised texture without having to seal the bird before cooking when roasting at a high temperature, but it is more foolproof to take the time to seal the skin first.

1 × 1.2 kg pheasant	extra virgin olive oil, for cooking
finely chopped rind and juice of 1 orange	sea salt flakes
6 juniper berries, crushed	verjuice (optional), for cooking
2 sprigs thyme	125 ml Golden Chicken Stock (optional)
gin (optional), for marinade	(see page 181), for cooking

To prepare the pheasant, cut the tips off the wings with a sharp knife and take the flesh off the wing joint to show bare bone. Because of the lack of fat in many pheasants (although not ours, which are especially raised on vegetarian grains), the wing is not a succulent part, and if the flesh is left on this part of the wing it inhibits the cooking of the breast. As a pheasant this size is perfect for two, to save the trouble of carving, keep the bird intact while cooking, then when ready to serve, simply cut it in half with a sharp cook's knife or kitchen scissors.

Place the pheasant in a dish with the orange rind and juice, crushed juniper berries and thyme. (If cooking more than one pheasant, use this quantity for each pheasant.) If you are feeling extravagant, slosh in a little good gin as well. Leave to marinate in the fridge for 3 hours.

Preheat the oven to 180°C. Remove the pheasant from the marinade and place in a large heavy-based frying pan. Mix the marinade with some olive oil and brush this on the skin of the bird.

Season the pheasant with salt and gently pan-fry over low–medium heat until the skin is a golden colour. Lay the bird on one side in a shallow roasting pan, then generously brush the oil and marinade over the skin once more.

Bake the pheasant for 10 minutes on one side, then turn the bird over and bake for another 10 minutes on the other side. Now turn the pheasant breast-side down, and bake for a further 10 minutes. By this stage the bird should be almost cooked through; check by pulling a leg away from the breast, making sure there are no signs of rawness anywhere. If unsure, insert a skewer into the thickest part of the breast – if any pink juices show, then it requires a little more cooking.

To rest, turn the bird so the breast is facing down in the roasting pan. Cover with foil and leave for 20 minutes. At this stage, if you wish to use the pan juices to make a sauce, splash the hot pheasant with verjuice, then add 125 ml warm, good-quality chicken stock to the pan while the bird rests.

The easiest way to serve the bird is to cut it in half, place each half on a plate, then spoon over the pan juices. Serve with roasted parsnips and a green salad.

WARM SALAD OF SMOKED PHEASANT   *Serves 6*

I have a special recipe for the older birds we fatten and smoke. They are so juicy that you would never guess they would otherwise have ended up in the stockpot. The first time I made this dish was at the Australian Symposium of Gastronomy in Adelaide, where they organised a huge 'Market to Table Fair' in Gouger Street. The whole street was blocked off and trestle tables stretched its length. About 25 restaurants participated, many of them cooking in the street. There was a queue from the minute we set up, and I prepared about 800 serves of this dish. The queue was so long my daughters kept offering tastings of our pâté to stop people from becoming restless. It was an exhausting, exciting day, cooking right there in the street with my customers talking to me as they waited – a great bit of street theatre.

1 cos lettuce, leaves separated and cut
    into large pieces
6 witlof (3 red and 3 white), bases trimmed
    and leaves separated
1 bunch rocket
½ cup (125 ml) extra virgin olive oil,
    plus extra for cooking
1½ tablespoons balsamic vinegar *or*
    vino cotto (see Glossary)

60 g butter
250 g Portobello mushrooms,
    trimmed and sliced
sea salt flakes and freshly ground
    black pepper
1 smoked pheasant *or* large smoked chicken,
    boned and thinly sliced
18 pieces Mustard Apricots (see page 182)

Wash and dry the salad leaves. Make a vinaigrette with the oil and vinegar. Heat the butter in a frying pan until nut-brown, then add a dash of olive oil to stop it burning. Add the mushrooms, season with salt and pepper and sauté until cooked, then add the pheasant and mustard apricots to warm them through. Toss in a little vinaigrette to just coat the ingredients.

Arrange the leaves on serving plates and dress with the vinaigrette. Divide the pheasant, mushroom and apricot mixture among the plates and serve.

PHEASANT WITH SULTANA GRAPES AND VERJUICE *Serves 6*

3 × 800 g young hen pheasants
juice of 1 lemon
extra virgin olive oil, for cooking
½ cup (125 ml) verjuice
9 sprigs thyme
sea salt flakes

60 g unsalted butter, plus 100 g unsalted
    butter, cubed and chilled, extra (optional)
1 cup (250 ml) reduced Golden Chicken
    Stock (see page 181)
2 cups sultana grapes, removed from
    the stems

Preheat the oven to 180°C. With a sharp knife, cut the tips off the wings and take the flesh off the wing joint to show bare bone. Squeeze a little lemon juice into the cavity of each bird, then moisten the birds with a little olive oil and 2 teaspoons of the verjuice. Sprinkle over the thyme and season with salt.

Heat the 60 g butter in a large saucepan until nut-brown, adding a dash of olive oil to stop it burning. Brown the birds gently on all sides over low–medium heat until they are a golden colour. Place them on their sides in a shallow roasting pan.

Bake the pheasants in the oven for 10 minutes, then turn them onto the other side and bake for another 10 minutes; at this stage the skin should be golden all over and the birds cooked through. Check by pulling a leg away from the breast, making sure there are no signs of rawness anywhere. If unsure, insert a skewer into the thickest part of the breast – if any pink juices show, then it requires a little more cooking.

Remove the birds from the oven and transfer to another dish, each breast-side down, and rest, covered with foil, for 20 minutes. »

To make the sauce, deglaze the roasting pan with the rest of the verjuice, then add the stock and reduce by half over high heat. When ready to serve, cut the pheasants in half with a sharp cook's knife or kitchen scissors. Bring the sauce back to the boil then, if you wish, whisk in the extra butter to finish. About 40 seconds before serving, toss in the grapes, then pour over the sauce.

PHEASANT PIE

Serves 8

We now serve this pie regularly at the Farmshop, accompanied by a simple rocket and preserved lemon salad. This is also the game pie we once tried to launch on the Sydney market. It seemed the perfect product: we had pheasants to spare after the restaurant closed and we had lemons from our small grove at the Riverland vineyard. We even planted 36 thyme plants outside the pâté room but never managed to produce enough for the weekly pie orders. We made the mixture in our kitchen, then flew it up to Sue Patchett of Patchett's Pies in Sydney who made the pastry, cooked the pies and delivered them to David Jones. The pies were wonderful, if I do say so myself, but their shelf-life was so short and the ingredients so expensive that we were unable to sustain production.

If you can't get game birds for this pie, really good free-range chicken can be used instead. You need a total of 750 g meat off the bone – about 450 g breast meat and 300 g leg meat.

2 × 1 kg pheasants
250 g minced veal
250 g minced pork
250 g minced pork fat
125 g sugar-cured bacon, rind removed
   and finely chopped
2 cloves garlic, very finely chopped
finely chopped rind of 4 lemons
½ teaspoon juniper berries, bruised
sea salt flakes and freshly ground
   black pepper

150 g poultry livers, trimmed
   and finely chopped
butter, for cooking
500 g button mushrooms, chopped
1½ tablespoons thyme leaves
extra virgin olive oil, for cooking
1 × quantity Sour-cream Pastry
   (see page 177)
cream, for brushing

Remove the thigh meat from the pheasants and cut into small dice, then mix it with the minced veal and pork, pork fat and bacon. Add the garlic, lemon rind, juniper berries, 3 teaspoons salt and 1 teaspoon pepper, and mix well.

Toss the livers in a frying pan with a knob of butter over high heat until sealed, then season with salt and pepper and tip onto a plate to cool. In the same pan, toss the mushrooms and thyme with another knob of butter over medium–high heat until softened, then remove to a plate to cool. Reduce the juices in the pan over high heat to a glaze, then cool.

Cut the breast meat of the pheasant into 1 cm dice and sprinkle with a little olive oil. In a large bowl, combine the meat mixture, liver, mushrooms, glaze and, lastly, the breast meat. Cover and leave in the refrigerator overnight for the flavours to infuse.

Next day, make and chill the pastry as instructed. Cut out 8 pieces to fit 8 individual pie moulds, and another 8 for the lids. Line the pie moulds with the chilled pastry and spoon the filling into the pastry case. Top with the lids, pinching the edges to create a good seal. Brush the pies with cream and chill in the refrigerator for 20 minutes.

Preheat the oven to 230°C and cook the pies for 10 minutes, then lower the temperature to 210°C and cook for another 10 minutes. Rest the pies for 10 minutes before serving. They are fabulous eaten at room temperature and are great cold too.

POMEGRANATES

 POMEGRANATES ARE FREQUENTLY OVERLOOKED BECAUSE people don't know how to eat them, and they are often only grown for the ornamental beauty of the trees when laden with fruit in autumn. However, I love the crunch of the brilliant red seeds and the tartness their juice provides as much as the beauty of their waxy skins, which blush from gold to deep rosy-pink, and are topped with a crown-like calyx.

Pomegranate trees are really tough. During a heatwave in January 1999 we were away and weren't able to water our trees and plants. On our return we found only a few plants had survived, and the only one to continue to thrive was the pomegranate – and it was growing against a garden wall, which would have exacerbated the already scorching temperatures.

Heartened by this, I planted forty more pomegranate trees (they are formally trees, but look more like a bush) the next month, to make a hedge against a couple of walls at the farm – one in full sun and the other shaded by gum trees. A year later, the plants in the sunny position were 1.5 metres tall and full of fruit, while the shaded trees had a lot less fruit and were a little more spindly, but they made up for this as their leaves were lush enough to hide a very pedestrian fence, and their fruit found many uses. I found I had ordered about ten more plants than were needed at the farm, so I put them in at home to hedge a new deck. I kept them in pots for months before planting them out, and within two years they had reached the height of the decking (1 metre), spreading to become a hedge with fruit.

Pomegranates have long been grown in the Riverland of South Australia and Victoria and are finally becoming of more interest to commercial growers. They will grow in almost all climates, although the perfect choice is a sunny, dry one (Mediterranean, in fact). There are many varieties, including some truly ordinary in flavour, so do your homework before going to a nursery and only buy those that are known.

The larger fruit is the most popular and is often bought for floral art and religious ceremonies. My grower in the Riverland has a hundred trees of ten varieties. He thinks the brilliantly crimson Wonderful is the best all-rounder, but he also has a paler variety with softer seeds that is very popular, as the seeds can be swallowed whole rather than spat out. I find these bland, with virtually no flavour – I'd prefer to put up with the inconvenience of the seeds to be sure of getting that wonderful tartness. My favourite of all varieties is the Azerbaijani, which is deep-red, large, sweet and sour, and can be purchased from Daley's Fruit Tree Nursery.

It is hard to tell a ripe pomegranate by colour alone, since different varieties colour in different ways. If you have a pomegranate plant in your garden, you're perfectly placed to observe the hairline crack that appears in the waxy skin when the fruit is ripe. If relying on your greengrocer, buy one pomegranate first and cut into it to test for ripeness before planning a special pomegranate feast, as they are disappointing when under-ripe. Never buy fruit with mould in the crack as these pomegranates are already spoilt.

The pomegranate originated in Persia, and whereas it mostly featured in Persian, Russian or Greek cookbooks in the past, there are now many great Australian cooks who use and write about this intriguing fruit. You can imagine people buying whole pomegranates just for show, as cut in half they reveal a wonderful display of red, crystal-like seeds. These can be used in many different ways, but first need to be separated from their yellowish membranes, which harbour the astringency or tannin that can make a dish unpalatable. The seeds can be used simply as a dessert fruit – perhaps on a plate of autumn fruits with persimmon and tamarillo. Or savour the crunch the seeds add when tossed into late autumn and early winter salads, such as one of ripe figs, prosciutto and goat's

cheese. I love the crunchy texture of the brilliant red seeds in a dish, although some people may find them difficult as they are similar to the pips of the grape. If serving hummus, top with a little extra virgin olive oil and some pomegranate seeds.

To juice a pomegranate, simply cut in half, then squeeze in a citrus juicer. If not ripe, a great deal of tannin can be released when squeezing, so the juice needs to be tasted as it may be too astringent (often a little sugar syrup needs to be added, made by boiling equal parts sugar and water for 20 minutes). A large ripe pomegranate yields about 250 ml juice.

Pomegranate juice would make a very grown-up soft drink if you could get enough of it. But if you've only a little freshly squeezed juice, try it with gin – you won't need too much for that. For a cocktail, add a shot of Cointreau to a cocktail glass of pomegranate juice and finish with a few pomegranate seeds. For a non-alcoholic version, sweeten the pomegranate juice with a little sugar syrup, dilute with mineral water and top with a sprig of mint.

Like lemon juice, pomegranate juice contributes a significant sharpness to sauces, but it is more rounded, with a bittersweet characteristic that cuts the richness of game, pork, lamb or good poultry. Pomegranate juice and seeds lose colour when heated, so even though they give a brilliant lift of flavour to a sauce, it is worth holding back some of the seeds to add to the dish just before serving. I choose the ripest pomegranates in my pile and separate a tablespoon or so of seeds per person to add to the sauce at the very last moment so that it has crunch and colour.

I also make a warm vinaigrette to serve with partridge. I mix almond or walnut oil with pomegranate juice and seeds and chopped herbs (particularly mint), then pour this over the hot birds as they rest.

In the Middle East, a traditional soup combines spinach, leeks, rice or lentils, coriander, flat-leaf parsley and lots of pomegranate juice, with a final addition of fresh mint. Sugar is stirred in at the last moment, if required.

The first time I tasted pomegranate flesh I took one bite, spat it out and didn't try it again for years. Now I eagerly await the season to team the fruit with duck, pheasant or guinea fowl. I don't usually belong to the 'fruit with meat' school of thought, but there are exceptions! Certainly, lemon and orange are ideal with game, and the old-fashioned yet exotic pomegranate has a tartness that complements rich dishes extremely well.

Grenadine syrup was originally made from pomegranates, though sadly now it is chemically manufactured as 'nature identical' (as they say in the food-manufacturing trade to describe an ingredient made in a laboratory to mimic the natural product). Very popular in France with fruit salad or served with grapefruit instead of sugar, grenadine syrup is also used to make cordials, ices and jellies.

Pomegranate molasses is another by-product of this vibrant fruit. Available from Middle Eastern grocers, it can be used instead of fresh pomegranates when they are not in season; use it sparingly, adding water or verjuice to thin it down if necessary. It goes particularly well with poultry, lamb or game, so try adding it to a game or poultry sauce, or brushing it with extra virgin olive oil onto a rack of lamb before roasting.

POMEGRANATE SAUCE (SAVOURY)   *Serves 4*

This is a simple sauce we created in the restaurant to team with roasted mallard duck. It has a Persian influence and can also be used with quail, chicken, pheasant or guinea fowl.

1 onion, finely chopped

1 pomegranate, seeded carefully to avoid
   yellow membrane

pinch ground cardamom

pinch ground turmeric

freshly ground black pepper

pinch sugar

dash red-wine vinegar

juice of 1 lemon

100 ml Golden Chicken Stock
   (see page 181)

sea salt flakes

Sweat the onion and pomegranate seeds until translucent in a saucepan with olive oil over low–medium heat. Add spices and continue to stir. Add sugar and vinegar to taste, then stir until caramelised. When almost catching, add lemon juice and reduce. Finally, add chicken stock and reduce again to desired consistency. Season to taste with a little salt before serving.

WALNUT AND POMEGRANATE SALAD   *Serves 4*

1 pomegranate

2 slices walnut bread

2 teaspoons walnut oil, plus extra
    for brushing

2 punnets lamb's lettuce (mâche)

½ cup mint leaves

½ cup flat-leaf parsley leaves

2 tablespoons snipped chives

2 tablespoons walnuts

130 g fromage blanc *or* fresh ricotta

½ teaspoon rosewater

2 teaspoons extra virgin olive oil

sea salt flakes and freshly ground
    black pepper

Cut the pomegranate in half, then hold over a bowl, cut-side down, and tap each half with a wooden spoon to release the seeds into the bowl. Remove any bits of yellow membrane that have fallen into the bowl with the seeds.

Preheat the oven to 200°C. Brush the walnut bread with walnut oil, then tear into bite-sized pieces. Toast the walnut bread on a baking tray in the oven until golden, then set aside.

Assemble the lamb's lettuce, herbs, walnuts, fromage blanc and pomegranate seeds in a salad bowl. Mix the rosewater, olive oil and the 2 teaspoons of walnut oil together to make a vinaigrette, then pour over the salad. Top with the croutons, then season with salt and pepper and serve.

POMEGRANATE SAUCE (SWEET)   *Makes 250 ml*

3 pomegranates

juice of ½ good-sized lemon

100 g sugar

Cut one of the pomegranates in half, then hold over a bowl, cut-side down, and tap each half with a wooden spoon to release the seeds into the bowl. Remove any bits of yellow membrane that have fallen into the bowl, and reserve the seeds.

Cut the remaining pomegranates in half and squeeze them in a citrus juicer. Boil the resulting juice, along with the lemon juice and sugar, in an enamelled or stainless steel saucepan over high heat for 2 minutes or more to reduce a little.

Cool and add reserved seeds. Serve with desserts such as a rich chocolate cake.

PUMPKIN

 MY MOTHER INTRODUCED ME TO OUR LOCAL GREENGROCER when I was very young. The reason was to teach me how to choose a perfect pumpkin. It was something to be taken very seriously and we would only buy one if we were sure of getting a good thing.

In those days the only pumpkin variety we knew was the Queensland Blue. Once cut, the deep-ochre centre was revealed, but I knew not to be dazzled by it as I had been told to look out for a bluey-green tinge on the edge of the flesh that promised good flavour.

We relied on the greengrocer to have a large blade strong enough to cut through the massive pumpkin – there were no dried-out bits of packaged pumpkin then. The knife was like a cane cutter's blade: long and curved and ever-ready. We didn't have today's array of sophisticated stainless steel knives and, like most families, had only a carving knife to perform all tasks. Years later, when I lived in Europe, my requests for pumpkin were met with contempt, as there it was only considered for the animals.

There are pumpkins and then there are pumpkins, so it is well worth taking the time to find the best. A great Queensland Blue is still amazing, but harder to find in perfect condition than it used to be. Reject pale-fleshed specimens – these often turn out to be watery and tasteless. Woodiness, easily evident in pre-cut pumpkins, is also to be avoided at all costs. Butternuts are a dependable variety, but need to be a deeper colour to be ripe. But also look for new varieties, among them the Kent or jap, a boldly striped green pumpkin, or the Crown prince, which has smooth grey skin. Both are full of flavour and easy to peel.

I have three pumpkin vines this year – luckily garden space is not an issue for me. One of them has yielded lots and lots of male flowers and looks lustrous, but has only one pumpkin to show for itself. I really don't mind as the others are laden. And pumpkin flowers, though a little larger than zucchini flowers, can be stuffed and deep-fried as a starter or as part of an antipasto platter (as they are in Italy; turn to a good Italian cookbook for a batter recipe or stuffing suggestions). I tend to use one flower per person and stuff it generously, making sure that any cheese used is either soft goat's curd or cut quite small to ensure it melts in the short time it takes to deep-fry the battered flower in hot olive oil. Make sure you are ready to serve the moment they are golden – crisp is the word here.

Early in March 2006 we were filming an episode of the ABC TV series *The Cook and The Chef* when pumpkins were at the peak of their season. This coincided with the Tanunda Agricultural Show, and I was asked to be a judge for the best pumpkin at the show. I felt

so incredibly proud of the Barossa, with the different entries in the show hall and various stewards and judges taking their assessment of produce so seriously.

With the cameras rolling, I talked with some of the characters of the show – indeed, characters of the Barossa. It was hard to confine the filming just to pumpkins as the show was probably the best I'd seen in the thirty-three years we've lived in the Valley. This was partly because 2006 was a good year – we had great winter rains in 2005 that continued into spring, and this showed in the bountiful produce – but also because of the energies of that year's committee.

I left the show with half of the winning Queensland Blue under my arm. Filming a few days later, we had the wood fire going, and while my co-presenter Simon Bryant cooked a Beggar's Chicken, I made a huge Pumpkin Risotto (see page 122) out in the courtyard.

Baked pumpkin with the weekly roast was a childhood favourite of mine (always cooked with the skin on, by the way). Over the years I've learnt that pumpkin is also great par-cooked and finished on the barbecue grill plate, brushed with olive oil. For soup, I love to slow-roast chunks of pumpkin in the oven, just moistened with oil, to heighten their flavour. This technique is also good when making pumpkin pie.

During my long pumpkin-less European sojourn, I should have discovered the delights of Italy's pumpkin-filled pasta, which comes from the Modena region in particular. There, freshly baked pumpkin is mixed with crushed amaretti biscuits, egg and breadcrumbs to fill tortelli. Little pillows are made by cutting rounds from a sheet of pasta, then putting some of the pumpkin mixture in the middle before moistening the edges. The pasta is folded over the stuffing to make half-moon shapes and the edges are pressed together to ensure a tight seal. The tortelli are poached in water for a few minutes only and then served with nut-brown butter and freshly grated Parmigiano Reggiano. Another favourite from Italy is pumpkin-filled ravioli served with mustard fruits, burnt butter and sage – a wonderful marriage of flavours. My first experience of this dish was prepared by Sydney chef Franca Manfredi at Bel Mondo and has never been equalled. The pasta, made fresh daily, had an incredible silky texture and we ate it in spectacular surroundings overlooking the harbour – magical.

CHICKPEA AND ROASTED PUMPKIN SALAD   *Serves 4*

4 baby beetroot

sea salt flakes

400 g pumpkin, seeded and cut into wedges (skin on)

2 red onions, quartered

extra virgin olive oil, for cooking

freshly ground black pepper

2 heads Treviso radicchio, washed and dried

1 avocado, peeled and cut into chunks

lemon juice, for drizzling

1 × 140 g can chickpeas, rinsed and drained

freshly chopped flat-leaf parsley, to serve

VINAIGRETTE

¼ cup (60 ml) extra virgin olive oil, or to taste

1 tablespoon red-wine vinegar, or to taste

Preheat the oven to 180°C. Place the beetroot in a saucepan of cold water and bring to the boil. Add a little salt then simmer over low–medium heat for 30 minutes or until almost cooked. Drain, cool, then peel and cut in half.

Meanwhile, place pumpkin and onions on a baking tray lined with baking paper, drizzle with olive oil and season with salt and pepper. Roast for about 30 minutes or until cooked through and caramelised. Toss the halved beetroot with olive oil, then place on another baking paper-lined baking tray and roast for 15 minutes.

Heat a chargrill pan over high heat. Slice the radicchio into quarters, removing as much of the core as possible while keeping the quarters intact. Toss with olive oil and chargrill on both sides for about 2 minutes each, or until caramelised. Remove from heat and set aside.

Drizzle the avocado chunks with lemon juice. Combine all the ingredients in a large bowl. For the vinaigrette, mix olive oil and vinegar together to taste, and add to the salad.

PUMPKIN PICNIC LOAF   *Serves 6*

I love picnics no matter what time of the year, and am constantly thinking of ways to make them as simple as possible. Nothing spoils a picnic more than having to carry a lot with you, particularly when you choose spots you can only access by climbing through fences or over rocks – and aren't the best spots always just a little inaccessible?

The other thing I have become a lot smarter about is the packing away and cleaning up once you are home. There is something about picnics that induces such relaxation, which can quickly dissipate if the chores upon return require any more effort than throwing the leftovers to the chooks.

This pumpkin loaf makes great autumn picnic fare and would work with many variations of loaf shape – it is the quality of the bread that is important. Optional extras include pitted olives, anchovies or capers.

3 medium-sized very ripe red capsicums,
trimmed, seeded and quartered

¾ cup (180 ml) extra virgin olive oil

500 g good-quality pumpkin like Queensland
Blue *or* jap, seeded, peeled and cut into
large chunks

1 sprig rosemary, leaves stripped

sea salt flakes and freshly ground
black pepper

100 ml verjuice

3 medium-sized zucchini, cut into
1.5 cm chunks

1 × 16 cm-diameter round loaf
wood-fired bread

¼ cup flat-leaf parsley, coarsely chopped

175 g Gruyère, thinly sliced

6 slices prosciutto

Preheat the oven to 220°C. Rub the capsicum skins with a little of the olive oil and place on a baking tray or enamel plate (I have a collection of such plates bought from a hardware store that I use continually for such jobs). Roast for 20 minutes or until skins blacken; alternatively, blacken over a naked flame. Let the capsicums cool for just a few minutes, then place in a plastic bag to sweat.

Meanwhile, blanch the pumpkin in a saucepan of boiling water for 5 minutes. Drain, then drizzle with a little of the olive oil, scatter with rosemary and season with salt and pepper. Bake in a shallow roasting pan for 10 minutes or until cooked through and caramelised. Pour 70 ml of the verjuice over the pumpkin, then return it to the oven and cook for another 2–3 minutes.

Halfway through cooking the pumpkin, place the zucchini in another shallow roasting pan and drizzle with a little olive oil. Bake the zucchini for 5–10 minutes or until cooked but still firm and green. Pour the remaining verjuice over the zucchini, then return to the oven for another 2 minutes.

Peel the capsicum and keep them moist in a dish with their juices. Cut the loaf in half widthways and take out sufficient bread from both the base and the lid to allow the vegetables and other ingredients to be generously housed. Crisp the hollowed-out bread in the oven. Add the parsley to the cooling zucchini and check if it needs seasoning.

Fill the base of the loaf with the roast pumpkin, then top with the sliced Gruyère. Lay prosciutto slices over that. Layer the capsicum and then the zucchini in the hollowed-out loaf top. Put the two halves together, then bake for 15 minutes to melt the cheese. Remove from the oven, then weigh down using cans from the pantry, and leave at room temperature to cool for 15 minutes before wrapping for a picnic.

Pumpkin picnic loaf (see page 119)

PUMPKIN PIZZA WITH OLIVES AND BOCCONCINI *Makes 6 individual pizzas*

For another great version of this pizza, lightly fry some sage leaves in nut-brown butter and olive oil and scatter them over the cooked pizza in place of the olives.

¼ Queensland Blue pumpkin, peeled, seeded
    and cut into 1 cm cubes

½ cup (125 ml) extra virgin olive oil

sea salt flakes and freshly ground
    black pepper

¼ cup (60 ml) verjuice

about 1 cup (250 ml) tomato sugo *or* passata
    (see Glossary)

6 bocconcini, cut into quarters

75 g pitted kalamata olives, roughly chopped

DOUGH

15 g fresh yeast *or* 1½ teaspoons
    dried yeast

500 g strong flour (see Glossary)

1 teaspoon castor sugar

1–1½ cups (250–375 ml) warm water

2 teaspoons salt

1 tablespoon extra virgin olive oil,
    plus extra for greasing

To make the dough, combine the yeast, 1 teaspoon of the flour, castor sugar and warm water in a large bowl and whisk together. Stand this mixture in a warm place for 5–10 minutes or until the yeast activates and froths up. Slowly add the rest of the flour and salt and combine to make a stiff dough. Turn the dough out onto a floured surface and drizzle with olive oil. Knead the dough until it is shiny and bounces back to the touch. Place in a bowl, cover and set aside to rise for 30 minutes.

Meanwhile, preheat the oven to 200°C. Toss the pumpkin in olive oil and season with salt and pepper. Transfer to a baking tray and spread out so the pumpkin pieces have room around them. Roast for 10–15 minutes or until the pumpkin is cooked and golden brown. Drizzle the verjuice over the pumpkin, then return to the oven and cook for another 5 minutes. Remove from the oven and leave to cool.

Increase the oven temperature to 220°C. Turn the dough out onto a floured bench, divide into 6 even pieces, then roll each to a 5 mm thickness and place on a well-oiled heavy-based baking tray. You can top each with about 2 tablespoons of your favourite tomato sugo or passata if you are traditionally minded. Par-bake for 15 minutes or until pale golden.

Remove the pizzas from the oven, drizzle with a little extra virgin olive oil, then top with bocconcini, pumpkin and olives. Return to the oven for 5–10 minutes or until the cheese begins to melt.

PUMPKIN, VERJUICE AND EXTRA VIRGIN OLIVE OIL RISOTTO *Serves 4*

It was my friend Stefano de Pieri who asked me why I didn't use verjuice in risottos, as he thought it perfect for them. As I have such a fondness and respect for Stefano I immediately acted upon his advice and have been using verjuice in my risottos ever since, particularly when making vegetable or seafood ones. I now wonder why it took so long for me to open my eyes to the idea.

I have a huge enamelled paella pan I use for risottos when I'm cooking for a crowd. It's perfect for cooking outdoors, and holds enough to feed twenty to thirty people, depending on whether the risotto (or paella) is an accompaniment or main dish. Pumpkin and verjuice are such a magical combination, and when you add them to risotto (the perfect vehicle for both) it's the easiest way I know to cook for a large group.

2 cups (500 ml) Golden Chicken Stock
    (see page 181)
2 tablespoons extra virgin olive oil
500 g jap pumpkin, peeled and cut
    into 2 cm cubes
50 g unsalted butter
1 onion, finely chopped

1¼ cups (250 g) Arborio rice (see Glossary)
100 ml verjuice
sea salt flakes and freshly ground
    black pepper
60 g freshly grated Parmigiano Reggiano
freshly chopped flat-leaf parsley and
    extra virgin olive oil, to serve

Heat the stock in a saucepan, then keep warm. Heat the olive oil in a wok over high heat and sauté the pumpkin until tender.

Heat the butter in a shallow, wide-based, large saucepan, add the onion and sauté over low–medium heat until golden. When the onion is cooked, add the rice and stir to coat with the onion mixture. Cook for 1–2 minutes then increase the temperature to high. Make a well in the centre of the rice and add the verjuice, continuing to stir until the liquid evaporates. Season with salt and reduce heat to low, then add a ladle of hot stock and stir until absorbed.

Continue adding the stock, a ladleful at a time, stirring until each has been absorbed, until half of the stock has been used; it should take 10 minutes. Add the pumpkin and its juices, then add the remaining stock, a ladleful at a time, until the rice is cooked.

Remove the pan from the heat and stir in the Parmigiano Reggiano. Serve topped with flat-leaf parsley and drizzled with olive oil.

QUINCES

THIS WONDERFULLY EVOCATIVE FRUIT WAS MY FIRST LINK TO
the land in a sense, as when we were looking for a place in the Barossa, more
years ago than I care to remember, we looked at many farmhouses and, even
at the most derelict of places, where the gardens and orchards had been left
untended for years, there would be a surviving quince tree.

With the fervour of the city-turned-country-dweller, I quickly learned to love the quince
tree in all its seasons, so much so that we planted our own quince orchard at a time when
most people were throwing quinces away.

I started dreaming about planting the quince orchard after I read a piece written by
Stephanie Alexander in which she talked about drinking quince wine on a frappé of ice in
France. At the time I had Steve Flamsteed, a passionate young wine-making student,
working with me, so I threw him the challenge of making a quince wine and he was happy
to give it a try.

Finding the quinces for our trial wasn't a problem as, like most properties in the Barossa,
we have a sprawling quince tree in the creekbed that runs through our vineyard. Totally
untended, this tree is abundant with small quinces that are incredibly intense in flavour.
Ever the optimist, I could see the quince wine becoming a huge success, and decided that
planting my own orchard was the only way I could have control over availability.

We planted some 350 quince trees at the Pheasant Farm, then two more quince orchards
as part of our Barossa and Riverland Vineyards, which we own with Colin's brother and
wife – the spring blossom makes a beautiful sight. Just recently another orchard was
planted at home with six new varieties. Not surprisingly, we've had our mishaps. Although
we ordered the Smyrna variety we actually ended up with about fifty pineapple quince
trees, and it wasn't until after harvesting the first crop that we realised. The flavour of the
much larger pineapple quince doesn't suit my requirements. The Smyrna is more 'quince'
in flavour and, very importantly, does not break up in long cooking. (Once you've tried the

Pot-roasted quinces (see page 132)

Pot-roasted Quinces on page 132 you'll understand the significance of this: these quinces need to hold their shape during cooking.)

We've had several vintages of quince wine now, and it's still looking 'interesting'. Remember that we were guided by a whim, never having tasted quince wine before – between us, Steve and I had decided that it should be an apéritif with some spirit. If we had been more 'structured' people, we would have done more research, for it is very difficult to extract juice from mashed-up quinces, and juice is what we needed. We ended up blanching the quinces, then mashing them in a large commercial food processor before putting them through a basket press. It was a performance, with lots of physical work, and left a dreadful mess to clean up!

Steve Flamsteed was one of a core of incredibly talented people who worked for me during the restaurant days, and who are still part of our extended family. Steve is a bit of a one-off, having first trained as a chef then studied wine-making at Roseworthy during the time he worked for us. He then learnt to become a cheese-maker in France, with a Queen's Fellowship. Having excelled in all three fields, he is back to wine-making now, although he still has a great interest in food, particularly cheese – a very special mix of talents in one very special person.

Whilst the making of the quince paste began with whatever fruit we could find from the early 1980s, in 1995 we started to make it on a larger commercial scale. It was Steve who produced the first thousand wooden boxes of paste, making it in three 20-litre pots at a time, day after day. Once the paste reached the right consistency (which required up to five hours of careful stirring, with lots of burns and splatters to show for it) it then needed to be dried out. For this, we ended up sterilising our pheasant incubator (the season being over, I hasten to add) and using it to dry the paste overnight in moulds. We had a side project of quince jelly on the go too, and the perfume of the quinces used in both preparations permeated for weeks.

By 1996 we were making 5 tonnes of quince paste a year. Now, twenty years later, our own trees are in full production, as are those of eight orchardists that grow for us, and we probably make about 150 tonnes per year. It is the one product we have been able to upscale and cook in large batches, the absolute opposite of every other product we make, and I can truly say it gets better and better.

Quince paste has since became one of my signatures, and while its main use is to serve with cheese, particularly a sharp crumbly cheddar or a creamy, slightly stinky, waxed rind, that is only the beginning. Roll half teaspoonfuls of quince paste in melted bitter couverture chocolate. Cut it into small squares and dust all over with a mixture of cinnamon and sugar, then serve with coffee. Use leftover pieces to melt over roasting legs of lamb or add a teaspoon to a sauce for duck, venison or leg of mutton.

Quince trees bear really well, and one tree will have you making quincey things for the whole neighbourhood by the time the tree is five years old. Here in the Barossa we pick our quinces in April, and even in the coolest places in Australia, May would be the latest time for harvesting. So the wide availability of quinces on greengrocers' shelves in winter is due to the quinces being stored in cool-rooms.

There is no end to the quince's versatility. While quince paste is our hero quince product, we also make the quince wine (some years), small amounts of quince jelly and pickled quinces, quince vino cotto, quince glaze for Christmas, and many more quince ideas to come.

The tartness of quince when peeled, cored and sautéed in nut-brown butter is the best antidote to rich and fatty food. If you are ever lucky enough to have fresh foie gras, try pan-frying slices of it with quince and you'll understand the joys of one of the greatest food combinations ever. (You'll need to be in Europe or the United States to have access to fresh foie gras, so you could instead use slices of fresh livers of very well-brought-up chooks, geese or ducks. If all else fails, team with pork or duck meat for much the same effect – though these options lack the silkiness of the livers.)

Quince purée can be served with duck, quail, guinea fowl, partridge or pheasant, or even a great-tasting chook. Cook chopped and peeled quince in a little water in a covered saucepan until it is just soft enough to purée in a food processor or to put through a food mill. You may have to add a little sugar to the purée – but only a couple of tablespoons per kg of fruit. A certain tartness is desirable, but it shouldn't be so intense that it puckers your mouth. The purée will be a light-apricot colour (not the deep red of slow-cooked quince, a process which gives such complexity of flavour). This paler hue is, by the way, the colour of most European quince paste, which is not cooked as long as mine is. Cooking quince

changes its colour due, I believe, to an enzymatic reaction. It begins at pale yellow and goes through stages of pale orange to pink when cooked for a short period. To obtain the deep-red colour, it takes hours and hours of cooking.

Puréed quince can also be used as a dessert by adding more sugar and a vanilla bean during cooking. As figs are in season at the same time as quinces, try serving pan-fried or oven-baked figs in a pastry case with warm quince purée and a scoop of vanilla ice cream alongside.

Pickled quince can be teamed with pickled pork, lamb chops or barbecued kangaroo, or added to a Smoked Duck Breast Salad (see page 131). The cuisines of Morocco and the Middle East feature quinces in savoury dishes, too, particularly with couscous and in tagines, where sweet is mixed with sour. In her book *Mediterranean Cooking*, Paula Wolfert writes about a fish couscous that includes quinces, raisins and baharat (a mixture of 2 parts ground cinnamon to 1 part ground dried rosebuds). How exotic!

You can bake small quinces fresh from the tree. Peel and core the quinces, then stuff them with walnuts, butter and brown sugar or honey and bake, covered, for 45–60 minutes at 220°C, with a little verjuice in the bottom of the baking dish to prevent the juices burning.

Bake quartered or sliced quinces brushed with butter in a 160°C oven with a little verjuice or water in the baking dish for a couple of hours. Try then baking this with pastry or brioche as you would your favourite apple pie. Make a flat quince tart in the same style

as a traditional French apple tart. Follow the instructions for preparing the pastry for the Quince and Prune Tart on page 133. While the pastry is still warm, brush quince or loquat jelly over it. Peel and core quinces, then arrange super-thin slices on the pastry and brush with more jelly. Bake the tart at 180°C for 15–20 minutes, being careful the quince doesn't burn.

Preserving fruit or vegetables is a most satisfying occupation. I often don't put the fruits of my labours away in cupboards or the pantry for ages as I love gloating over them – until I can't cook for the clutter on the benches and one of my tidying frenzies comes upon me. Even then, the top of my huge stainless steel fridge holds masses of bottles (it dates from circa 1950 and in its previous life held specimens in a university laboratory!). The soft late-afternoon sun catches the colours of the preserved quinces and they glow like jewels. The jars on show are the last of the year's harvest to be used, a constant reminder of how clever I have been – and that a new season's bounty is waiting in the cupboards!

Preserving quinces as a breakfast fruit was my first experiment in bottling without adding a sugar syrup. They are delicious, and I now see no reason to use sugar with any fruit when preserving.

Quinces are wonderful to make jelly from as they have such a high pectin content – and the highest amount of pectin is to be had from new-season, just-picked, slightly under-ripe fruit that hasn't been refrigerated. Rosemary goes particularly well with quinces: add a sprig of rosemary to the boiling syrup – this is great brushed over a leg of lamb or fillets of pork before baking. If the jelly is too sweet, add a touch of red-wine vinegar before brushing it over the meat. You can also add allspice berries or black peppercorns to the quince in its initial cooking if you want to use the jelly mainly with savoury dishes.

Quince jelly takes my husband Colin back to his childhood. He toasts doorstops of white bread and adds unsalted butter (a modern-day refinement) before dolloping on the jelly. If there's cream in the fridge, and I'm not looking, he smothers the jelly with it.

To store fragrant quinces, rub the down off them carefully and place them in a wide-necked jar. Pour honey over them. This form of storage produces a wonderful liquid with the taste of honey and quince. We have a friend who for several years kept his beehives on our land and this was a favourite way to use the honey he kindly left for us. The same can be done with brandy to make a quince liqueur.

Pick the last quinces off the tree and when you can neither cook nor give away any more, put them in a basket in the mustiest part of your house – a cellar, store cupboard, or a room with no ventilation – and the perfume of the quince will transform it.

QUINCE PASTE
Makes one 28 × 22 cm scone tray

This quince paste is made just like a jam. It follows a traditional method, with the addition of a little lemon juice so it is not too sweet. I actually use less sugar in my quince paste to allow the quince flavour to shine, but that is because I do not have much of a sweet tooth. You can vary the sugar according to your taste – my paste uses 30 per cent sugar and 70 per cent fruit. You will need to wear a fair amount of armour to stop yourself from being burnt. The end result is worth the effort – every time you serve a beautifully ripe and creamy brie, this paste will be testimony to your determination.

2 kg quinces
castor sugar, to equal the weight
  of the purée when cooked

juice of 2 lemons

Wash and quarter the quinces. Keep the cores, wrap them in some muslin and cook them with the quinces. In a large heavy-based saucepan, pour just enough water over the quinces to cover them, and bring to a boil, simmering over low heat for about 30 minutes or until they are tender enough to purée easily. Drain the quinces, discard the cores and purée the fruit in a food processor or using a food mill, then weigh the purée.

Place the purée and an equal weight of sugar in a very deep, heavy-based saucepan. Add the lemon juice and cook over low heat, stirring almost continuously, for up to 4 hours or until the mixture thickens. (At this stage it is advisable to wrap a tea towel around your arm to protect it, and to use as long a wooden spoon as possible. The mixture will explode and pop and turn a dark red, and only by constant stirring will you prevent it from burning.) Cook until you can hardly push the spoon through the paste.

Remove the paste to a scone tray lined with baking paper and spread it out to a 12 mm thickness. When it cools, wet your hands and flatten the surface as you would when shaping polenta. Place the tray in an oven on the lowest possible setting (in a gas oven, the pilot light would be sufficient) and leave to dry overnight. When it has set enough to be cut into squares with a hot knife, it is ready to be cooled and stored. Pack the quince paste between layers of baking paper and store in an airtight container for up to 1 year.

FLO BEER'S PICKLED QUINCES

Flo Beer, my very special mother-in-law, shared this recipe with me the first time Colin took me home to Mallala to meet his family, only three weeks before our wedding – 45 years ago now. That first meal we had together, Mum (as I used to call her as well as my own mother) served these pickled quinces with pickled pork, and they remain a sentimental favourite. As a lover of pickles, I never miss making a batch every year, and I think of her every time. They are wonderful with ham and terrines or grilled meats, particularly duck or game. Adding some of the juices to a beef or poultry sauce, which is then reduced to a glaze, also works brilliantly.

This recipe is written to work equally well for those who have bought a kilo of quinces from the greengrocer and those wondering what to do with boxes and boxes of the fruit. The volume of liquid required is enough to just cover the cut quinces. You can establish this at the beginning by covering the cut quinces with water, measuring the water used, and using this amount of vinegar.

quinces	castor sugar
lemon juice	whole cloves
white-wine vinegar (the better the quality, the better the final product)	black peppercorns

Wash, peel and core the quinces and cut into quarters or eighths, depending on the size, retaining the skins and cores. Put the cut quinces immediately into water to which lemon juice has been added, to prevent discolouration.

For each 600 ml vinegar, add 440 g sugar, 1 teaspoon cloves and 1 teaspoon peppercorns. Heat the vinegar in a large heavy-based saucepan, then pour in the sugar in a stream to dissolve. Bring to the boil, then add the cloves and peppercorns and boil rapidly to begin forming a syrup. Turn the heat down to low and cook for 15 minutes.

Place the reserved peels and cores in a muslin bag and add to the syrup; it will immediately take on a rosy glow. Add the sliced quinces and cook for about 15 minutes or until they have turned pink and are soft but not mushy.

Store in clean airtight jars with the quinces well-immersed in the liquid. The colour of the quinces will deepen in the jar. Leave for several weeks before opening.

QUINCE ALLIOLI

Makes about 250 ml

I found references to quince allioli in books about Spanish food, and as I'm always interested in anything to do with quince, I experimented with the idea. Then one year, a friend brought me a jar of quince allioli from Spain. I didn't think quickly enough to note the ingredients listed on the jar, but was delighted by the fresh flavour, so once again I started playing around with ingredients and quantities and this is the result.

100 g Maggie Beer Quince Paste

2 tablespoons verjuice

1 clove garlic

sea salt flakes

1 dessertspoon finely chopped rosemary

½ cup (125 ml) extra virgin olive oil

lemon juice (optional), to taste

Melt the quince paste slowly with the verjuice (I find a microwave set on defrost works well for this; otherwise use a pan over very low heat). Leave to cool. Crush the peeled garlic clove and a pinch of salt on a chopping board with the flat side of a knife to make a paste. Transfer the garlic paste, quince paste mixture and chopped rosemary to a food processor and blend. With the motor running, slowly add the olive oil, starting a drop at a time until the mixture emulsifies; after about one-third of the oil has been absorbed, you can start to pour it in a thin, steady stream. (As this is quite a small quantity for many food processors, you might need to scrape the sides of the processor bowl with a rubber spatula now and then to make sure all the ingredients are combined.) Taste and adjust seasoning, squeezing in a little lemon juice if necessary.

Serve with barbecued chicken or rack of lamb, or cold pickled pork.

SMOKED DUCK BREAST SALAD WITH PICKLED QUINCE AND VINO COTTO DRESSING

Serves 4

2 smoked duck breasts

1 tablespoon unsalted butter

50 g Pickled Quinces, including pickling
    liquid (see opposite)

1 head radicchio, leaves separated,
    washed and dried

2 witlof, bases trimmed and leaves separated

1 bunch rocket, washed and dried

1 tablespoon lemon juice

½ cup (125 ml) extra virgin olive oil

vino cotto (see Glossary), to taste

3 golden shallots, thinly sliced

1 tablespoon thinly sliced ginger

1 tablespoon flat-leaf parsley leaves

sea salt flakes and freshly ground
    black pepper

Heat a chargrill plate over high heat. Carefully cut the skin of the duck breasts (not the meat) in diagonal lines, then sear them skin-side down for a couple of minutes – the time will depend on the thickness of the meat – to render the fat and crisp the skin. Turn and seal the other side until just brown, then set aside to rest.

Melt the butter in a sauté pan over medium–high heat, then add the drained quince and brown.

Combine the salad leaves in a large bowl. Make a dressing with a little of the pickled quince liquid, lemon juice, olive oil and vino cotto to taste. Add the quince, shallots and ginger to the salad bowl, then toss with the dressing. Thinly slice the duck breast, then add to the salad, along with the parsley. Season to taste with salt and pepper and serve.

LAMB NECK WITH QUINCES
Serves 2–4

Lamb neck is delicious and full of flavour when cooked slowly. You'll need to ask your butcher to leave the neck whole, as when it is cut into sections it's much more likely to dry out during cooking.

I often cook this the day before I want to serve it, as the easiest way to separate the fat is to refrigerate the lamb overnight then skim the solidified fat from the surface.

1 tablespoon extra virgin olive oil

½ knob ginger (2 cm), peeled and roughly chopped

2 cloves garlic, roughly chopped

8 onions, roughly chopped

1 × 850 g–1 kg large lamb neck, whole

1 large quince, washed, peeled, cored and roughly sliced

1 tablespoon sherry vinegar

1 teaspoon coriander seeds, crushed

½ teaspoon ground turmeric

1 teaspoon ground cumin

1–2 cups reduced Golden Chicken Stock (see page 181)

1 tablespoon Quince Pickling Liquid (see page 130)

2 quarters Pickled Quince (see page 130), thinly sliced

⅓ cup coriander leaves, chopped

Preheat the oven to 120°C. Heat the oil over medium heat in a heavy-based enamelled casserole dish with a tight-fitting lid. Toss in the ginger, garlic and onions and fry until golden. Add the lamb neck and brown evenly, then add the fresh quince slices. Deglaze the pan with the sherry vinegar and add the spices. Pour in enough stock to half-cover the lamb neck, place the lid on and transfer the casserole to the oven to cook for approximately 3½ hours or until the lamb is very tender. Set aside to cool, then place in the fridge overnight.

On the day of serving, remove the lamb from the fridge and skim off the fat, then warm the lamb slowly in the casserole over low heat. Once heated through, remove the lamb neck from the pan and set it aside, wrapped in plastic film to keep it moist. Add the quince pickling liquid to the casserole, turn the heat to high and bring to the boil. Carefully remove the meat from the bone of the neck, then add this to the casserole along with the pickled quince slices. The sauce should glisten invitingly.

Scatter with the chopped coriander and serve with creamy polenta.

POT-ROASTED QUINCES
Serves 6

Dessert is my least favourite part of the meal, but this dish, passed on to me by Hazel Mader, the mother of my friend, Jenny Beckmann, is one of such simplicity that it's a favourite of mine at this time of year. The effect of the long cooking is that the quinces change from bright yellow to a deep ruby-red. They remain whole, but are so well cooked you can even eat the cores! These baked quinces can be cooked and kept frozen in their juices, to bring out in the middle of winter. If you are lucky enough to have picked the quinces yourself and left the stem on with a few leaves still attached, there is nothing more to do after cooking than to serve them unadorned to revel in their own majesty.

This recipe works for small–medium quinces that will not fall apart when cooked for a long time. Avoid super-large or pineapple variety quinces for this dish.

6 quinces, picked with stems and leaves intact, if possible	**4 cups (880 g) sugar** **juice of 3 lemons**

Rub the down off the quinces and wash them. Pack them tightly in a heavy-based saucepan with the sugar and 1.5 litres water. Boil at a reasonably high temperature until a jelly starts to form, then reduce heat to low and simmer for up to 5 hours (I often use a simmer pad to control the temperature). The quinces should be turned at least 4 times during the cooking process so that the deep-ruby colour goes right through to the core. Add lemon juice at the last stage of the cooking to remove any excessive sweetness.

Serve the quinces whole or sliced with a little of the jelly and fresh cream or Crème Anglaise (see page 39).

QUINCE AND PRUNE TART
Serves 6

150 g pitted prunes	**juice of 1 lemon**
150 ml verjuice, plus 1 tablespoon for cooking	**1 × quantity Sour-cream Pastry (see page 177)**
1 tablespoon finely chopped lemon rind	**1 tablespoon quince paste**
3 large quinces (to yield 450 g peeled, cored, sliced quinces)	**1 egg, lightly beaten** **mascarpone *or* double cream, to serve**

Soak prunes in the 150 ml verjuice overnight (or microwave prunes and verjuice on low for 5 minutes), then add the lemon rind and leave for 15 minutes; the prunes will plump and absorb the verjuice. Either mash, roughly chop or purée the prunes in a food processor and set aside.

Peel and core the quinces, then cut into slices, placing them in a bowl of water acidulated with lemon juice as you go, to prevent discolouration. Blanch the drained quince slices in a saucepan of boiling water for 7 minutes or until partially cooked, then drain and transfer to a baking tray to cool.

Make and chill the pastry following the instructions. Roll out to a 3 mm thick rectangle to fit a scone tray, reserving the excess pastry. Chill the pastry on a tray in the refrigerator for 20 minutes.

Preheat the oven to 200°C. Prick the pastry all over with a fork, then cover with foil and pastry weights and blind bake for 15 minutes. Remove foil and weights and bake for another 5 minutes. Leave the tart shell to cool. »

Spread the puréed prunes evenly over the cooled pastry base. Overlap the quince slices like roof tiles over the prunes. Melt the quince paste with the extra verjuice in a small saucepan over low heat until it reaches a spreadable consistency, stirring to combine.

Reset oven to 180°C. Brush quince paste mixture over the quince slices and bake for 10 minutes. Meanwhile, roll the reserved pastry off-cuts, then cut into strips. Increase the oven temperature to 210°C, arrange pastry strips in a lattice pattern over the quince, brush pastry with beaten egg and bake for another 15 minutes or until the pastry is golden.

Serve warm slices of the tart with mascarpone or double cream.

QUINCES AND PEARS POACHED IN VERJUICE   *Serves 6*

3 quinces

juice of 1 lemon

sugar, to taste (optional)

3 cups (750 ml) verjuice

1 kg beurre bosc pears, peeled,
cored and quartered

Preheat the oven to 180°C. Peel and core the quinces, then cut each one into 8 wedges, putting the cut quince into a bowl of water acidulated with lemon juice as you go to prevent discolouration. If you are using sugar, simmer it with the verjuice on a medium heat for approximately 20 minutes to begin to form a syrup. Poach the quince and pears in the oven with the verjuice and sugar (if using), in a large, flat baking dish until cooked through. (The cooking time will depend on the variety and ripeness of the fruit.) The fruit should be soft to the touch but still intact and will not be the deep ruby-red of long-cooked quince. Once cooked, put the quince with the syrup into a pan and, over high heat, reduce the verjuice until both the fruit and verjuice caramelise – turn the slices of fruit over once the first side has caramelised. Serve with mascarpone or fresh cream, or with a delicate Italian lemon biscuit.

RHUBARB

 ALTHOUGH RHUBARB IS USED ALMOST ENTIRELY AS A FRUIT, botanically it is a vegetable. It is available all year round (spring is when it shoots forth), but the largest rhubarb grower in South Australia tells me that the best rhubarb is actually to be had from May to June, as it grows more slowly then and the stalks are a deeper red.

If you have the room, rhubarb is worth growing at home as it is not always the staple it should be on greengrocers' shelves, considering what an established food plant it is (it is now deemed old-fashioned, and has to compete with so many more 'fashionable' fruit and vegetables).

No matter what time of the year, you should only select young and slender pinky red stalks of rhubarb (unless they are of the green variety available now). Large green–pink rhubarb is older and will be tough, stringy and acidic. Those of you who grow rhubarb will know from experience that it needs to be picked regularly – if you don't, you need to be strong-willed enough to throw the oversized stalks on the compost and not be tempted to cook them. I know people who pick young rhubarb straight from the garden, breaking off the stalks and eating them raw, although most would dip them in sugar first. I am told fresh uncooked rhubarb tastes like very sharp sorrel, which doesn't surprise me, since it is related to that wonderful bitter herb. Remember never to eat rhubarb leaves, though, as they contain poisonous oxalic acid.

In the main, rhubarb sometimes needs little stringing and this should only be considered if the rhubarb is large and therefore more likely to be old. Keep in mind that stringiness equates to acidity, which can be countered by adding a little more sugar when cooking. I say only 'a little more' as my main complaint with rhubarb is that it tends to be served over-sugared and waterlogged. Little, if any, juice or water needs to be added to rhubarb, as it gives off so much moisture as it cooks, but the amount of sugar required is open to negotiation. I do not have a sweet tooth and like to taste the tartness of the rhubarb, so I tend to err on the side of adding very little sugar or honey. Start sparingly, adding extra sweetness if necessary. The amount of sugar needed will differ every time you cook it.

Remove any signs of browning from the base of the stalks and chop into 2.5–3 cm lengths. Cook in an enamelled, earthenware or stainless steel casserole with a tight-fitting lid (never cook rhubarb in aluminium as its acidity will react with the metal and give the fruit a metallic taint). The size of the container is important: it should be just large enough to accommodate the rhubarb snugly. If you're nervous that the rhubarb might burn add a tablespoon of verjuice or orange juice rather than water, or instead add 60 g butter for every 500 g trimmed rhubarb. Drizzle with a little honey or sprinkle brown sugar on top – try ¼ cup sugar to 500 g trimmed rhubarb – then put the lid in place. Cook the rhubarb for about 10 minutes at 200°C, then check it for sugar and doneness (the cooking time will depend on the pot you are using). Cooked this way, the rhubarb will collapse but not become a mush.

It was very rare for us to have dessert in our house as I grew up, but rhubarb from the garden was a favourite. For special occasions Mum would make a rice pudding flavoured with nutmeg and served with stewed rhubarb alongside. The rhubarb was also brought out for breakfast, when we had it chilled from the refrigerator on Weetbix with hot milk.

The piquancy of rhubarb is a perfect foil to rich meat such as liver, duck, pork or lamb and, surprisingly to some, fish (particularly oily fish like tommy ruffs). Try cutting fresh young rhubarb into tiny dice and adding it to calf's liver cooking in a pan of nut-brown butter just as you prepare to turn the liver. The liver takes only a couple of minutes a side to cook, and the rhubarb should still have a crunch. Drizzle a little top-grade balsamic vinegar over the dish at the last moment.

I once had a truly remarkable quince tart made by Jennifer Hillier, of the wonderful Uraidla Restaurant in the Adelaide Hills, for the 1984 Symposium of Gastronomy. She had used a brioche recipe from a book very dear to her, *The Auberge of the Flowering Hearth* by Roy Andries de Groot. It presented like a tarte tatin, and the fragrant juices were taken up by the brioche when the tart was inverted. This would work so well with rhubarb, tossed in butter with brown sugar and cinnamon over medium heat to just soften. There is no doubt that one idea can lead to another, and every recipe should be seen as just a starting point.

RHUBARB, STRAWBERRIES AND CRÈME FRAICHE *Serves 4–6*

500 g ripe rhubarb stalks,
    trimmed, washed and
    cut into 2.5 cm lengths
finely chopped rind of 1 orange
    and 3 tablespoons juice
½ cup brown sugar
1 cup ripe strawberries

balsamic vinegar *or* vino cotto
    (see Glossary), for drizzling
    (optional)
1 cup crème fraiche
3 tablespoons cream
pinch freshly grated nutmeg
lemon juice, to taste (optional)

Place the rhubarb, orange rind, orange juice and brown sugar in a small pan with a tight-fitting lid. Bring to a gentle simmer with the lid on, then remove the pan from the heat, take the lid off and stir. Depending on the age of the rhubarb, you may only need to stand it in the hot saucepan for a few minutes more to cook it through, but if it needs further cooking, heat over low heat with the lid off for another 3 minutes. Transfer to a bowl and refrigerate, covered, for several hours.

Hull strawberries and cut into thin vertical slices. If the strawberries are not as ripe as they could be, drizzle the tiniest bit of vino cotto or balsamic over them.

Fold the crème fraiche and the cream together in a bowl, and then fold in the rhubarb and the grated nutmeg. Chill, covered, for another hour. Fold strawberries in at the last moment. Adjust the flavour if necessary with a squeeze of lemon.

RICE PUDDING WITH POACHED RHUBARB AND ORANGE   *Serves 6–8*

6 eggs	POACHED RHUBARB AND ORANGE
3 tablespoons castor sugar	750 g ripe rhubarb stalks, trimmed,
5 cups full-cream milk	washed and cut into 2.5 cm lengths
½ cup cream	finely chopped rind of 1 orange
pinch freshly grated nutmeg	¼ cup orange juice
½ cup (115 g) short-grain rice	¼ cup (110 g) brown sugar
3 tablespoons chopped candied orange peel	
1 tablespoon butter	

For the pudding, preheat the oven to 160°C. Beat the eggs and castor sugar together in a bowl, then add the milk, cream and grated nutmeg and mix together. Stir in the rice and candied orange peel.

Butter a ceramic soufflé mould (I use one that is 19 × 9 cm), pour in the mixture and bake for 1¾–2 hours, depending on the height of the dish, until cooked with a brown crust on top.

Meanwhile, to make the rhubarb, take a small pan with a tight-fitting lid and add the rhubarb, orange rind, orange juice and brown sugar. Bring to a gentle simmer with the lid on, then remove the pan from the heat, take the lid off and stir. Depending on the age of the rhubarb, you may only need to stand it in the hot saucepan for a few minutes more to cook it through, but if it needs further cooking, heat over low heat with the lid off for another 3 minutes. Once cooked, remove the pan from the heat and set aside to cool for a few minutes, then transfer the rhubarb to the refrigerator to chill.

Allow the pudding to cool a little and spoon a good serving into a dish with the chilled rhubarb and perhaps some runny cream.

CHOCOLATE ORANGE BROWNIE PUDDING
WITH RHUBARB AND MASCARPONE

Serves 8–10

I decided I liked the idea of rhubarb and chocolate together, and as the marriage of rhubarb and orange works so well, I thought I'd combine the lot. Then I found a packet of my friend Noëlle Tolley's glacé cumquats and took it one step further.

150 g dark chocolate, chopped

200 g butter

2 large eggs and 2 egg yolks, beaten

300 g brown sugar

120 g plain flour

40 g unsweetened cocoa (see Glossary)

1 teaspoons baking powder

¼ teaspoon salt

100 g glacé cumquat *or* orange peel

mascarpone, to serve

RHUBARB

1.5 kg ripe rhubarb stalks, trimmed, washed and cut into 4–5 cm pieces

finely chopped rind of 1 orange

½ cup orange juice

½ cup (110 g) brown sugar

Preheat the oven to 160°C. To prepare the rhubarb, spread it out over a baking dish, and add the orange rind, juice and brown sugar, then bake for about 15–20 minutes, or until collapsed and tender. Allow to cool, then refrigerate.

For the pudding, grease and line a flat 26 × 16 cm slice tray. Melt the chocolate and butter together in the microwave on medium heat for 40 seconds at a time, repeating this 3 times (be careful not to overcook) stirring until smooth. Alternatively, you can use a double boiler, or a heatproof bowl that fits snugly over a pan of boiling water.

Using an electric mixer, beat the eggs with the sugar until thick and pale. Fold in the remaining ingredients, except the mascarpone, with a wooden spoon, stirring until well combined.

Spread the batter into the prepared tray and bake for 35 minutes. The pudding should still be moist and springy in the centre. Allow to cool a little, in which time it will 'cook' a little further.

Serve the pudding whilst still warm, with the chilled rhubarb and mascarpone.

RHUBARB CRUMBLE

Serves 4

What could be more old-fashioned than rhubarb crumble? I leave the rhubarb a little tart – the sweetness of the crumble provides the balance. A variation is to add chopped almonds to the crumble topping.

For this recipe, you'll need a dish that is around 26 × 18 cm, and not too deep, or the crumble will become soggy.

1.5 kg ripe rhubarb stalks, trimmed,
    washed and cut into 4–5 cm lengths
½ cup orange juice
½ cup (110 g) castor sugar
2 tablespoons unsalted butter
finely chopped rind of 1 orange
double cream, to serve

CRUMBLE
1 teaspoon ground cinnamon
80 g dark-brown sugar
125 g plain flour
140 g unsalted butter, cut into
    cubes and chilled

Preheat the oven to 200°C. Spread the rhubarb out in a baking dish, add the orange juice and castor sugar, dot with butter and bake for about 10 minutes or until rhubarb is just cooked.

To make the crumble, mix the cinnamon, dark-brown sugar and flour in a bowl. Work the butter into the flour mixture with your fingertips.

Place the cooked rhubarb in a buttered soufflé mould (or 4 individual ramekins), then sprinkle with orange rind and top with the crumble mixture. Bake for 15–20 minutes or until golden. Serve with rich double cream.

VERJUICE

IN THE FOURTEENTH AND FIFTEENTH CENTURIES VERJUICE WAS so familiar to Parisian cooks that, writing in *Winestate* in 1984, Barbara Santich suggested: 'the flask of verjuice was probably always within the cook's easy reach and as frequently used as soy sauce in a Chinese kitchen today'.

Verjuice (or verjus) is made from the juice of unripe grapes. Its flavour has the tartness of lemon and the acidity of vinegar without the harshness of either. It lends a subtle hint of grapes and is a marvellous addition to almost any dish.

In the Middle Ages verjuice was used with wild duck, chicken, capon, goose and roasted pork and was also an important ingredient in sauces. In the eighteenth century, the son of a Dijon master vinegar-maker instituted a small but revolutionary change when he substituted verjuice for vinegar in his mustard. The supremacy of Dijon mustards is still evident today, and mustard made with verjuice is particularly fine, being slightly less acidic and pungent than that made with vinegar.

Even though it is a staple of French cooking, verjuice is rarely seen for sale commercially in France. Households once made their own, as they did vinegar. Certainly restaurants in France still make verjuice, either when grapes are in season, freezing the grapes or juice for later use, or stabilising the verjuice with alcohol (although this method masks its true flavour).

It was while reading about verjuice in books on French provincial cooking that I was first encouraged, as a cook and grape grower, to try making it myself. My first attempt, with the assistance of friend Peter Wall, was in 1984. I believe we were the first in the world to make verjuice commercially available all year round by using modern wine-making techniques. It took years before the next commercial trial, mainly because the only people who knew about our verjuice were the restaurateurs we were selling it to, including Stephanie Alexander and Lew Kathreptis, then of the Adelaide restaurant Mezes. This was our first lesson in marketing, and it took ten more years to really get it off the ground – now I'm pleased to say that the best gourmet delis across Australia have a regular supply of not only my verjuice, but many others as well, and ours is so popular it's also available in supermarkets. We also export to Japan, the United States, the United Kingdom, Dubai and Hong Kong.

Having led the way in making verjuice commercially in a form suitable to be stored is something that I am enormously proud of, yet it's also important that others have followed, both legitimising verjuice as an important ingredient in the serious cook's pantry and making it relatively accessible.

Since our early days of production, verjuice has become not only indispensable to my own cooking, but also to that of many chefs and home cooks alike. This in turn prompted me to write a book totally dedicated to the subject, *Cooking With Verjuice*, in an attempt to share just how versatile this product is. I never stop discovering new ways with verjuice and try to continually add ideas to my website. With so many ideas, I had to write another verjuice cookbook in 2012, this time with beautiful photographs to stimulate the appetite.

Every year the choice of wine grapes for my verjuice varies with the season, but when I was offered some sangiovese grapes in 2000 for making verjuice I was keen to have a go and decided to crush them. I was delighted that they resulted in a beautiful rose-coloured product with a sweet fruitiness, which was offset by the grapes' natural acidity; so now, each year we make a small amount with these. While the sangiovese verjuice can be used in any of the recipes featuring verjuice in this book, I've found that using it when poaching soft fruits like nectarines or peaches and then setting the syrup as a jelly with the fruit suspended in it gives a wonderful flavour, as well as a colour that truly sparkles. When making a sangiovese verjuice sabayon, once again, its pale-pink colour becomes the defining character of the dish.

We make a non-alcoholic drink based on verjuice. It started out as an idea for an adult soft drink, but as I progressed with the idea I found it had more potential than I could have imagined. At first I called it Sour Grapes, a name I was inordinately proud of, since to me it seemed a perfect name for a drink based on verjuice. However, I found that those who understood the verjuice connection saw the humour in it, but those who felt the use of 'sour' was negative dismissed it out of hand. For once in my life I listened to others' opinions and renamed it Desert Pearls, a name my friend Gayle Gray helped me come up with (when drinking it, the bubbles feel like pink pearls, and, as we make Desert Pearls from the cabernet grapes in our Riverland vineyard, the Riverland is a desert climate and a pearl begins with a grain of sand, it all fell into place). Particularly as our first export market was Dubai, a desert climate, and the name seemed perfect there – and we also export it to Japan, a country where pearls are much revered. Whilst I loved the name, it failed to tell the story behind it, so our final name says exactly what it is – Sparkling Ruby Cabernet.

As to how it's made, I'm not going to give away any trade secrets here as it is a patented product. I was very proud to receive a worldwide patent, as I have used very different methods to come up with a wonderfully refreshing and fruity (yet not sweet) non-alcoholic drink that feels like you are drinking a glass of champagne. It is a very sophisticated drink, with the hues and bubbles of a rosé champagne, and is incredibly popular with those who

Verjuice vinaigrette with oysters (see page 145)

prefer not to drink alcohol, as they truly don't feel left out. All other non-alcoholic drinks I have tried are made from de-alcoholised wines, and are often very sweet and lack freshness.

In a culinary context, Sparkling Ruby Cabernet can be used for making a sorbet or jelly. My good friend Simon Bryant, my co-presenter on the ABC TV program *The Cook and The Chef*, made a jelly of it and poached pear (with the addition of chilli – I suspect just to have a go at me as I'm the chilli wimp of all time), which made for a really zesty and refreshing dessert.

If you have difficulty finding verjuice and you grow your own grapes, it can be made at home. While it is traditional to use wine grapes, any grapes picked 'green' (meaning sour), before they swell to ripeness, can be used. It takes about 4 kg grapes to produce 1 litre verjuice. I've found that the most practical method for home cooks is to first wash the grapes well, then pluck them from their stems and purée them in a food processor. Strain or pick out the seeds, then freeze the resultant juice in ice blocks to add to recipes calling for verjuice.

A dash of verjuice added to vine-ripened tomatoes pan-fried in nut-brown butter and seasoned with sea salt flakes and freshly ground black pepper balances the sweetness of the tomatoes. Or brush wild mushrooms with walnut oil and grill them for a couple of minutes a side before drizzling them with verjuice (and maybe a little more walnut oil to balance the vinaigrette) and seasoning for a true celebration of the best of autumn. I like to cook the mushrooms on our open grill over vine cuttings from the winter prunings for the extra flavour they add.

Try roasting pumpkin wedges with some extra virgin olive oil, bay leaves or rosemary and salt in a 200°C oven until caramelised and cooked through. Deglaze the roasting pan with verjuice and return it to the oven for a few more minutes – it's just wonderful.

Walnut oil seems to have a particular affinity with verjuice, as do grapes, of course. A simple vinaigrette can be made by combining 3 parts walnut oil to 2 parts verjuice, then adding 1 teaspoon Dijon mustard and seasoning with sea salt flakes and freshly ground black pepper. Toss the dressing, along with some grapes, through salad greens.

Verjuice and seafood make the finest of marriages. Make a simple sauce by deglazing the pan in which seafood has been cooked with verjuice, or use reduced verjuice to make a beurre blanc instead of white wine or vinegar. Verjuice also makes a hollandaise sauce without peer. While talking seafood, make a simple vinaigrette for freshly opened oysters by finely chopping golden shallots and pouring verjuice over, then adding some fresh chervil if you have it – a stunning accompaniment, with so little effort.

Then there is game, another autumn ingredient. Pheasant, rabbit, hare, quail, guinea fowl and partridge all benefit from being partnered with verjuice. Quail and partridge lend themselves to being wrapped in vine leaves and poached slowly in verjuice; reconstitute sultanas, raisins or dried currants in verjuice to add to the finished sauce.

Try pot-roasting chicken, first browned in goose fat (or just plain nut-brown butter), with heads of garlic, a sprig of rosemary and 125 ml each of verjuice and chicken stock, for 40–60 minutes. (Goose fat is available in tins from good delicatessens or, if you cook a goose, collect it from the pan afterwards.) Turn the chicken occasionally and add more verjuice or stock, as necessary – a syrupy glaze will develop around the chook.

In countries in which duck or goose foie gras is available, verjuice added to pan-fried foie gras provides the most marvellous balance to the richness of the liver. In Australia, fresh blond livers from mature free-range chooks will have to suffice. (The more fat in the liver, the paler they are, hence the term 'blond'.) Sweetbreads and verjuice are an exceptional combination. Pan-fry blanched pressed sweetbreads in nut-brown butter and deglaze the pan with verjuice.

Try grilling tender young veal very quickly on the barbecue, first moistened with olive oil to save it from sticking, and then drizzle with verjuice while it rests after cooking. A sauce Barbara Santich found in her research from the sixteenth and seventeenth centuries still stands today as a good one to serve with grilled meat: reduce equal quantities of verjuice and good strong stock with finely chopped golden shallots, then season the finished sauce with sea salt flakes and freshly ground black pepper.

I add verjuice to sauces, soups, and when braising vegetables (particularly fennel and globe artichokes). I also use it to reconstitute dried fruit or for poaching soft fruits. I soak summer-caught riverfish in verjuice to rid it of its 'muddy' flavour. Verjuice also becomes a preserving agent for tropical fruit – the pH is low enough to extend the fruit's shelf-life without overtaking the flavour.

If all these seem a little fancy for everyday occasions, the easiest and most startling way to use verjuice is probably with chicken breasts or cubed chicken thigh meat (skin on, of course!) pan-fried in nut-brown butter. Wait until the chicken is almost cooked, then pour off any excess butter and turn up the heat as you add a good glug of verjuice. Loosen any residue in the pan with a spatula and reduce the verjuice to a syrup; the chicken will caramelise a little as the sauce reduces (you can also extend the sauce with some stock, if you like). I can promise you that this is the best way I know to give a boost to the flavour of a supermarket chook.

SEARED RAZORFISH ON SPINACH WITH
VERJUICE BUTTER SAUCE

Serves 8 as an entrée

The following recipe is another created by Urs Inauen, Tom Milligan, Cheong Liew and me for the Seppelts Menu of the Year competition in 1991. Razorfish is a wonderful local mollusc not well known except among fishermen. If you can't find it, substitute with scallops.

16 razorfish hearts *or* 24 raw scallops

50 g unsalted butter

250 g baby spinach leaves, stalks removed, washed and dried

sea salt flakes and freshly ground black pepper

freshly grated nutmeg, to taste

2 teaspoons extra virgin olive oil

finely chopped rind and juice of ½ lime

finely chopped lemon rind, to serve

SAUCE

4 golden shallots, thinly sliced

1 cup (250 ml) verjuice

sea salt flakes

2 tablespoons cream

250 g unsalted butter, chopped

juice of 1 lemon

freshly ground black pepper

First, make the sauce. Cook the golden shallots and verjuice with salt in a small saucepan over high heat until reduced and syrupy. To help stabilise the sauce add the cream, gently warm and then gradually whisk in the butter, maintaining a medium–high heat through the cooking, but do not bring to the boil. Finish the sauce with lemon juice and adjust the seasoning. Set aside in a warm place.

With a paring knife, clean the razorfish hearts of all skin and remaining shell pieces or trim the scallops. Heat 30 g of the butter in a saucepan until just brown. Add the spinach, season with salt, pepper and nutmeg and stir well. Take out the spinach and place on kitchen paper. Wipe out the pan, then heat the olive oil with the remaining butter. Season the fish or scallops with salt, lime rind and juice, then sear in the pan for a few seconds only on each side and place on kitchen paper.

Divide the spinach evenly between 8 warmed plates. Place 2 razorfish hearts or 3 scallops on top of the spinach in the middle of each plate, leaning one on the other. Garnish with lemon rind. Pour the sauce around the spinach and grind over some pepper.

OCEAN TROUT IN VERJUICE JELLY

Serves 16 as a small entrée

This entrée is beautiful – it sparkles on the plate and palate. I first made it for a dinner for 400 guests using Murray cod, as I wanted something very fresh to serve as an entrée with Rhine Riesling. While Murray cod worked wonderfully, it can be hard to obtain. Here I've used ocean trout fillets, but if they aren't available, try salmon fillets instead.

unsalted butter, for cooking

2 × 750 g ocean trout fillets, skin off
    and pin-boned

1 bulb fennel

sea salt flakes and freshly ground
    black pepper

20 sage leaves

extra virgin olive oil, for cooking

2 stalks lemongrass, finely chopped

½ bunch flat-leaf parsley, leaves picked
    and finely chopped

1 bunch chervil, leaves picked
    and finely chopped

½ bunch chervil, leaves picked, to garnish

VERJUICE JELLY

6 × 2 g leaves gelatine (see Glossary)

3 cups (750 ml) verjuice

2 teaspoons castor sugar

Preheat the oven to 180°C. Liberally grease two sheets of baking paper, each large enough to wrap one of the fish fillets. Top each sheet of baking paper with a piece of fish, then scatter some fennel fronds over each fillet and salt well. Dot the fillets with some more butter and fold over the edges to seal the parcels. Carefully transfer the parcels to a baking tray and bake for 10 minutes on one side, then turn the fillets over and bake for another 5–8 minutes, depending on the thickness of the fillet. The fish should be just set and will continue to cook while it cools. Once the fish has cooled, remove from the baking paper and carefully cut into bite-sized pieces.

Now, make the jelly. Soak the gelatine leaves in cold water for 5 minutes. Meanwhile, warm the verjuice and the sugar in a stainless steel saucepan to dissolve the sugar; don't allow the mixture to boil or it will become cloudy. Remove the softened gelatine sheets from the water and squeeze out any excess moisture before dropping them into the warm verjuice mixture. Stir gently over low heat until the gelatine dissolves. Set aside to cool a little.

Melt a knob of butter in a frying pan over high heat until nut-brown, then crisp the sage leaves in the butter and drain on kitchen paper. Wipe out the pan and add a little extra virgin olive oil. Finely chop the fennel bulb and sauté, along with the lemongrass, in the oil, then remove the pan from the heat and add the parsley and the chopped chervil (this preserves the colour and flavour of the herbs). Season with salt and pepper and set aside to cool.

Pour just enough gelatine mixture to coat the bottom of the mould (in the finished dish the jelly layer should be just a little deeper than the thickness of the fish). Cover the mould with plastic film and refrigerate for 30–45 minutes or until set. Keep the remainder of the gelatine mixture in a warm place until required. »

As soon as the first layer of jelly has set, arrange the pieces of fish in a layer over the jelly, then top with the fennel and herb mixture, distributing it evenly over the fish. Arrange the crisped sage leaves evenly over the top. Pour over the remaining gelatine mixture, then refrigerate until set as before.

To serve, dip the base of the mould in hot water and quickly invert the jelly onto a plate. To present the herb-side uppermost, carefully invert the jelly onto another plate. Cut into portions using a hot, dry knife. Serve immediately, drizzled with a fruity extra virgin olive oil, seasoned with salt and garnished with chervil leaves. This jelly is great served with grilled Asparagus and a verjuice hollandaise or a side salad of avocado, chervil and extra virgin olive oil.

KANGAROO CARPACCIO WITH CUMQUATS, GREEN PEPPERCORNS AND VERJUICE
Serves 4

I first made this dish for a masterclass in Melbourne in 1994 and have used it so often since, not only with kangaroo but also venison or beef. It would be fabulous made with fillet of wagyu beef. A friend from the Riverland, Noëlle Tolley, had provided me with the most wonderful dried cumquats. These days I dehydrate my own in a small dryer I bought in an organic food store. It sits on the kitchen bench and is one of the kitchen toys really worthy of its position. When I can get hold of fresh green peppercorns I preserve them in verjuice – they last for months. Otherwise they can be macerated, as here. If you can't do either, rinse green peppercorns preserved in brine and steep them in verjuice overnight, at least.

1 teaspoon fresh green peppercorns

1 tablespoon verjuice,
 plus extra for soaking

⅓ cup dried cumquat slices

1 × 300 g kangaroo fillet

⅓ cup (80 ml) extra virgin olive oil,
 plus extra for brushing

lemon juice, to taste

2 tablespoons coriander leaves

Macerate the green peppercorns in a little verjuice overnight. Next day, reconstitute the dried cumquats in verjuice for 30 minutes.

If you have a double fillet of roo (the best cut), follow the sinew down the middle with a sharp knife and separate the 2 pieces. Trim off all sinew, brush the meat with a little olive oil to minimise oxidation, then wrap the meat in plastic film to form a 'log'. Freeze the meat for about 20 minutes until it has firmed up (this will aid slicing). Finely slice the meat, then gently flatten each slice between pieces of plastic film with a wooden mallet (until it is as thin as prosciutto) or roll between 2 sheets of plastic film with a rolling pin. Arrange the meat on serving plates, with each piece just touching the next.

Combine the olive oil, 1 tablespoon verjuice and a squeeze of lemon juice to make a vinaigrette, then toss in the drained cumquats and green peppercorns and add the coriander. Dress the kangaroo and serve immediately.

VERJUICE SABAYON WITH GRILLED FIGS *Serves 6*

I like to serve this with olive oil brioche made with bitter orange peel instead of candied Seville orange peel. If you can't buy brioche, try accompanying this with toasted and buttered slices of panettone.

1½ cups (375 ml) sangiovese verjuice
1 × Olive Oil Brioche (see page 180)
    or bought brioche
100 g unsalted butter, melted

3 free-range egg yolks
50 g castor sugar
12 figs

Heat the verjuice in a small saucepan over high heat, then simmer until reduced to 150 ml. Leave to cool. Bring some water to a simmer in a medium-sized saucepan.

Preheat the oven to 200°C. Cut the brioche into 2 cm-thick slices, then brush with melted butter and toast on a baking tray in the oven until golden brown. Keep warm.

Combine the egg yolks and castor sugar in a heatproof bowl that will sit over the saucepan of simmering water without touching the water, or use a double boiler. Whisk the egg yolks and sugar over the simmering water, slowly adding the cooled reduced verjuice, a little at a time, until the mixture is cooked and thick enough to form ribbons when the whisk is lifted. Keep the sabayon warm while you prepare the figs.

Cut the figs in half and brush with melted butter, then grill under a hot griller. Serve with the warm sabayon poured over them and the toasted brioche alongside.

VINEGAR

WHEN YOU THINK ABOUT IT, THE VINEGAR THAT HAS LONG BEEN made here in South Australia is a natural adjunct to the wine-making for which the state is so famous. And good vinegar is something I urge all cooks to investigate.

As a cook you need a variety of vinegars for different purposes. My favourite vinegars to use for cooking and making vinaigrettes are red-wine sherry vinegars, made by the traditional Orléanais method (see page 153), or top-class balsamics, depending on the dish. Vino cotto is a traditional Italian seasoning made from the juice of grapes and it has a unique sweet and sour flavour, known as *agrodolce* in Italy. We now make our own version of this, finished with our red-wine vinegar so it's truly sweet and sour. It is a delicious alternative to balsamic vinegar and adds piquancy to both sweet and savoury dishes.

It is a little extravagant to use these vinegars for making sauces and chutneys when there are many good-quality vinegars and spiced vinegars available for this purpose. However, we use our traditional red-wine vinegar in all our sauces and chutneys, and the results speak for themselves. In the early days of the Pheasant Farm Restaurant we produced pickled quail eggs virtually by the tonne using Seppelt's spiced vinegar, and I was very proud of them.

Malt vinegars were the flavour of my childhood, and it is no wonder that I was never a fan of my mother's cucumber and onion salad. Made today with a red-wine vinegar, it is a different dish altogether! For me, malt vinegar simply lacks the flavour and aroma of traditionally made wine vinegars.

A good-quality balsamic is a wonderful vinegar, but unfortunately not all balsamics are made to a high standard. To be awarded the *aceto balsamico tradizionale* tag, the vinegar must be made according to a traditional process, which takes twelve years. It is made exclusively from the unfermented musts (juices) of crushed grapes that are boiled and concentrated in copper pots. No flavourings and additives are permitted. The musts go through a gradual fermentation and acetification process in a series of casks made from

chestnut, mulberry, oak, cherry, acacia, ash and sometimes juniper. The juice is slowly decanted from one barrel to the next, each one smaller than the last since evaporation concentrates the liquid. This syrupy, dark-amber to honey-coloured vinegar has an amazing sweet–sour note to the nose and palate.

Naturally, you pay dearly for true balsamic, and justifiably so, but it should be used sparingly – an eye dropper or two of aged vinegar (twenty years or so – the age of the vinegar will be declared on the bottle) is all you need. I've actually tasted a balsamic that was a century old. Like Para Port, the 100-year-old liqueur made by Seppelt's, it was incredibly intense – more like an essence. When balsamic vinegars first hit the markets in Australia and the United States they became instantly fashionable, causing a shortage of traditionally made vinegar (not surprising, given the number of years required to make it). Specialised suppliers and the best gourmet food shops do offer some excellent aged balsamics that haven't reached the age required for *tradizionale* vinegars, but there are also many on the market with none of the same complexities. I find it a shame that so many cooks take the 'easy fix' with ordinary, very sweet balsamic vinegars, and ignore wonderful Australian red-wine vinegar with its toasty, aged flavours that add dimension to dishes without overpowering them.

I believe that we should be taking our red-wine vinegars very seriously – I prefer them most of the imported red-wine vinegars I have come across. I urge you to think Australian, particularly when we have products of such outstanding quality.

On my doorstep, red-wine and sherry vinegars are being made using the traditional Orleans method by Yalumba under the Hill Smith label, and we also have one under our own label. Further south, Coriole is using the same technique, as are a small number of wineries around Australia, all producing red-wine vinegar on a small scale (Coriole has also released small quantities of an aged sweet vinegar). This is a natural offshoot of the wine industry, and as the public becomes more aware of traditionally made vinegar, more wine companies will no doubt start to make their own.

In the Orléanais method, the vinegar bacteria are grown in a half-filled barrel containing a 'mother', or culture. The base always begins with good-quality wine, and the process is long and slow. Wine vinegars made this way have great depth of flavour – in fact, they share the flavours of the wine from which they are made.

Red-wine vinegar ages like red wine, and the unstable pigments drop out of the solution, leaving the vinegar reddish brown. As with wine, vinegar softens over time if unopened, and once opened will slowly oxidise. If you have a bottle of red-wine vinegar with sediment in it, decant it – the clear vinegar left will be wonderful.

Some time ago I took part in a vinegar-tasting at Yalumba where twenty-four vinegars were put to the test. Only a handful were really worthy of mention. We tasted both young and aged South Australian red-wine and sherry vinegars (all of which were great), French and Spanish red-wine vinegars, and malt, balsamic (but no *tradizionale*), rice and even coconut vinegars. Those vinegars brought to the tasting already open, some for a long time, were positively horrid (although it must be said that some others freshly opened for the occasion were just as bad!). Vinegar oxidises at varying speeds according to the conditions it's kept in once opened. (The trick is to buy a small bottle, use it regularly and keep it stored in cool conditions.)

Red-wine vinegar can, of course, be made at home. It is the perfect fate for any leftover red wine, as long as it was a good bottle in the first place. Remember, life's too short to drink bad wine; and the older and better the wine, the better the vinegar. Most good red wines include natural vinegar bacteria as they have not been sterile-filtered, a process that is sometimes used to remove anything that could spoil the wine but also ends up taking out some of the flavour, among other things. Cask wines have been sterile-filtered and are also highly sulphured, so avoid these. Good wine is clarified through traditional methods of extended maturation and racking in barrels, so it does not require filtering.

You can purchase a stone jar with a loose-fitting lid from wine-making shops for making vinegar, but I prefer to use wood as it gives a more appealing colour, aroma and flavour to the vinegar. Geoff Linton, my expert tutor from Yalumba, also prefers to keep away from ceramics when making vinegar, purely because he can't be sure that all the glazes are lead-free. He also worries about storing very acidic products in enamelled containers. Glass, however, is fine.

There are several ways you can acquire a vinegar 'mother'. You can make your own from scratch by simply putting some premium wine into a wooden half-open barrel. Of course, you could also beg, borrow or steal a vinegar mother from someone already making vinegar. Or you could try starting your mother by crumbling several thick slices of stale sourdough bread (made without preservatives) into an open jar and then pouring in half a bottle of good aged red wine (note that if the bread develops mould you must throw out the lot and start again, as the mould produces a toxin). Whichever option you choose, cover the container with muslin to keep out the vinegar flies. You know you are on the way when a filmy growth appears on the surface of the wine and it starts to smell like vinegar – this film is acetic acid bacteria and, in time, it will become so heavy that the mass sinks to the bottom of the barrel: this is your mother. Remember that the greater the surface area the better, as the vinegar needs aerobic activity to operate.

I was lucky enough to be given a mother by a vinegar-maker, and I keep it in an old 20-litre Yalumba port barrel that was shaved out by the coopers. It sits on a wooden cradle right next to the stove (maintaining warmth is important when making vinegar). Three holes (about a centimetre in diameter) are drilled in a line across the top of the barrel, which I never have more than two-thirds full because the vinegar must be open to the air to convert the alcohol in the wine to vinegar. The top is loosely covered with muslin. The barrel has a tap just up from its base from which to pour the vinegar – it is important that there is sufficient vinegar for the mother to swim in and that the tap is above the level of sediment so that it doesn't pour off when the vinegar is extracted.

Whichever way you start when making your own vinegar, enjoy the process, and make sure you smell, taste and look at it every month or so. Just draw off enough in a saucer to check what's happening. After three or four months it will have become quite vinegary, but it is probably best to leave it until it has been in the barrel for at least six months before you start to draw any off for everyday use – even longer is better, if you can be patient. (Starting with premium wine in a wooden barrel without an existing mother could require waiting twelve months before you can use it.) When your vinegar tastes strong, you can assume the microbiological changes have ceased and it is ready to use. In this case, you need to bottle some of the vinegar so that it isn't exposed to as much air – you don't want it to oxidise after waiting so patiently. Topping up the barrel with more wine will set the process in motion again.

Once your vinegar is well and truly established it is probably worth cleaning out the container and dividing your mother. A mature mother is a large rubbery mass, and if it gets too large it gets starved of oxygen and can become inactive. Pour off the vinegar and decant it into flagons, then flush out the barrel with hot water (no detergents). Divide the mother and return one portion to the barrel (give the other to a friend), along with the settled vinegar, and you're away again. The vinegar mother remains good for years and years.

If you had thought that a good vinegar was an imported one, please look again at the top-quality Australian red-wine vinegars now on the market and compare them with the plethora of imported ones. Obviously vinegar should be acidic but it should also have

Vinaigrette of red-wine vinegar, extra virgin olive oil and lemon thyme

a fruity nose (once you have gotten over the gasping effect if you have been too vigorous in your smell test!). Vinegar lovers, me included, will taste vinegar by the spoonful to ascertain its qualities. Years ago, in Tokyo, I was presented with elegant vinegar-tasting glasses – fragile, hand-blown, the size of a thimble on a long stem – and gingerly carried them back in my cabin luggage. A good red-wine vinegar is my first everyday option, but there are also incredibly complex vinegars made from sherry, champagne and, of course, vino cotto. Like my choice of oil, the choice of vinegar depends on what I'm preparing.

There is such a world of difference in quality. True artisan-made aged balsamic results in a vinegar so intense and syrupy it needs to be treated with great reverence. This vinegar, sold for exorbitant prices, is only added by the dropful at the last moment, perhaps to hot poached salmon, poultry or vegetables. Or try vino cotto or balsamic vinegar when deglazing roasted vegetables, particularly onion, or when pan-frying liver, duck or beef.

A good vinegar can be used in many ways: a salad of sliced sun-ripened tomato is enhanced further by a splash of red-wine vinegar. And a generous dash of good vinegar adds piquancy to a stew, soup or sauce in the same way as verjuice, but the result is much stronger.

I love adding vinegar to hare, venison or goat dishes. I was once sent a recipe for a Greek kid dish that required red-wine vinegar. Whereas I usually cook very young kid extremely slowly, this recipe was for a larger animal and called for a kettle barbecue to be used to cook the leg or shoulder. The meat was rubbed with olive oil, dried oregano and freshly ground black pepper and studded with garlic cloves and then cooked on a rack over a bed of onions and tomatoes. (I recommend cooking the kid at a lower heat than you would a leg of lamb, and for half as long again.) The meat was basted regularly with red-wine vinegar, but it had to be watched carefully so that it didn't burn. I tried it myself – and it was wonderful!

Don't think that vinegar should only accompany savoury things. For example, not-quite-ripe strawberries sprinkled with aged balsamic vinegar or vino cotto are a surprisingly successful combination. And old-fashioned honeycomb made with sugar and bicarbonate of soda relies on a good vinegar for flavour.

During the pheasant season I would be allowed to use any blue-coloured eggs for cooking, as Colin knew they wouldn't hatch. A favourite way to cook them was to poach them with a touch of red-wine vinegar in the water. I'd render cubes of sugar-cured bacon (from Schulz's Butcher in the Barossa), then toss baby spinach leaves in the same pan; the eggs were served on the spinach and bacon with shavings of fresh Parmigiano Reggiano and a vinaigrette of extra virgin olive oil, my red-wine vinegar, sea salt flakes and freshly ground black pepper. Croutons were used to dip into the poached eggs (just like toast soldiers) – a wonderful Sunday night meal.

I am constantly amazed at how often I am asked how to make a good vinaigrette. No culinary question is more easily answered, and nothing is more special if you have the best-possible extra virgin olive oil and vinegar to hand, than to place them in glass cruets on the table with a dish of sea salt flakes and a good pepper grinder, and let people help themselves. Then no one can say the dressing is too acidic or oily. A good vinaigrette will only ever be as good as its ingredients.

MORE TIPS FOR VINAIGRETTES

+ For me, the first step in preparing a standard vinaigrette is to rub the bowl I am using with a clove of freshly cut garlic.

+ Pour fresh (not rancid – check first) extra virgin olive oil into the base of the salad bowl (how much depends on the size of the bowl and the salad, but use an oil-to-vinegar ratio of 4:1). Vinegar is added next, then a few flakes of sea salt and freshly ground black pepper.

+ Lettuce and herbs must be washed and well dried (use a salad spinner). Keep the salad leaves separate from the dressing until the very last moment.

+ Be sparing with the amount of dressing. When ready, toss the leaves through the dressing, preferably using your fingers to check that the vinaigrette has just 'touched' the leaves.

+ While many variations are possible, you might add mustard, sugar, cream, fresh herbs or preserved lemon, to name a few. Try making an anchovy vinaigrette by adding chopped anchovy fillets and flat-leaf parsley or torn basil to the vinegar and olive oil.

+ If you have been using balsamic vinegar in your vinaigrettes, you might try vino cotto, or better still, a quality red-wine vinegar with a dash of vino cotto which, like balsamic, has to be used judiciously.

PETER WALL'S RASPBERRY VINEGAR   *Makes 500 ml*

Peter Wall, a great friend of mine, is a former wine-maker and fascinated by vinegar. His raspberry vinegar should be used with gusto – it is particularly good for deglazing, especially when cooking calf's liver. Be careful when buying the base vinegar for this: it must be at least 6 per cent acetic acid, which is stronger than many. A vinegar as strong as this will stop fermentation from occurring – and you can generally equate strength with quality.

200 g fresh *or* frozen raspberries   **400 ml red-wine vinegar (6 per cent)**

If you are using frozen raspberries, defrost them, then wash any remaining frost off and dry them well with kitchen paper. Blend the raspberries and vinegar in a food processor, then bottle and leave for 3 months. Pour the vinegar through a paper filter (like those used in a coffee machine) into a sterilised bottle (see Glossary) and discard any solids.

OLIVE TAPENADE WITH RED-WINE VINEGAR   *Makes 300 ml*

This recipe works brilliantly with either kalamatas or good-quality green olives, and it's the combination of olives and orange that I love so much.

You must use top-quality red-wine vinegar, though – the end result here is heavily dependent on the quality of the ingredients.

250 g pitted kalamata olives

1 clove garlic, chopped

1 tablespoon baby capers, rinsed

1 tablespoon chopped lemon thyme leaves

1 teaspoon chopped marjoram leaves

1 teaspoon chopped rosemary

1 tablespoon finely grated orange rind

2 tablespoons good-quality red-wine vinegar

80 ml extra virgin olive oil

Place all the ingredients in a food processor and pulse until roughly chopped and well combined, but not a smooth paste.

BABY BEETS IN VINO COTTO WITH ROCKET, WALNUTS AND GOAT'S CHEESE   *Serves 4*

1 bunch baby beets (around 12 baby beets)

1 teaspoon red-wine vinegar

¼ cup vino cotto (see Glossary)

½ cup extra virgin olive oil

sea salt flakes and freshly ground
   black pepper

100 g walnuts

1 bunch rocket

150 g firm goat's cheese, cut into pieces

Place the beets in a pan with enough cold, salted water to cover them, and bring to the boil, then turn the heat down and simmer with the lid on until the beets are cooked through (the cooking time will depend on the age of the beets). Remove the beets from the pan and set aside to cool, then peel them and cut them in half.

Preheat the oven to 200°C. In a small bowl, combine the red-wine vinegar, vino cotto and olive oil, and season with salt and pepper to taste. Toss the beets through the dressing, then transfer the mixture to a roasting pan and roast for 10 minutes.

Meantime, roast the walnuts on a baking tray for 10 minutes. Remove and, whilst still warm, rub their skins off with a clean tea towel then sieve away the skins.

Combine the walnuts, rocket and baby beets in a bowl. Mix through the pan juices from the roast beets, then top with goat's cheese and serve.

WALNUTS

 IT DOESN'T SURPRISE ME THAT WALNUTS AREN'T AS POPULAR AS they deserve to be. It is simply because so few people have access to the new season's crop. A rancid walnut, as they so often are if stored badly, would make anyone think twice about eating them.

But there is nothing more delicious than picking, shelling and eating walnuts that are just about to drop (these nuts are described as being 'wet') – particularly if you're lunching under a walnut tree, as we used to many years ago at Kilikanoon, a restaurant in South Australia's Clare Valley, when Janet Jeffs and Susan Ditter owned it. The beauty of the tree and the delicacy of the just-fallen nuts, which we duly added to the cheese plate, encouraged me to plant my own grove.

My vision for my own walnut grove was inspired by a visit to a grove in the Napa Valley in California. Perched on the side of a hill, it was an extraordinary sight as the canopies of the mature trees touched to form a shaded sanctuary from the harsh sun. Here, however, very hot summers and years of drought, along with fierce gully winds, have meant that my walnut trees have struggled. As recently as 2005 I transplanted four of the surviving trees to better position them (I am still determined to have my mini-grove, even though the chestnuts I planted alongside them are obviously more suited to the conditions, as they are thriving). With so few trees, I'm not banking on a huge crop or turning it into a commercial enterprise, but the grove is in keeping with our philosophy that any tree we grow must produce food.

The most exciting prospect for me as a walnut grower is the multitude of uses to which I can put the bounty of this tree. The young fresh leaves can be used to make a wine, as they do in the south of France. Then comes the green walnuts, from which the French and Italians make a liqueur. Picked in late November or early December before the husks form, the nuts retain their wonderful colour and crisp texture, quite unlike blackened pickled walnuts that, interesting as they are, both fall apart and taste more of the vinegar than the nut.

My great friend Peter Wall taught me how to pickle green walnuts. Put the nuts, interspersed with fresh vine leaves, into a glass container, or even a large plastic bucket. Pack the container with extra vine leaves, then cover completely with white vinegar and leave for three weeks. Pour off the vinegar and discard the leaves, then re-fill the jar with the nuts and new vine leaves as before, cover with fresh vinegar and leave for another two weeks. Remove the vine leaves and pack the nuts back into the washed and dried jar. In a large stainless steel saucepan, combine 3 litres commercial wine vinegar with enough salt so that an egg will float in it. Add 30 g each of ground cloves, ground mace and ground allspice to the pan, then grate in two whole nutmegs. Simmer this mixture for a minute and immediately pour it over the nuts to cover. Seal the container and leave the walnuts to mature for three months before using them. The nuts remain green, although will turn more of an olive-green, and stay deliciously crisp. Pickled walnuts are a great partner to rillettes of pork, hare or rabbit, and are also good with rich duck or pork dishes or a really sharp cheddar.

Right through the season the leaves of the walnut tree can be used to wrap fish for cooking on the barbecue. The pungency of the cloudy, freshly pressed walnut oil I've tasted in France may well be too strong for the faint-hearted, but even when it needs toning down with a more neutral oil, it is still incredibly special. Compared with a standard walnut oil of indeterminate age purchased from the delicatessen, you may suspect the latter has been watered down, such is the difference in flavour. At present, you can only buy these top-class oils from really good providores, but I eagerly await the day when walnut oil of this quality is made by Australian growers.

Autumn is the time to be on the lookout for fresh nuts. A passionate farmer clears any debris from around the tree just before harvest and mows the grass so that the nuts can be picked up daily as they fall, just like eggs. Sadly, I know that this is hardly feasible on a commercial scale. Those growers large enough will machine-pick or trunk-shake harvest about ten days before the nuts are due to fall, taking the whole crop off at once. These nuts are then dried in ovens, as they turn black and rancid if stored without first being dried (traditionally they were dried in the sun).

As the walnut is full of oil, its potential for rancidity is high. It is not possible to detect a rancid nut by the colour of its skin – a dark skin does not automatically signify a rancid nut, as different varieties produce darker or lighter skins. The skins will also be lighter if the nuts have been harvested before maturity.

It is really only on tasting that you will know whether the nut is fresh or rancid. There should be some natural bitterness – this comes from the tannin that protects the nut from rancidity – but it should be in balance with the 'meat' of the walnut, and a rich nutty flavour should be left in the mouth. You can dry-roast walnuts back to life if they are old, even rancid, in a hot oven (220°C) for 6–8 minutes, before rubbing off the skins with a clean tea towel. This will take away the acute bitterness and produce a mellow-flavoured nut that is well worth using, but the flavour still won't touch the intensity of the fresh walnuts of the new season.

Proper storage is extremely important if rancidity is to be avoided. The best way is to store the nuts, dried in their shells, in the coolest possible place. Make sure there are no cracks in the shells and no mould present before storing. The next best thing is to keep shelled walnuts in an airtight container in the refrigerator, or even the freezer. Once opened, a bottle of walnut oil can be kept refrigerated for quite some time, and doesn't solidify as extra virgin olive oil does when chilled.

Walnuts have figured a great deal in my menus over the years, both in the restaurant and at home: rabbit with walnuts and pancetta; warm salad of pheasant confit, waxy potatoes and walnuts; guinea fowl stuffed with walnuts, liver and sugar-cured bacon; smoked rack of lamb with pickled walnuts; Duck Egg Pasta (see page 179) with Walnut and Parsley Pesto (see page 183); brains with a duxelle of walnuts and mushrooms; walnut cake with prunes in Sauternes with Sauternes custard; and the humble but wonderful combination of walnuts, slices of pear and Parmigiano Reggiano – all of these

using fresh walnuts or roasted ones with the skins rubbed off.

Walnuts make a great pasta sauce. In his book *The Fruit, Herbs and Vegetables of Italy*, Giacomo Castelvetro writes of an *agliata* sauce, made from pounding walnuts and garlic together using a mortar and pestle, that can also be used to thicken a sauce or stew or to make a hearty soup. Stale white bread which has been soaked in meat stock is then mixed in, along with some of the stock, which thins the sauce. Treated this way, a good game or Golden Chicken Stock (see page 181) would make an excellent soup; it would be a mushroom-pink colour and would only need a salad of bitter greens to make a meal.

I combine walnuts, bacon and herbs when making poultry stuffings, or prunes and walnuts if cooking goose. I love walnuts in salads, particularly with freshly cooked green beans in a creamy dressing. I add walnuts and grapes to a green salad, or stir them into a bath of walnut or olive oil in which a cooked, hot bird is rested to soak up the juices (grilled quail is superb this way).

Walnut bread is probably my first choice to serve with cheese, especially if a grainy flour is mixed with the bread flour. Or toss shelled walnuts and freshly picked rosemary in a little nut-brown butter, then add a little sea salt before serving warm with drinks. They're utterly addictive!

I only wish that a date stamp appeared on packaged walnuts so that everyone could enjoy the standard of walnut to which I have become accustomed. But just a use-by date wouldn't suffice: what I really want to know is when the walnuts were picked and shelled.

I believe that demand for walnuts would increase if everyone was able to taste the 'perfect' nut, and then people would be prepared to pay a premium for the new nuts of the season.

I bought the most wonderful walnut oil on a trip to France a few years ago. I had a week in Périgeux and spent it immersed (well, almost) in truffles, foie gras and walnut oil. It was one of the great privileges of my life. I am an inveterate note-taker and on this trip my notepad was so full that every page was used. Then that horror of horrors happened: I misplaced the notepad somewhere in Milan airport. Devastated though I was, as my camera is ever-present in my shoulder bag, at least I had the photographs from the trip so all was not lost.

Thumbing through these photographs now, I can almost smell the heady scent of walnuts crushing in the ancient mill at Moulin de la Tour, near Sarlat. Powered by a waterwheel (with a fair bit of human effort), the mill crushes hazelnuts and almonds as well as walnuts. The day I was there the small sales outlet was crammed with locals waiting for their walnuts to be crushed – it was a fascinating experience. Precious though luggage space always is, I managed to find room for a sample of each oil (sold in tins rather than bottles, fortunately).

While good nut oils are a thing of joy, those made with the passion and integrity demonstrated at the Moulin de la Tour are in a different league altogether. But all nut oils are incredibly susceptible to rancidity; once opened, they're generally best used within a week unless you refrigerate them. If you have an opened bottle of nut oil, make sure you smell it before using it again to make sure it's not rancid. Rancidity is easy to detect – just think of what butter left uncovered in the refrigerator smells like. Discard the oil if it is rancid.

The first time I tried walnut oil in France was with the simplest salad of green leaves, with a mound of soft goat's curd in the centre. The oil was drizzled over and a grind of black pepper finished off the dish. There was enough salt and acid in the cheese not to require anything else. What could be easier? If you have a really good walnut oil you must use it with discretion – you may even need to use another oil with it so you don't overpower the dish, but this will depend on your palate. The only way to find out is to try.

Walnut oil changes in character depending on the acidulant you use with it – be it wine vinegar, lemon juice or verjuice. A stronger acidulant should be used with stronger flavour bases. So, if you were using radicchio, watercress and walnuts (roasted and rubbed of their skins, if not from the current season), for example, you might use walnut oil and red-wine vinegar. If making a salad of cos lettuce hearts, avocado and grapes, you might use walnut oil and verjuice, then break down the intensity of the walnut oil with some grapeseed oil or mellow but still fresh extra virgin olive oil. And if you were combining rocket, witlof and fennel with roasted walnuts, you could use walnut oil, lemon juice and a little finely chopped lemon rind.

Walnut oil can add flavour to other dishes, too. If grilling chicken, rabbit or quail, make a sauce by slowly adding walnut oil to a large dollop of wholegrain mustard as if you were making a mayonnaise. Add a dash of walnut oil when making an *omelette aux fines herbes*, or toss mixed mushrooms with a touch of walnut oil before adding it to the eggs. Drizzle walnut oil over slices of stale but good bread before spooning rustic bean soup over the bread, then sprinkle with chopped flat-leaf parsley. And if you make a walnut cake, add a little walnut oil to the batter.

SASKIA'S WALNUT, MUSHROOM AND PROSCIUTTO TART   *Serves 8*

My daughter Saskia just loves to cook, and from a very young age would delight me by taking a dish I'd made at the restaurant, changing it around and making it hers, as with this dish.

1 × quantity Sour-cream Pastry
   (see page 177)
100 g dried boletus mushrooms
¼ cup (60 ml) verjuice
2 cups (400 g) shelled walnuts
2 slices white bread, with crusts on
   (about 75 g)

½ cup (125 ml) milk
10–12 slices prosciutto, thinly sliced
2 cloves garlic, finely chopped
1 kg button mushrooms, chopped
butter, for cooking
sea salt flakes and freshly ground
   black pepper

Make and chill the pastry as instructed, then use to line a 20 cm tart tin with a removable base. Chill the pastry case for 20 minutes.

Reconstitute the dried boletus mushrooms in the verjuice for 30 minutes. Meanwhile, preheat the oven to 200°C. Line the pastry case with foil and pastry weights, then blind bake for 15 minutes. Remove the foil and weights and return the pastry case to the oven for another 5 minutes. Remove from the oven and reset the temperature to 220°C.

Dry-roast the walnuts on a baking tray for 6–8 minutes, then rub off their skins with a clean tea towel. Toast the bread in the oven until golden, cut it into cubes and soak in the milk until softened, then squeeze out the milk. Blend the soaked toast, prosciutto, garlic and walnuts in a food processor to make a paste, then set it aside.

Sauté the button mushrooms in a frying pan in a little butter over quite a high heat (do them in batches so that they don't stew), then season well and set aside. Toss the reconstituted boletus mushrooms in the pan in a little more melted butter, then season and purée them in a food processor.

To assemble the tart, spread the walnut and prosciutto paste in the bottom of the pastry case, then brush with the boletus purée and arrange the sautéed button mushrooms on top. Bake for about 20 minutes or until the edge of the pastry case is golden brown. Serve warm or at room temperature.

SALAD WITH WALNUT OIL VINAIGRETTE

Serves 4

Choose a mixture of sharp, peppery, crisp salad leaves and herbs.

12 shelled walnuts

2 handfuls mixed lettuce leaves and herbs,
   washed and dried

175 g seedless grapes

2 tablespoons top-quality walnut oil

2 tablespoons neutral vegetable oil
   (try grapeseed oil)

3 tablespoons verjuice

sea salt flakes and freshly ground
   black pepper

Preheat the oven to 220°C. Dry-roast the walnuts on a baking tray for 6–8 minutes, then rub off their skins with a clean tea towel.

Place the salad leaves and herbs in a salad bowl and add the grapes. Mix the remaining ingredients in a jar and pour over the salad leaves. Add the walnuts and toss thoroughly.

WALNUT FLATBREAD

Serves 6–8

I like to serve this flatbread with Pheasant Farm Pâté, as well as caramelised onions, warmed in a stainless steel saucepan to just above room temperature.

1 cup (250 ml) full-cream milk

7 g dried yeast (1 sachet)

½ cup (180 g) honey

1 cup (150 g) unbleached plain flour
   (see Glossary)

½ teaspoon ground ginger

1¼ cups (150 g) chopped walnuts

3 teaspoons sea salt

2 tablespoons extra virgin olive oil,
   plus extra for brushing

1⅔ cups (250 g) wholemeal flour
   (see Glossary)

finely chopped rind of 1 orange
   (optional)

Warm the milk in a microwave for 1 minute on high and then place in a large bowl. Whisk in the yeast, honey and 100 g of the unbleached flour. Let stand for 15 minutes, after which it should start to bubble.

Add the ginger, walnuts, salt, olive oil and orange rind (if using) to the yeast mixture and gradually incorporate most of the two flours. When the mixture becomes a bit stiff, remove it from the bowl and knead in the remaining flour on a bench; the dough should bounce back and be reasonably firm.

Roll the dough out to a 30 × 40 cm rectangle, approximately 5 mm thick, and brush with olive oil. Rest the dough for 1 hour, covered with plastic film to prevent dryness.

Preheat the oven to 180°C. Place the dough on a baking tray and bake for approximately 20 minutes or until golden. Remove bread from the oven and place on a wire rack to cool.

Cut the bread into 2 cm squares or triangles to serve. Leftover bread can be frozen and then warmed before next use.

CHOCOLATE SWEETMEATS *Makes 25*

The prunes can be replaced with the same quantity of diced quince paste; in that case, soak in Cointreau rather than port. The chocolate mixture must be cool before the quince paste is added, otherwise the paste will melt.

150 g prunes, pitted and chopped
port, for soaking
1½ cups (150 g) shelled walnuts
400 g bittersweet couverture chocolate
   (see Glossary), chopped

200 ml cream (35 per cent fat)
   (see Glossary)
dutch-process cocoa (see Glossary),
   to serve

Soak the chopped prunes in port for several hours. Preheat the oven to 220°C. Roast the walnuts on a baking tray for 6–8 minutes, then rub off the skins with a clean tea towel and coarsely chop the nuts.

Heat the chocolate gently with the cream in the top of a double saucepan over boiling water. (If you don't have a double boiler, use a heatproof bowl that fits snugly over a pan of boiling water.) Remove from the heat before all the chocolate has melted. Stir continuously off the heat to finish melting the chocolate, then cool. Fold the drained soaked prunes and chopped nuts into the cooled chocolate mixture, then roll into balls and dust with cocoa.

WILD DUCK AND DUCK FAT

AUTUMN IS THE TIME FOR WILD GAME AND, AS THE WEATHER becomes cooler, slow-cooked dishes become more tantalising. The wild duck season usually runs from mid-February to mid-June in South Australia (unless it is cancelled altogether due to climatic conditions). Wild duck is a wonderful food but, as with most game, can be tricky to cook until you master the principles. It cannot be sold but, if shot with a licence, can certainly be shared with friends.

As with all wild game, it is hard to determine the age of a wild duck, so it is certainly safer to use slow-cooking methods. However, I have read, particularly in American books, of the practice of spit-roasting wild duck rare, in much the same way as I cook pheasant. Having tested this with young mallard (grown as a domestic duck), I can assure you it is effective if the bird is young. There are various tests you can use to determine the age of a wild duck, but some are quite hit and miss. So unless you are sure of the duck's age, I would suggest using slow-cooking methods – pot-roasting, pressure cooking (with a simmer mat under the pot to slow it down as much as possible), or roasting in an oven bag at a very low temperature.

The mallard is the most common wild duck in Europe and America, and most domestic ducks are descended from this breed. In Australia the mallard has caused a problem by breeding with native ducks and 'shandying' the breeds. In South Australia we have mainly black ducks, teals and wood ducks. The teal and black duck are considered the best for eating – the teal is small and succulent and the black duck is stronger and gamier. The duck's flavour is dependent on its breeding ground and, certainly in some parts of the world, can be 'fishy'. In such cases, the duck is precooked for a few minutes with onion in salty water to eliminate this. In Europe, particularly, they hang their wild duck, whereas in Australia most people do not bother.

One of the best food memories of my life was a wild duck dinner cooked by my friends the Walls, when Peter was still with Yalumba. Both Peter and Judith are great cooks and well understood the principle of slow pot-roasting for many hours. In this instance, they made a liver and sage *panade* (stuffing) for the duck, then wrapped it in bacon or back fat (I think – my memory is a bit hazy!), and kept it moist with stock and wine added as it cooked. It was the first time I had eaten wild duck and, washed down with some great Yalumba reds, it was magnificent.

It was the sort of experience that is hard to replicate – as with so many food memories, it is linked to the people the meal is shared with, the mood of the night and so on. I mention it because of the influence of a very special man, Alf Wark, who was Yalumba's company secretary from 1945 to 1971, and whom I was privileged to meet when we first came to live in the Barossa in 1973.

Alf Wark had a tremendous impact both in Yalumba and across Australia and he was passionate and knowledgeable about food. His influence on the Hill Smiths – founders of Yalumba and a very special family which has helped South Australia develop enormously – is evident. Alf was a keen hunter and fisherman and also a conservationist, as are his son and grandson today, who continue the tradition with their love of game. James, Alf's son, is a member of the South Australian Field & Game Association, whose members come from all walks of life. They are not only responsible hunters but are committed to conservation. One such member, at his own expense, has undertaken a rehabilitation program of wetland areas on his land that had been drained and dried out for farming. They now boast a flourishing and increasing population of many species of water birds.

In 1969, Alf wrote a tiny book, *Wine Cookery*, featuring recipes and ideas he had developed over the years through his long association with good food and wine. With the kind permission of his family, I give you his two recipes for wild duck on the following page.

I have cooked wild duck smothered in pork back fat and stuffed with olives and thyme, or simply stuffed with onion, apple and a few herbs, using about 12 mm of stock in the bottom of the baking dish, and a lid so that condensation helps to keep the bird moist. If pot-roasting duck in a roasting pan or heavy-based saucepan, I prefer to do it on top of the stove as I am reminded to check whether it needs more liquid, and the aroma of the food is so much greater than when enclosed in the oven – it creates a lovely atmosphere in the kitchen. If you don't have any stock to use as a braising medium, try water or sweet white wine and water combined with a little lemon juice.

Both orange and lemon marry very well with duck, as they do with most game. Tart jellies such as redcurrant, crabapple or native currant also go very well.

One last tip with duck is to remove the 'preen glands' (or oil glands) before cooking. In a wild duck they can impart a strong, musky flavour and in a domestic duck they can be bitter. They are located on either side of the duck's tail and are about the size of an elongated pea, with the consistency of kidney.

WILD DUCK POACHED IN WINE SAUCE   *Serves 4*

225 g butter

2 tablespoons Worcestershire sauce

300 ml burgundy (remembering that we used
   to call all red wine burgundy or claret
   when Alf wrote this book in 1969)

⅓ cup redcurrant jelly

finely chopped rind of 1 orange

4 teal duck breasts

¼ cup (60 ml) port

Melt the butter and add all ingredients, except the duck and port, and simmer. Add the duck breasts, then cover the pan and simmer over low heat as gently as possible for 20 minutes. (I would then take the breasts out of the pan.) Season to taste. Add the port and reduce the sauce to the desired consistency before serving.

BLACK DUCK AND ORANGE SAUCE   *Serves 4*

2 wild black ducks, with giblets intact

sea salt flakes and freshly ground
   black pepper

extra virgin olive oil, for cooking

2 medium-sized white onions,
   1 roughly chopped, 1 quartered

2 sticks celery, 1 roughly chopped,
   1 cut into 5 cm lengths

30 g butter

clarified butter, for cooking

⅓ cup (120 g) honey

4 oranges

½ cup (125 ml) port

Preheat the oven to 180°C. When cleaning the ducks, save the giblets, and make sure the cavity is well cleaned of blood from shot wounds. Rub salt and pepper inside and leave for some time before cooking. Over low–medium heat, simmer the giblets in a saucepan with just enough water to cover them, olive oil and the roughly chopped onion and celery pieces for stock. In the body cavity, place the quartered onion and long celery pieces. Add the butter to the cavity. Close the cavity with a skewer and smear the breast of each duck with clarified butter.

Pour 2 tablespoons of the honey (which has been diluted with some of the stock from the giblets) into a roasting pan, then add the duck and roast in the oven for 1½ hours or until cooked (soft to the touch). Baste with the pan juices a few times during the cooking, taking care that the juices do not dry out – add more stock or water if it looks like they are.

Squeeze the juice from 2 of the oranges and mix with port and the remaining honey. When the bird is nearly cooked, baste the breast frequently with this mixture to glaze it. Grate the orange rind from the other 2 oranges and cut the flesh into thin slices.

When the duck is cooked, place it on a hot plate and cover to keep warm. Add the remaining stock to the pan juices and boil until it reduces and thickens, then add the grated orange rind and pour over the duck. Garnish with the thin slices of orange and, with poultry scissors, cut the birds into 4 pieces and serve.

DUCK FAT

I first started using duck fat when I collected the excess from a bird I had cooked. Needing more for the restaurant, I bought it in 10 kg batches from Luv-a-Duck in Nhill, Victoria (through their South Australian distributors), and rendered it myself. These days they sell it in 1 kg tubs ready to use. It keeps for months and has myriad uses.

The easiest way of all to use duck fat is to bake it with potatoes (particularly waxy potatoes) that have first been boiled whole in their jackets and then sliced, with a little rosemary in a heavy-based roasting pan. Heat about 5 mm duck fat with the rosemary before adding the potato slices. They will take about 15 minutes in a hot oven, and the potato slices should be turned over as soon as the first side is golden brown. The moment the second side is golden, the potatoes should be slid out of the baking dish on to kitchen paper. If you wish to season them, sprinkle with sea salt flakes and freshly ground black pepper. Eat immediately! This is a more-ish snack and a great vegetable accompaniment to almost any dish. It cannot be done in advance and should be served crisp and straight out of the oven. There is absolutely no comparison in flavour to potatoes done similarly in oil or butter or a combination of the two – try it.

I first read about duck fat in Elizabeth David's books, but it was Paula Wolfert's *The Cooking of South West France* that converted me to using it as a cooking medium. I was so seduced by the flavour that it wasn't difficult for Paula also to convince me that it is healthier than other fats. She says that the US Department of Agriculture states that rendered poultry fat (goose, duck and chicken) contains 9 per cent cholesterol, lard contains 10 per cent, and butter contains 22 per cent. She continues, 'Since one needs less poultry fat, oil or lard than butter to sauté meat or vegetables, one will ingest far less saturated fat if these cooking media are used instead of butter. One needs less of these because butter breaks down and burns at high temperatures whereas poultry fat, lard and oil do not.'

As I have said, there is no doubt in my mind of the flavour benefits of cooking in duck fat, but that doesn't mean you have to serve fatty foods when you use it. The actual flavour component in the duck fat is water-soluble and can be separated from the fat itself, so the food can be served almost fat-free yet with all the advantages of the increased flavour.

Rillettes de canard (see page 173)

Braising meat at a very low temperature in duck fat to make confit is a foundation of the cuisine of southwest France, and is a technique I use with old game. I am very careful never to let the meat 'move' at anything more than a simmer, and always use the heaviest saucepan in my kitchen (with a tight-fitting lid). I often use a simmer mat between the pan and the flame to be sure there is virtually no movement. This method ensures that the food being cooked is totally immersed in the duck fat throughout.

When such low temperatures are used, the cooking fats mingle but do not incorporate with the wine or juices used in the cooking, and the 'fat' is therefore easy to remove by degreasing the dish after cooking. Where possible, I chill the dish overnight to allow the fat to settle in an easily removable slab – I have always found it difficult to totally degrease freshly cooked dishes. Flavours of slow-cooked dishes always improve by slowly reheating them the next day anyway.

If you want to render duck fat yourself, take a heavy-based stockpot or similar and place the duck fat and skin on the bottom. Some people cut up the skin into small pieces or even purée the fat and skin but, as time tends to be such a consideration now, unless you plan to use the skin for a salad, I suggest you simply add a few bay leaves and juniper berries and cover the fat with water. Cook slowly for about an hour until the fat turns clear, making sure that none of the skin sticks to the bottom and burns.

Strain while still hot, pour into a container and cool before refrigerating or freezing. If you wish to make the skin into crackling, slowly reheat the pieces of skin in another pot until they turn golden brown, stirring to avoid burning. Drain and sprinkle with sea salt flakes, then use in salads.

QUATRE-ÉPICES   *Makes 1 tablespoon*

This spice mixture is used for pâtés, rillettes and terrines. Although meant to be made of four spices, it can be modified to suit personal taste. Spices are much better freshly roasted and used straightaway than stored for a long period.

10 cloves

1 tablespoon white peppercorns

1 cinnamon stick

¾ teaspoon ground ginger

¾ teaspoon freshly grated nutmeg

Grind all ingredients to a fine powder in a spice mill.

RILLETTES DE CANARD
(COMPOTE OF SHREDDED DUCK)

Serves 6–8

I have adapted Paula Wolfert's recipe for duck rillettes, but you can also use rabbit, hare, pork or pigeon in exactly the same way. This recipe should be prepared one week in advance. It takes 30–45 minutes of active cooking time and unattended cooking time of 4–5 hours. Duck breast is not used, as it would dry out too much.

1½ cups duck fat, chilled

4 duck marylands (thigh and drumstick)
 or 6 pigeon legs *or* front and back legs
 of 2 large hares

340 g pork shoulder, cut into 2 cm cubes

duck carcass and wings (not breast),
 chopped

sea salt flakes and freshly ground
 black pepper

190 ml unsalted Golden Chicken Stock
 (see page 181)

190 ml dry white wine

1 bay leaf, crushed

1 teaspoon thyme leaves

1 large clove garlic, halved

2 golden shallots, peeled

½ teaspoon Quatre-Épices (see opposite),
 plus extra to taste

2 tablespoons Armagnac *or* brandy

Moisten the bottom of a crockpot, heavy-based cast-iron casserole or camp oven with a little of the duck fat, place the duck marylands in and cover with pork pieces. Add the chopped duck carcass and wings to the pan, then season with 1 teaspoon each of salt and pepper. Add the stock, wine, herbs, garlic, shallots and quatre-épices.

Cook over the lowest possible heat at barely a simmer, uncovered, until the meat falls off the bone (4–5 hours). Stir from time to time to prevent sticking – the liquid in the pan will evaporate.

Strain the pork and duck through a colander set over a deep bowl and set aside until it is cool enough to handle. Pick out all the bones and gristle, leaving aside the moist pieces of meat. Set aside ½ cup of the rendered fat.

Using a fork (not a food processor), shred the meat and add the remaining chilled duck fat, the cooked garlic and shallots and the Armagnac or brandy. Taste for seasoning, adding more salt, plenty of pepper, thyme and quatre-épices to taste. It should be very peppery.

Spoon the rillettes into clean stoneware or glass dishes, leaving about 1 cm at the top. Seal with the reserved fat from the cooking. Chill and keep refrigerated for a week for the flavours to develop.

Serve with rounds of crusty bread, cornichons (see Glossary), lots of black pepper and a glass of chilled Sauternes.

BASICS

Makes enough to line a 20–24 cm tart tin

This recipe makes a very short, flaky pastry with a light, melt-in-the-mouth texture. It is a great all-rounder and can be used in a whole variety of dishes, both sweet and savoury. I like to chill the pastry case in the freezer, as this ensures it is really well-chilled before it goes in the oven.

This pastry rises beautifully and is really light and flaky, which is great if you're making a tart or a pie, but if you want a flat pastry, like a thin pizza dough, a good trick is to 'inhibit' the pastry as it cooks. To do this, carefully open the oven halfway through the cooking (when the pastry is beginning to rise), take out the tray for a moment and press down on the pastry with a similar-sized tray or a clean tea towel, then return the tray to the oven. This will stop the pastry rising too much.

200 g chilled unsalted butter, chopped into small pieces

250 g plain flour
120 g sour cream

Put the butter and flour into the bowl of a food processor, then pulse until the mixture resembles coarse breadcrumbs. Add the sour cream and pulse again until the dough just forms a ball. If shrinkage worries you, gather the dough into a ball with your hands and bounce it on the bench. Carefully wrap the dough in plastic film and leave to rest in the refrigerator for 15–20 minutes.

Roll out the dough until it is 5 mm thick, then use it to line a 20 cm tart tin with a removable base. Chill the pastry case for 20 minutes.

To blind bake, preheat the oven to 200°C. Line the pastry case with foil, then cover with pastry weights. Blind bake the pastry case for 15 minutes, then remove the foil and pastry weights and bake for another 5 minutes.

CHOUX PASTRY-STYLE
GLUTEN-FREE PASTRY

Makes enough to line a 24 cm tart tin

As a friend who is a coeliac confided to me, the thing she most missed after being diagnosed was the lack of a luscious pastry. So, along with Victoria Blumenstein, my chef at the Farmshop at the time, I set about finding something to fit the bill.

This pastry browns beautifully, has a nice crispness and holds in moisture; it also has a lovely potato-ey undertone which is very pleasant. It is great for any type of pie and keeps well in the refrigerator for up to five days.

You could add 2 teaspoons of icing sugar to make a sweet pastry for fruit pies and other pastry-based desserts.

Xanthan gum is derived from corn sugar and acts as a binding agent in gluten-free pastry. It is available from most health food stores.

2 teaspoons salt

90 g unsalted butter

150 g gluten-free flour (I use a mix of
    potato flour, rice flour and maize flour),
    plus ½ cup extra for dusting

2 g xanthan gum

3 × 57 g eggs

In a heavy-based saucepan, combine the salt, butter and 250 ml water. Bring to a simmer over medium–high heat and add the flour and xanthan gum gradually, stirring with a wooden spoon. Reduce the temperature to low and continue to cook until the pastry is well combined and is coming away from the sides of the pan. Remove from heat and allow to cool to room temperature.

Whisk eggs to combine, then slowly add them bit by bit to the pastry mixture, incorporating fully before adding the next bit; you may not need all the egg mixture.

Turn the pastry out onto a bench that has been dusted with ½ cup gluten-free flour to assist rolling, then knead until shiny. Try to incorporate as little flour as possible so the pastry does not become too crumbly.

Chill the pastry for 20 minutes, then, using a rolling pin, roll the pastry between 2 pieces of baking paper which have been greased on both sides. Roll the pastry until it is 5 mm thick, then use it to line a 24 cm tart or pie tin.

To blind bake, preheat the oven to 200°C. Line the pastry case with foil, then cover with pastry weights. Blind bake the pastry case for 15 minutes, then remove the foil and pastry weights and bake for another 5 minutes.

ROUGH PUFF PASTRY

450 g plain flour, plus extra for dusting

450 g chilled unsalted butter,
cut into 1.5–2 cm cubes

1 teaspoon salt

1 cup (250 ml) water *or* 300 ml cream

To make the pastry, tip the flour onto a cool bench and make a well in the centre, then add the butter and salt. Using the tips of your fingers or a pastry scraper, rub or cut the butter into the flour. Add three-quarters of the water or cream and mix into the flour mixture, but do not knead it. Add the remaining water or cream if necessary; the dough should still be lumpy with small knobs of butter.

Generously flour the bench and roll the dough out to a 1.5 cm-thick rectangle. Use your hands to even up the rectangle to make folding and rolling easier. Brush any flour from the pastry, then fold one end into the centre (brushing the flour off is important, as any extra flour will toughen the pastry). Repeat this on the other side, then fold the dough in half, creating four layers of pastry. This is your first double turn. Roll out the pastry and repeat this process twice more. If the dough becomes too difficult to manage, refrigerate it for 15–20 minutes between turns. Wrap the finished dough in plastic film and rest it in the refrigerator for 20 minutes.

Roll out the chilled pastry and use it to line a 20 cm tart tin with a removable base. Prick the base of the pastry case all over with a fork. Refrigerate the pastry case for at least 20 minutes.

DUCK EGG PASTA

(makes 500 g)

3⅓ cups (500 g) strong flour (see Glossary)

4–5 duck eggs, depending on their size

To make the pasta, tip the flour onto a bench and make a well in the centre. Whisk the eggs together and pour into the well, and gradually incorporate them into the flour, following the method described on page 57. Add an extra yolk if needed. Knead the pasta dough until it forms a shiny ball and is firm to the touch. Cover the dough with plastic film and rest it in the refrigerator for 30 minutes. Cut the pasta dough into about 8 equal portions.

Before beginning to roll the pasta, bring a large saucepan of salted water to the boil. Set the pasta machine on a bench, screwing it down firmly. Working in batches, take one piece of dough and press it as flat as you can with the palm of your hand, then feed it through the rollers set on their widest aperture. Fold the rolled dough in thirds, and then pass the narrow end through the machine again. Repeat several times, preferably until you hear a sound that I can only describe as a 'plop' – this is the tension of the dough releasing as it goes through the rollers. »

Adjust the machine to the next setting and pass the dough through. Repeat this with every setting until you get to the second to last. As the dough moves through each setting it will become finer and finer and the sheets will become longer and longer; you may need to cut the sheets to make them more manageable. Adjust the machine, selecting the widest cutter, and run the pasta through to cut into strips. Hang the pasta ribbons over the back of a chair to dry.

Slide the pasta gently into the boiling water, then partially cover with a lid to bring back to a rapid boil. Stir the pasta gently to keep it well separated. Fresh pasta only needs to cook for 3 minutes or so. Drain the cooked pasta, reserving a little of the cooking water in case you need it to moisten the completed dish. Do not run the pasta under water or you will lose the precious starch that helps the sauce or oil adhere. Generously drizzle the pasta with olive oil immediately.

OLIVE OIL BRIOCHE WITH CANDIED SEVILLE PEEL *Makes 2*

1 cup (250 ml) warm water	3 teaspoons salt
1½ teaspoons castor sugar	1 cup candied Seville peel (see page 105),
15 g fresh yeast *or* 1 teaspoon dried yeast	roughly chopped
675 g unbleached strong flour (see Glossary)	1 free-range egg yolk
3 × 55 g free-range eggs	1 tablespoon milk
¼ cup (60 ml) extra virgin olive oil	

In a bowl, combine the warm water, castor sugar, yeast and 2 tablespoons of the flour and whisk to combine. Set aside for 5–10 minutes or until frothy.

Whisk the eggs, then add the olive oil and stir to combine. Combine the remaining flour and the salt in a large bowl and make a well. Combine the yeast and egg mixtures and pour into the well. With your hands, gently fold in the flour until everything is combined and the dough starts to form a ball. Add the candied peel to the dough.

Turn the dough out onto a floured bench and knead for 10 minutes until soft and satiny, adding a little extra flour if it becomes too sticky. Return the dough to the bowl and cover tightly with plastic film, then refrigerate for 12 hours until doubled in volume.

Remove the dough from the refrigerator and let it return to room temperature (this will take about 1 hour). Knead the dough lightly for 1–2 minutes, then divide it into 2 portions and put into greased loaf tins or large brioche moulds. (This dough does not need to be knocked back – dough with a higher fat content struggles to rise again if knocked back.) Leave to rise in a draught-free spot for about 40 minutes or until it is 1½ times its original volume.

Preheat the oven to 220°C. Mix the egg yolk with the milk and brush this over the tops of the loaves. Bake for 10 minutes, then reduce the temperature to 180°C and bake for another 20 minutes. Turn the loaves out onto a wire rack and leave to cool.

GOLDEN CHICKEN STOCK

Makes about 2 litres

I just can't cook without a good stock, and a chook stock is the one I use most of all. While there are a few good stocks on the market, usually made by small producers, for me nothing touches the homemade. There is something incredibly rewarding about having a pot of stock simmering on the stove, especially knowing that, either reduced or frozen, it might keep you going for a month. It takes so little work and adds so much to your cooking that I urge you to do it.

The better the quality of the original chook the better your stock will be. The skin and bones (with a generous amount of meat still attached) of a mature, well-brought-up bird has not only better flavour but more gelatinous quality. It's truly important not to overcook a stock; your benchmark should be that the meat on the bones is still sweet. An overcooked stock has all the goodness cooked out of it, and the bones have a chalky flavour.

I tend to make my stock in a large batch and then freeze it in 1-litre containers. Using fresh 'bright' vegetables rather than limp leftovers, and roasting the bones and veg before simmering them, gives the stock a wonderful golden colour and a deeper flavour. You only need use enough water to cover the bones and veg by about 7 cm in your stockpot (this way in most cases your stock won't need reducing). Never allow your stock to boil, just bring it to a good simmer, and don't skim it as you'll take the fat – and the flavour – off with it (you can remove the fat easily after the cooked stock has been refrigerated.) Don't let the stock sit in the pan once it is cooked: strain it straight away, then let it cool before refrigerating.

1 large boiling chicken (about 2.2 kg), cut
    into pieces (if you are using bones only,
    you will need 3 kg)

2 large onions, unpeeled and halved

1 large carrot, roughly chopped

extra virgin olive oil, for cooking

100 ml white wine (optional)

1 large leek, trimmed, cleaned
    and roughly chopped

1 stick celery, roughly chopped

1 bay leaf

6 sprigs thyme

6 stalks flat-leaf parsley

1 head garlic, halved widthways

2 very ripe tomatoes, roughly chopped

Preheat the oven to 200°C. Place the chicken pieces, onion and carrot in a roasting pan and drizzle with a little olive oil. Roast for 20 minutes or until chicken and vegetables are golden brown.

Transfer the chicken and vegetables to a large stockpot, then deglaze the roasting pan with wine over high heat, if using. Add the wine with the remaining vegetables and herbs to the pot, and cover with about 2.5 litres water. Simmer, uncovered, for 3–4 hours.

Strain the stock straight away through a sieve into a bowl, then cool by immersing the bowl in a sink of cold water. Refrigerate the stock to let any fat settle on the surface, then remove the fat.

The stock will keep for up to 4 days in the refrigerator or for 3 months in the freezer. To reduce the stock, boil in a saucepan over high heat until it is reduced by three-quarters. When the reduced stock is chilled in the refrigerator, it should set as a jelly; if not, reduce again. Jellied stock will keep in the refrigerator for 2–3 days, and in the freezer for 3 months.

MUSTARD APRICOTS   *Makes 1 litre*

This recipe uses dried apricots; however it can also be made using very firm fresh apricots, peaches, small figs, cherries or glacé fruit. I serve these mustard fruits with pâtés, terrines, rillettes or cold meats, especially legs of sugar-cured ham or baked hands of pork.

400 g dried apricots	1 cinnamon stick
¾ cup (180 ml) boiling water	3 sprigs lemon thyme
50 g Keen's dried mustard powder	2 cups (440 g) sugar
1⅔ cups (410 ml) lemon juice	1 tablespoon finely grated horseradish
finely grated rind of 1 lemon	

Sterilise two 500 ml-capacity jars (see Glossary). Put the apricots in a bowl with the boiling water and leave to soak for 1 hour. Drain the apricots and transfer to a large bowl, reserving ⅓ cup (80 ml) of the soaking liquid.

Put the mustard powder, lemon juice, lemon rind, cinnamon, lemon thyme, sugar and the reserved soaking liquid in a saucepan and bring to the boil, then simmer over low heat for 10 minutes. Stir the horseradish in to this syrup, and pour immediately over the soaked apricots, then transfer straightaway to the sterilised jars.

Leave to mature for at least 1 week before using. Unopened jars of mustard apricots will keep for up to 12 months, although the apricots will darken a little.

BRAISED CAVOLO NERO

Serves 4

1 bunch cavolo nero, washed and
    roughly chopped
½ cup (125 ml) extra virgin olive oil

1 clove garlic
2 anchovy fillets

Blanch the chopped cavolo nero by plunging it briefly in a saucepan of boiling water until just tender, then drain immediately and set aside.

Heat the olive oil over low–medium heat, then sauté the garlic. Add the anchovy fillets and cavolo nero and season with a little salt and pepper. Sauté slowly for about 5 minutes, until the cavolo nero is tender on the tooth.

I like to serve this as an accompaniment, and it works especially well with a slow-roasted oyster blade.

WALNUT AND PARSLEY PESTO

Serves 4

If your garden is overflowing with parsley, try this variation of pesto, using parsley and walnuts ground with garlic and extra virgin olive oil, to serve with pasta and shaved Parmigiano Reggiano. This pesto is also delicious with smoked tongue.

2 cups (200 g) shelled walnuts
2 cloves garlic
1 cup firmly packed flat-leaf parsley leaves

100 ml extra virgin olive oil
2 teaspoons sea salt flakes
freshly ground black pepper

Preheat the oven to 220°C. Dry-roast the walnuts on a baking tray for 6–8 minutes, then rub off the skins with a tea towel and sieve away any remaining bitter skin. Allow to cool, then grind all the ingredients using a mortar and pestle or by pulsing in a food processor. The pesto will keep for a few days, covered with a film of oil, in a jar in the refrigerator. I invariably have difficulty preventing my pesto from oxidising after a few days, finding the recommendation to cover it with a film of oil never quite sufficient (although a splash of lemon juice will help if you are planning to store it). For this reason, when basil is abundant, I often resort to making a paste with the basil, pine nuts and oil and then freezing it in tiny plastic pots with a good seal. The pots can be defrosted in hot water and then mixed with the grated cheese and garlic (garlic shouldn't be frozen as its composition will change) and perhaps a little more oil and seasoning.

GLOSSARY

Wherever possible, I've explained any less familiar ingredients and techniques in the relevant recipes, but I've also included brief notes here on some ingredients and procedures that are used throughout the book.

Arborio rice

What distinguishes this pearly-white, short-grained rice is the amount of starch it releases during cooking, and it is this starch that makes a risotto creamy. Arborio rice should be cooked until it is *al dente*, which takes about 20 minutes, depending on the quality of the rice.

Blind baking

Baking a pastry case 'blind', or without its filling, helps to stop the filling from making the pastry soggy. Lining the pastry case with foil and holding it down with pastry weights prevents the pastry case from rising and losing its shape as it cooks. Special pastry weights are available at kitchenware shops, but dried beans work just as well.

Cheese

see Gorgonzola; Parmigiano Reggiano

Chocolate

The flavour of chocolate is determined by the amounts of chocolate liquor and cocoa solids it contains.

Bitter chocolate has the highest percentage of cocoa liquor and no added sugar, so it has a strong chocolate flavour, which adds depth to savoury dishes.

A good bittersweet chocolate may contain 65–70 per cent cocoa solids, and the best even more. Because it has sugar added, it is mostly used for sweet dishes – or eating.

Couverture chocolate is the name given to high-quality chocolate that melts well and dries to a glossy finish, making it perfect for covering cakes and for making fine desserts. It can also be used in any recipe calling for chocolate, since its high cocoa butter content gives it a fine flavour and texture.

Cornichons

Cornichons are tiny, crisp gherkins pickled in the French manner: picked when they are 3–8 cm long, and pickled in vinegar or brine. They are crunchy and salty, and are perfect to serve with rillettes, pâtés or terrines, to accompany a charcuterie plate, or as part of a ploughman's lunch.

Cream

In Australia, most cows are kept to produce milk rather than cream, so the fat content of their milk needs to be supplemented at various times of the year to bring it up to the 35 per cent fat content that is needed for pure cream. With nothing else added, this cream is good for enriching sauces.

Any cream labelled 'thickened cream' also has a thickener such as gelatine added. Because of the extra stability that the thickener provides, this is the best cream for whipping – just remember that reduced-fat thickened cream (with around 18 per cent fat) cannot be whipped successfully.

Double cream is very rich, with a fat content of 45–60 per cent. Some of the thicker ones are perfect for spooning alongside a dessert. Try to find farmhouse versions that have been separated from unhomogenised milk.

Flour

Strong flour, also known as bread flour or baker's flour, is my staple flour. What differentiates strong flour is its high gluten content, which allows dough to stretch rather than break during kneading and rolling, making it particularly suitable for making pasta and bread. The gluten in strong flour also helps to ensure an extensive and even rise in bread.

Flours are further classified according to the percentage of wheat grain present. Wholemeal flour contains the whole grain, and so has a wonderful nutty taste, while brown flour contains about 85 per cent of the grain and white flour between 75 and 80 per cent. The flour industry is moving to predominantly unbleached flour; bleached flour must be specially requested. I prefer unbleached flour as it contains slightly more nutrients; it also has a more robust texture, which works well in breads and pizza bases.

Self-raising flour is plain flour with baking powder and salt added during the milling process, in the proportions of about 1¼ teaspoons of baking powder and a pinch of salt for every cup of flour.

It is used for making pancakes, cakes and muffins.

Gelatine

Gelatine leaves have a better flavour and texture than powdered gelatine. However, confusion can arise from the fact that the gelling strength of gelatine leaves is measured by their 'bloom' rather than their weight. All my recipes have been developed using Alba brand Gold-strength leaves, which weigh 2 g each and have a bloom of 190–220 g.

As gelatine will set more firmly over time, you may be able to use less gelatine if you can make the jelly the day before it is needed. A couple of other things to note: gelatine takes twice as long to dissolve in cream or milk as it does in water; and sugar can inhibit setting, so the higher the sugar content, the softer the set will be.

Gorgonzola

This Italian blue cheese comes in sweet (*dolce*) and spicy (*piccante*) versions. Gorgonzola dolce is soft and ripe, with a creamy, spreadable texture.

Gorgonzola piccante is earthier in flavour, firmer, and has a more powerful aroma, having been washed repeatedly in brine during its year or more of cave-ageing.

Oils

As you will probably have gathered by now, I use extra virgin olive oil liberally in my cooking, and consider it vital to my food – and, indeed, my life. The only other oils I occasionally use are nut oils to flavour a salad dressing, and refined grapeseed oil in dishes where a more neutral-flavoured oil is desirable, such as in desserts, or to combine with extra virgin olive oil when making mayonnaise, to avoid a bitter after-taste.

Parmigiano Reggiano

Authentic aged parmesan cheese made in Italy according to specific traditional practices, Parmigiano Reggiano is my first choice for use in risottos, polenta, soups, and sauces such as pesto. I also love it as part of a cheese board or freshly shaved in salads. Grana Padano has a similar flavour to Parmigiano Reggiano, but has not been aged for as long, so can be a useful, less expensive alternative.

Pastry weights *see* Blind baking

Rice *see* Arborio rice

Sterilising jars and bottles

To sterilise jars that are to be used for storing or preserving food, wash the jars and lids in hot, soapy water, then rinse them in hot water and place them in a 120°C oven for approximately 15 minutes to dry out. This method also works for bottles.

Sugar syrup

Sugar syrup is a simple solution of 1 part sugar dissolved in 1–2 parts water (depending on its intended use) over low heat. It is great to have on hand if you are keen on whipping up your own cocktails at home!

Tomato sugo and passata

These dense, slow-cooked tomato sauces originate from Italy. They are usually made with just tomatoes, but herbs and spices may also be added. Sugo is coarser as it is made from chopped tomatoes, whereas the tomatoes for passata are sieved, making it more like a purée. Both can be used in soups, stews sauces, or any dish where a tomato flavour is desired, but without the texture of acidity of fresh tomatoes.

Vino cotto

Literally meaning 'cooked wine' in Italian, this traditional Italian preparation is made by simmering unfermented grape juice until it is reduced to a syrup. The one I produce is finished with traditional red-wine vinegar to make it truly *agrodolce* (sweet–sour). With a much softer flavour than vinegar, vino cotto can be used to make sauces for meat or salad dressings or even drizzled over strawberries. In fact, it can be used anywhere you would normally use balsamic vinegar.

LIST OF SOURCES

The author and publisher would like to thank the following people and companies for allowing us to reproduce their material in this book. In some cases we were not able to contact the copyright owners; we would appreciate hearing from any copyright holders not acknowledged here, so that we can properly acknowledge their contribution when this book is reprinted.

Extracts

Andrews, Colman, *Catalan Cuisine*, Headline, London, 1989; von Bremzen Anya and Welchman, John, *Please to the Table: The Russian Cookbook*, copyright C 1990 by Anya von Bremzen and John Welchman, used by permission of Workman Publishing Co., Inc., New York, All rights Reserved; Castelvetro, Giacomo (trans. Gillian Riley), *The Fruit, Herbs and Vegetables of Italy*, Viking, New York, 1990; Gray, Patience, *Honey from a Weed*, Prospect Books, London, 1986; Grigson, Jane, *Jane Grigson's Fruit Book*, Michael Joseph, London, 1982; Huxley, Aldous, *The Olive Tree*, Ayer, USA, reprint of 1937 edition; Santich, Barbara, 'The Return of Verjuice', *Winestate*, June 1984.

Recipes

Black duck and orange sauce, Wild duck poached in wine sauce: Alf Wark; Cheong's figs: Cheong Liew; Hare pie, Stephanie's partridge pies: Stephanie Alexander; Kylie Kwong's Chinese-style partridge with pomegranate-caramel sauce: Kylie Kwong; Margaret's persimmon bread: Margaret Lehmann; Peter Wall's raspberry vinegar: Peter Wall; Sandor Palmai's persimmon tarts: Sandor Palmai.

BIBLIOGRAPHY

Alexander, Stephanie, *The Cook's Companion* (2nd edition), Lantern, Melbourne, 2004.

—— *Cooking and Travelling in South-West France*, Viking, Melbourne, 2002.

—– *Stephanie's Journal*, Viking, Melbourne, 1999.

—— *Stephanie's Seasons*, Allen & Unwin, Sydney, 1993.

—— *Stephanie's Australia*, Allen & Unwin, Sydney, 1991.

—— *Stephanie's Feasts and Stories*, Allen & Unwin, Sydney, 1988.

—— *Stephanie's Menus for Food Lovers*, Methuen Haynes, Sydney, 1985.

Alexander, Stephanie and Beer, Maggie, *Stephanie Alexander & Maggie Beer's Tuscan Cookbook*, Viking, Melbourne, 1998.

Anderson, Ronald, *Gold on Four Feet*, Ronald Anderson, Melbourne, 1978.

Andrews, Colman, *Catalan Cuisine*, Headline, London, 1989.

The Barossa Cookery Book, Soldiers' Memorial Institute, Tanunda, 1917.

Beck, Simone, *Simca's Cuisine*, Vintage Books, New York, 1976.

Beck, Simone, Bertholle, Louisette and Child, Julia, *Mastering the Art of French Cooking, Volume One*, Penguin, Harmondsworth, 1979.

Beer, Maggie, *Maggie's Table*, Lantern, Melbourne, 2005.

—— *Cooking with Verjuice*, Penguin, Melbourne, 2003.

—— *Maggie's Orchard*, Viking, Melbourne, 1997.

—— *Maggie's Farm*, Allen & Unwin, Sydney, 1993.

Beeton, Mrs, *Mrs Beeton's Book of Household Management*, Cassell, London, 2000.

—— *Family Cookery*, Ward Lock, London, 1963.

Bertolli, Paul with Waters, Alice, *Chez Panisse Cooking*, Random House, New York, 1988.

Bissell, Frances, *A Cook's Calendar: Seasonal Menus by Frances Bissell*, Chatto & Windus, London, 1985.

Boddy, Michael and Boddy, Janet, *Kitchen Talk Magazine* (vol. I, no's 1–13), The Bugle Press, via Binalong, NSW, 1989–92.

Boni, Ada, *Italian Regional Cooking*, Bonanza Books, New York, 1969.

von Bremzen, Anya and Welchman, John, *Please to the Table: The Russian Cookbook*, Workman, New York, 1990.

Bureau of Resource Sciences, *Marketing Names for Fish and Seafood in Australia*, Department of Primary Industries & Energy and the Fisheries Research & Development Corporation, Canberra, 1995.

Carluccio, Antonio, *A Passion for Mushrooms*, Pavilion Books, London, 1989.

—— *An Invitation to Italian Cooking*, Pavilion Books, London, 1986.

Castelvetro, Giacomo, *The Fruit, Herbs and Vegetables of Italy*, Viking, New York, 1990.

Colmagro, Suzanne, Collins, Graham and Sedgley, Margaret, 'Processing Technology of the Table Olive', University of Adelaide, in Jules Janick (ed.) *Horticultural Reviews* Vol. 25, John Wiley & Sons, 2000.

Cox, Nicola, *Game Cookery*, Victor Gollancz, London, 1989.

David, Elizabeth, *Italian Food*, Penguin, Harmondsworth, 1989.

—— *An Omelette and a Glass of Wine*, Penguin, Harmondsworth, 1986.

—— *English Bread and Yeast Cookery*, Penguin, Harmondsworth, 1979.

—— *French Provincial Cooking*, Penguin, Harmondsworth, 1970.

—— *Summer Cooking*, Penguin, Harmondsworth, 1965.

De Groot, Roy Andries, *The Auberge of the Flowering Hearth*, The Ecco Press, New Jersey, 1973.

Dolamore, Anne, *The Essential Olive Oil Companion*, Macmillan, Melbourne, 1988.

Ferguson, Jenny, *Cooking for You and Me*, Methuen Haynes, Sydney, 1987.

Field, Carol, *Celebrating Italy*, William Morrow, New York, 1990.

Fitzgibbon, Theodora, *Game Cooking*, Andre Deutsch, London, 1963.

Glowinski, Louis, *The Complete Book of Fruit Growing in Australia*, Lothian, Melbourne, 1991.

Gray, Patience, *Honey From a Weed*, Prospect Books, London, 1986.

Gray, Rose and Rogers, Ruth, *The River Cafe Cook Book*, Ebury Press, London, 1996.

Grigson, Jane and Fullick, Roy (eds), *The Enjoyment of Food: The Best of Jane Grigson*, Michael Joseph, London, 1992.

Grigson, Jane, *Jane Grigson's Fruit Book*, Michael Joseph, London, 1982.

—— *Jane Grigson's Vegetable Book*, Penguin, Harmondsworth, 1980.

—— *Good Things*, Penguin, Harmondsworth, 1973.

—— *Jane Grigson's Fish Book*, Penguin, Harmondsworth, 1973.

—— *Charcuterie and French Pork Cookery*, Penguin, Harmondsworth, 1970.

Halligan, Marion, *Eat My Words*, Angus & Robertson, Sydney, 1990.

Hazan, Marcella, *The Classic Italian Cookbook*, Macmillan, London (rev. ed.), 1987.

Hopkinson, Simon with Bareham, Lindsey, *Roast Chicken and Other Stories*, Ebury Press, London, 1994.

Huxley, Aldous, *The Olive Tree*, Ayer, USA, reprint of 1937 ed.

Isaacs, Jennifer, *Bush Food*, Weldon, Sydney, 1987.

Kamman, Madeleine, *In Madeleine's Kitchen*, Macmillan, New York, 1992.

—— *The Making of a Cook*, Atheneum, New York, 1978.

Lake, Max, *Scents and Sensuality*, Penguin, Melbourne, 1991.

Manfield, Christine, *Christine Manfield Originals*, Lantern, Melbourne, 2006.

McGee, Harold, *The Curious Cook*, Northpoint Press, San Francisco, 1990.

—— *On Food and Cooking*, Collier Books, New York, 1988.

Ministero Agricoltura e Foreste. D.O.C. *Cheeses of Italy* (trans. Angela Zanotti), Milan, 1992.

Molyneux, Joyce, with Grigson, Sophie, *The Carved Angel Cookery Book*, Collins, 1990.

Newell, Patrice, *The Olive Grove*, Penguin, Melbourne, 2000.

del Nero, Constance and del Nero, Rosario, *Risotto*, Harper and Row, New York, 1989.

Olney, Richard, *Simple French Food*, Atheneum, New York, 1980.

Peck, Paula, *The Art of Fine Baking*, Simon & Schuster, New York, 1961.

Pellegrini, Angelo M., *The Food Lover's Garden*, Lyons & Burford, New York, 1970.

Pepin, Jacques, *La Technique*, Hamlyn Publishing Group, New York, 1978.

Perry, Neil, *The Food I Love*, Murdoch Books, Sydney, 2005.

Pignolet, Damien, *French*, Lantern, Melbourne, 2005.

Reichelt, Karen, with Burr, Michael, *Extra Virgin: An Australian Companion to Olives and Olive Oil*, Wakefield Press, Adelaide, 1997.

Ripe, Cherry, *Goodbye Culinary Cringe*, Allen & Unwin, Sydney, 1993.

Santich, Barbara, 'The Return of Verjuice', *Winestate*, June 1984.

Schauer, Amy, *The Schauer Australian Cookery Book* (14th ed.), W.R. Smith & Paterson, Brisbane, 1979.

Scicolone, Michele, *The Antipasto Table*, Morrow, New York, 1991.

Scott, Philippa, *Gourmet Game*, Simon & Schuster, New York, 1989.

Silverton, Nancy, *Nancy Silverton's Pastries from the La Brea Bakery*, Random House, New York, 2000.

Simeti, Mary Taylor, *Pomp and Sustenance*, Alfred A. Knopf, New York, 1989.

Stobart, Tom (ed.), *The Cook's Encyclopaedia*, Papermac, London, 1982.

Studd, Will, *Chalk and Cheese*, Purple Egg, Melbourne, 2004.

Sutherland Smith, Beverley, *A Taste for All Seasons*, Lansdowne, Sydney, 1975.

Sweeney, Susan, *The Olive Press*, The Australian Olive Association, Autumn 2006.

Symons, Michael, *One Continuous Picnic*, Duck Press, Adelaide, 1982.

Taruschio, Ann and Taruschio, Franco, *Leaves from the Walnut Tree*, Pavilion, London, 1993.

Time-Life Fruit Book, Time-Life, Amsterdam, 1983.

Wark, Alf, *Wine Cookery*, Rigby, Adelaide, 1969.

Waters, Alice, Curtan, Patricia and Labro, Martine, *Chez Panisse Pasta, Pizza and Calzone*, Random House, New York, 1984.

Waters, Alice, *Chez Panisse Café Cookbook*, Random House, New York, 1999.

—— *Chez Panisse Menu Cookbook*, Chatto & Windus, London, 1984.

Weir, Joanne, *You Say Tomato*, Broadway Books, New York, 1998.

Wells, Patricia, *At Home in Provence*, Scribner, New York, 1996.

Wells, Patricia and Robuchon, Joël, *Simply French*, William Morrow, New York, 1991.

Whiteaker, Stafford, *The Compleat Strawberry*, Century Publishing, London, 1985.

Wolfert, Paula, *The Cooking of the Eastern Mediterranean*, Harper Collins Publishers, New York, 1994.

—— *The Cooking of South-West France*, The Dial Press, New York, 1983.

—— *Mediterranean Cooking*, The Ecco Press, New York, 1977.

Zalokar, Sophie, *Picnic*, Fremantle Arts Centre Press, Perth, 2002.

ACKNOWLEDGEMENTS

This extract from *Maggie's Harvest* represents the culmination of a life's work to date, so how can I possibly conjure up all the people who have been instrumental in so many ways over the years?

My husband, Colin, is my rock – a true partner in every sense of the word. My daughters, Saskia and Elli, have grown into strong, independent women and we share regular boisterous meals with their partners and our much-loved grandchildren, Zöe, Max, Lilly, Rory, Ben and Darby.

The indomitable Julie Gibbs, originally suggested an update of *Maggie's Farm* and *Maggie's Orchard*, an idea which developed over time into *Maggie's Harvest*. I always had faith in Julie's extraordinary ability to know just what will make a book special.

Photographer Mark Chew effortlessly captured the essence of the produce in the book – it feels so Barossan! Daniel New, the book's designer, weaved his magic with the design. Marie Anne Pledger not only helped out on the shoots, but provided paraphernalia from her own kitchen and that of her friends for us to use.

There are so many in the team at Penguin I'd like to thank. My editors Kathleen Gandy and Virginia Birch and Nicole Brown for keeping us all on track, Anouska Jones for proofreading, and Jocelyn Hungerford and all at Penguin for eleventh-hour assistance.

Over the years I have had an incredible array of staff who have contributed so much to both my business and my life. First and foremost was the lovely Hilda Laurencis, who sadly died as I wrote the very last pages of *Maggie's Harvest*.

From the Pheasant Farm Restaurant days, Sophie Zalokar, Steve Flamsteed, Nat Paull and Alex Herbert remain part of our extended family, and more recently Victoria Blumenstein and Gill Radford have both done much to ease my daily life.

The friendly, hard-working team at the Farmshop are the public face of our business and help to keep the tradition of the farm alive. I have so much to thank them for. Our customers, from the early days of the Pheasant Farm Restaurant, to those who buy our products all over the world today, have believed in us and what we've done.

I would also like to thank the following people who have lent their expertise in specific areas: Louis Glowinski; Geoff Linton of Yalumba; Dr Rod Mailer, Principal Research Scientist at the NSW Department of Primary Industries (who I'm delighted to say works exclusively with the olive oil industry now); and Richard Gunner of Coorong Angus Beef, for his passionate endeavours and wealth of knowledge on beef and lamb.

INDEX

A

Aileen's Olive Bread 80
Alexander, Stephanie 2, 3, 61, 64, 76, 82, 87, 124, 141
allioli
Quince Allioli 130
almonds 2–10
~ bitter 4, 5
~ buying in the shell 4
~ fresh 4
~ green 2, 3
~ marzipan 5
~ paper-shell 4
~ roasting 5
~ soup 6
~ storing 4–5
~ sweet 4
~ as thickening agent 6
Almond and Garlic Soup with Grapes 48
Almond Macaroons 10
Almond Paste 8
Avocado, Ginger and Roasted Almonds with Pasta and Fresh Coriander 6
Orchard Cake 8
Pheasant with Almonds and Sherry 7
anchovy vinaigrette 83, 157
Andrews, Colman 54
apricots, dried
Mustard Apricots 182
Auricht, Ed 4
Australian Symposium of Gastronomy 108
Avocado, Ginger and Roasted Almonds with Pasta and Fresh Coriander 6

B

Baby Beets in Vino Cotto with Rocket, Walnuts and Goat's Cheese 158
Baked Olives 79
balsamic vinegar 150, 152, 156
Fillet of Beef in Balsamic Vinegar or Vino Cotto 17
Barossa Vintage Festival 43–4
Beckmann, Jenny 132

beef 11–20
Carpetbag Steak 20
Coorong Angus Beef Pie with Red Wine, Fennel and Green Olives 14
Fillet of Beef in Balsamic Vinegar or Vino Cotto 17
Oxtail with Orange, Olives and Walnuts 18
Slow-braised Beef Cheeks in Barossa Shiraz 16
Slow-roasted Oyster Blade with Onion Cream and Braised Cavolo Nero 19
Beer, Colin 1, 52, 62, 74, 81, 82, 87, 88, 104, 106, 128, 130, 156
Beer, Flo 130
beetroot
Baby Beets in Vino Cotto with Rocket, Walnuts and Goat's Cheese 158
Biron, George 68
black duck 167
Black Duck and Orange Sauce 169
blancmange 5
blind baking 177, 185
Blumenstein, Victoria 178
Boni, Ada 63
Braised Cavolo Nero 183
Brandel, Catherine 27
bread
Aileen's Olive Bread 80
Almond and Garlic Soup with Grapes 48
Liver Crostini 54
Margaret's Persimmon Bread 101
Pumpkin Picnic Loaf 119
Schiacciata 48
Walnut Flatbread 165
brioche
Olive Oil Brioche and Candied Seville Peel 180
Bryant, Simon 118, 144
Burge, Grant 44
Burnt Fig Jam Slice 42
butters
~ almond 5, 6,
Cèpe Butter 57

C

cabbage
Partridge with Savoy Cabbage, Pancetta, Walnuts and Verjuice 85
cakes
Chocolate Cake with a Fig Centre and Ganache 40
Génoise Sponge 94
Orchard Cake 8
caramel
Pomegranate-caramel Sauce 86
Carluccio, Antonio 70
carpaccio
Kangaroo Carpaccio with Cumquats, Green Peppercorns and Verjuice 148
Carpetbag Steak 20
Carrodus, Bailey 59
Castelvetro, Giacomo 3, 162
Cave-Rogers, Robert 71
cavolo nero
Braised Cavolo Nero 183
Cèpe Butter 57
cheese
Pumpkin Pizza with Olives and Bocconcini 122
see also goat's cheese; gorgonzola
Cheong Liew 35, 59–60, 83, 107, 146
Cheong's Figs 35, 42
chicken
~ with verjuice 145
Golden Chicken Stock 181
Grape Grower's Chicken 49
chicken livers
Liver Crostini 54
Chickpea and Roasted Pumpkin Salad 119
Chinese Master Stock 86
chocolate
Cheong's Figs 35, 42
Chocolate Cake with a Fig Centre and Ganache 40
Chocolate Orange Brownie Pudding with Rhubarb and Mascarpone 139
Chocolate Sweetmeats 166
Ganache 40

Choux Pastry-style Gluten-free
    Pastry 178
Coates, Marjorie 81
Collins, Graham *77*
Colmagro, Suzanne *77*
Compote of Shredded Duck 173
Cooking with Verjuice 142
Coorong Angus Beef Pie
    with Red Wine, Fennel
    and Green Olives 14
coriander
    Avocado, Ginger and Roasted
        Almonds with Pasta and
        Fresh Coriander 6
cornichons 185
crabapples 21–5
    ~ with pheasant 22
    ~ varieties 22
    Crabapple Jelly 23, 24, 25
    Kathy Howard's Wild
        Crabapple and Sage Jelly 24
    Spiced Crabapples 23
cream
    double 185
    'thickened' 185
Crème Anglaise 39
crumble
    Rhubarb Crumble 139
cumquats
    Kangaroo Carpaccio
        with Cumquats,
        Green Peppercorns
        and Verjuice 148
custard
    Crème Anglaise 39
    Sauternes Custard 94

D

damson jelly 25
David, Elizabeth 5, 63, 70–1
de Groot, Roy Andries 136
de Pieri, Stefano 45, 122
de Rohan, Maurice 16
del Nero, Constance 73
Desert Pearls 47
di Marchi, Paolo 59
Ditter, Susan 159
dressings *see* mayonnaise;
    vinaigrette
Dried Fig Tapenade 37
Dried Pears Poached in Verjuice 93
duck
    Compote of Shredded Duck 173
    Smoked Duck Breast Salad with
        Pickled Quince and Vino Cotto
        Dressing 127, 131
    see also wild duck
duck fat
    ~ health benefits 170
    ~ rendering 170, 172
    Hare Cooked in Duck Fat 62
    Rillettes de Canard (Compote
        of Shredded Duck) 173
Duck Egg Pasta 179

E

eggs
    ~ beating 10
    ~ guinea fowl 53
    ~ leftover whites 10
    Duck Egg Pasta 179
Ellis, Margaret 90
escabeche 83
extra virgin olive oil 74
    Olive Oil Brioche with
        Candied Seville Peel 180
    Oxtail with Orange, Olives
        and Walnuts 18
    Pumpkin, Verjuice and
        Extra Virgin Olive Oil
        Risotto 118, 122

F

Farmshop 110, *177*
fennel 26–31
    ~ caramelised 29
    ~ choosing 26
    ~ fresh 26–7
    ~ peeling 26
    ~ poaching 27
    Coorong Angus Beef Pie
        with Red Wine, Fennel
        and Green Olives 14
    Fennel with Goat's
        Curd 27, 29
    Pasta with Caramelised
        Fennel, Preserved
        Lemon and Garlic 30
    Persimmon and Fennel
        Salad 100
    Tea-smoked Ocean Trout
        with Fennel 30
fennel oil 29
fennel seeds 26, 29, 35
figs 32–42
    ~ baked 35
    ~ caramelising 35
    ~ choosing 34
    ~ deep-fried 35
    ~ dried 35
    ~ grilled 36
    ~ ice cream 35
    ~ marinated 35
    ~ semi-dried 36
    ~ unripe 34
    ~ varieties 32
    Burnt Fig Jam Slice 42
    Cheong's Figs 35, 42
    Chocolate Cake with a Fig
        Centre and Ganache 40
    Dried Fig Tapenade 37
    Fig and Gorgonzola Tart 38
    Fig and Preserved Lemon
        Salad with Walnuts and
        Goat's Curd 37
    Figs in Puff Pastry with
        Crème Anglaise 39
    Fig and Walnut Tart 41

Fresh Fig and Prosciutto
    Salad 36
Pickled Figs, Farm
    Follies Style 38
Verjuice Sabayon with
    Grilled Figs 149
fig leaves 35
Fillet of Beef in Balsamic
    Vinegar or Vino Cotto 17
fish
    ~ Murray cod 69, 147
    Ocean Trout in Verjuice
        Jelly 147
    Tea-smoked Ocean Trout
        with Fennel 30
    see also tuna
Flamsteed, Steve 94, 124, 126
flat-leaf parsley *see*
    parsley (flat-leaf)
Flo Beer's Pickled
    Quinces 130
flour 186
foie gras with verjuice 145
Fresh Fig and Prosciutto
    Salad 36
fruit
    ~ poaching in verjuice 142
    see also specific fruits

G

game
    ~ braising in duck fat 172
    see also hare; pheasant
Ganache 40
garlic
    ~ keeping in oil 183
    ~ not freezing 183
    ~ roasting 27
    Almond and Garlic Soup
        with Grapes 48
    Onion, Garlic and
        Prosciutto Sofregit 54
    Pasta with Caramelised
        Fennel, Preserved
        Lemon and Garlic 30
    Quince Allioli 130
Garraffa, Vince and Anne 45
gelatine 186
Génoise Sponge 94
Gerard Madani's Mushroom
    Soup 72
gherkins (cornichons) 185
ginger
    Avocado, Ginger and
        Roasted Almonds
        with Pasta and
        Fresh Coriander 6
Glazed Pears with
    Mascarpone 96
Glowinski, Louis 2
gluten-free pastry 178
gnocchi
    Green Olive Gnocchi with
        Green Olive Sauce 79

goat's cheese
    Baby Beets in Vino Cotto
        with Rocket, Walnuts
        and Goat's Cheese 158
    Fennel with Goat's Curd 27, 29
    Fig and Preserved Lemon
        Salad with Walnuts and
        Goat's Curd 37
Golden Chicken Stock 181
goose fat 145
gorgonzola
    Fig and Gorgonzola Tart 38
grapes 43–51
    ~ juice extraction 50
    ~ pickled 47
    ~ removing pips 47
    ~ sultana grapes 45, 47
    ~ table grapes 45
    ~ for verjuice 142, 144
    ~ wine grapes 45, 48
    Almond and Garlic Soup
        with Grapes 48
    Grape Grower's Chicken 49
    Pheasant with Sultana
        Grapes and Verjuice 109
    Schiacciata 48
    Sherri's Rotegrütze 50
grapeseed oil 165, 186
Gray, Gayle 142
Gray, Patience 35
Green Olive Gnocchi with
    Green Olive Sauce 79
green peppercorns
    ~ preserved in verjuice 148
    Kangaroo Carpaccio
        with Cumquats,
        Green Peppercorns
        and Verjuice 148
grenadine syrup 114
Grigson, Jane 103
guinea fowl 52–8
    ~ bones for stock 58
    ~ carving 56
    ~ choosing 53
    ~ 'doneness' test 54
    ~ eggs 53
    ~ frozen 53
    ~ marinating 53
    Guinea Fowl with Cèpe Butter
        and Golden Shallots 57
    Guinea Fowl in Onion, Garlic
        and Prosciutto Sofregit 54
    Liver Crostini 54
    Stuffed Guinea Fowl with
        Red-wine Sauce 56
Gunner, Richard 12

H

Halliday, James 59
Hannaford, Belinda 34
hare 59–65
    ~ blood 60
    ~ fillets 61
    ~ hanging 59, 60
    ~ jointing 65
    ~ jugged (marinated) 60
    ~ saddle 60–1
    Hare Cooked in Duck Fat 62
    Hare Pie 61–2, 64
    Hare with Pine Nuts,
        Lemon and Sultanas 63
Harvey, Wendeley 71
Herbert, Alex 93–4
Hill Smith family 168
Hillier, Jennifer 136
hollandaise sauce
    Verjuice Hollandaise 144, 148
Howard, Jacqui 24
Howard, Kathy 24

I

ice cream, fig 35
Inauen, Urs 146

J

jam
    Burnt Fig Jam Slice 42
Jane's Persimmon Pudding 102
Jeffs, Janet 159
jelly
    ~ damson 25
    ~ quince 126, 127, 128
    Crabapple Jelly 23, 24, 25
    Kathy Howard's Wild
        Crabapple and Sage Jelly 24
    Verjuice Jelly 147
Jensen, Laurie 44

K

kangaroo
    Duck Egg Pasta with
        Smoked Kangaroo,
        Sun-dried Tomatoes
        and Pine Nuts 179
    Kangaroo Carpaccio
        with Cumquats,
        Green Peppercorns
        and Verjuice 148
Kathreptis, Lew 141
Kathy Howard's Wild
    Crabapple and Sage Jelly 24
kid 156
Kwong, Kylie 1, 82
Kylie Kwong's Chinese-
    style Partridge with
    Pomegranate-caramel
    Sauce 86
Kyritsis, Janni 35

L

lamb
    ~ rack 114, 131, 162
    Lamb Neck with Quinces 132
lard
    Stephanie's Lard Pastry 64

Lehmann, Margaret and
    Peter 84, 99, 102
    Margaret's Persimmon
        Bread 101
lemons
    ~ caramelising 100
    ~ marinade for offal 63
    Hare with Pine Nuts,
        Lemon and Sultanas 63
    see also preserved lemons
lettuce
    ~ cos 109, 163
    ~ drying 157
    ~ 'lamb's' (mâche) 84, 115
limes
    ~ candied 42
    Kylie Kwong's Chinese-
        style Partridge with
        Pomegranate-caramel
        Sauce 86
    Lime Sorbet 103
Linton, Geoff 153
Liver Crostini 54

M

macaroons
    Almond Macaroons 10
McGee, Harold 99, 100
Madani, Gerard 72
Mader, Hazel 132
Manfredi, Franca 118
Margaret's Persimmon Bread 101
marron 44, 69
marzipan 5
mascarpone
    Glazed Pears with
        Mascarpone 96
mayonnaise, oils for 186
meringue
    Almond Macaroons 10
    Fig and Walnut Tart 41
Milligan, Tom 146
Murray cod 69, 147
mushrooms 66–73
    ~ baking 70
    ~ cultivated 71, 72
    ~ drying 69, 70
    ~ native fungi 69
    ~ pan-frying 71
    ~ poisonous 68, 69
    ~ safe to pick 68
    ~ smoked 71
    Cèpe Butter 57
    Gerard Madani's
        Mushroom Soup 72
    Pigeon and Field
        Mushroom Pie 72
    Risotto with Mushrooms 73
    Saskia's Walnut, Mushroom
        and Prosciutto Tart 164
mustard
    ~ Dijon 141, 144
    Mustard Apricots 182
My Way of Cooking Pheasant 107

N

Newell, Patrice 77
nuts *see* almonds; walnuts
nut butter (almond) 5, 6
nut oils
~ rancidity 163
~ refrigerating 163
~ uses 186

O

Ocean Trout in Verjuice
Jelly 147
offal
~ grapes with 47
~ marinade for 63
Liver Crostini 54
oils
~ fennel 29
~ grapeseed 165, 186
~ for mayonnaise 186
~ uses 186
see also extra virgin olive oil;
nut oils
olives 74–80
~ baking 78
~ black 76
~ commercially-prepared 77
~ cooking with 78–9
~ deep-frying 79
~ dips 78–9
~ green 76, 79
~ kalamatas 77, 78
~ marinating your own 78
~ pickling 76, 77, 79
~ pitted 79
~ ripening 76
~ small producers 78
~ when to pick 76
~ wild 74, 76
Aileen's Olive Bread 80
Baked Olives 79
Coorong Angus Beef Pie
with Red Wine, Fennel
and Green Olives 14
Dried Fig Tapenade 37
Green Olive Gnocchi with
Green Olive Sauce 79
Olive Tapenade with
Red-wine Vinegar 158
Oxtail with Orange,
Olives and Walnuts 18
Pumpkin Pizza with Olives
and Bocconcini 122
Olive Oil Brioche and
Candied Seville Peel 180
onions
~ baby 13
~ caramelised 36, 165
Lamb Neck with
Quinces 132
Onion Cream 19
Onion, Garlic and
Prosciutto Sofregit 54

Oxtail with Orange, Olives
and Walnuts 18
see also shallots
oranges
~ candied peel 8, 180
~ juice 53, 57, 107, 136, 138
~ rind 78
~ Seville 180
Black Duck and Orange
Sauce 169
Chocolate Orange Brownie
Pudding with Rhubarb
and Mascarpone 139
Olive Oil Brioche with
Candied Seville Peel 180
Orange Sauce 169
Oxtail with Orange, Olives
and Walnuts 18
Poached Rhubarb and
Orange 138
Rice Pudding with Poached
Rhubarb and Orange 138
Orchard Cake 8
Oxtail with Orange, Olives
and Walnuts 18
oysters
Carpetbag Steak 20
Verjuice Vinaigrette 144, 145

P

Palmai, Sandor 103
pancetta
Partridge with Savoy
Cabbage, Pancetta,
Walnuts and Verjuice 85
parsley (flat-leaf)
~ stalks 18, 63, 181
Walnut and Parsley
Pesto 162, 183
partridge 81–2
~ breast 82
~ boning 83
~ grilling 82, 83
~ legs 82
~ marinating 82–3
~ roasting 83
~ spatchcocking 82, 83
~ stuffing 83
Kylie Kwong's Chinese-
style Partridge with
Pomegranate-caramel
Sauce 86
Partridge with Savoy
Cabbage, Pancetta,
Walnuts and Verjuice 85
Partridge 'Puddings'
with Sultanas and
Verjuice 84
Stephanie's Partridge Pies 87
pasta
~ home-made 179
Avocado, Ginger and Roasted
Almonds with Pasta and
Fresh Coriander 6

Duck Egg Pasta with Smoked
Kangaroo, Sun-dried Tomatoes
and Pine Nuts 179
Pasta with Caramelised
Fennel, Preserved
Lemon and Garlic 30
Walnut and Parsley
Pesto 162, 183
pasta machine 179–80
pastes
Almond Paste 8
Quince Paste 129
pastries
Burnt Fig Jam Slice 42
see also pies; tarts
pastry
~ blind baking 177, 185
~ gluten-free 178
~ 'inhibiting' 178
Choux Pastry-style
Gluten-free Pastry 178
Rough Puff Pastry 179
Sour Cream Pastry 177
Stephanie's Lard Pastry 64
Patchett, Sue 110
pâté spice mixture 172
Paull, Natalie 94
pears 88–96
~ caramelising 91
~ poaching 91
~ purée 91
~ ripening 90, 91
~ varieties 89–90
~ wine 88
Dried Pears Poached
in Verjuice 93
Glazed Pears with
Mascarpone 96
Poached Pears on Filo Pastry
with Mascarpone 93
Quinces and Pears Poached
in Verjuice 134
Sun-dried Pears Farm
Follies Style 91
Trifle of Pears, Prunes and
Sauternes Custard 93
Perry, Neil 12
persimmons 97–103
~ astringency 97, 99
~ cooking with 99
~ drying 99, 100
~ how to eat 99
~ paste 100
Jane's Persimmon Pudding 102
Margaret's Persimmon
Bread 101
Persimmon and Amaretto 101
Persimmon and Fennel Salad 100
Sandor Palmai's Persimmon
Tarts 103
Seared Tuna with Persimmon
and Fennel Salad 100
pesto
Walnut and Parsley
Pesto 162, 183

Peter Wall's Raspberry
    Vinegar 157
pheasant 53, 104–11
    ~ with crabapple 22
    ~ hanging 104
    ~ marinating 107
    ~ roasting 106
    ~ spatchcocking 107
    My Way of Cooking
        Pheasant 107
    Pheasant with Almonds
        and Sherry 7
    Pheasant Pie 110
    Pheasant with Sultana
        Grapes and Verjuice 109
    Warm Salad of Smoked
        Pheasant 108
Pheasant Farm
    Restaurant 93, 104–5, 150
picada 7
pickles and preserves
    ~ grapes 47
    ~ sterilising jars 186
    ~ tomatoes 187
    ~ walnuts 159, 161
    Flo Beer's Pickled
        Quinces 130
    Pickled Figs, Farm Follies
        Style 38
    see also jam; preserved lemons
pies
    Coorong Angus Beef Pie
        with Red Wine, Fennel
        and Green Olives 14
    Hare Pie 62, 64
    Pheasant Pie 110
    Pigeon and Field
        Mushroom Pie 72
    Stephanie's Partridge Pies 87
Pigeon and Field Mushroom
    Pie 72
pine nuts
    Hare with Pine Nuts, Lemon
        and Sultanas 63
pizza
    ~ fig topping 36
    ~ goat's cheese topping 36
    Dough 122
    Pumpkin Pizza with Olives
        and Bocconcini 122
Poached Pears on Filo Pastry
    with Mascarpone 93
Poached Rhubarb and
    Orange 138
poisonous fungi 68, 69
pomegranates 112–15
    ~ grenadine syrup 114
    ~ molasses 114
    ~ ripeness 113
    ~ varieties 112
    Pomegranate Sauce (savoury) 114
    Pomegranate Sauce (sweet) 115
    Pomegranate-caramel Sauce 86
    Walnut and Pomegranate
        Salad 115

pork sausages 26, 45
potatoes
    ~ in duck or goose fat 170
    ~ kipfler 44
    ~ waxy 50, 162, 172
    Green Olive Gnocchi with
        Green Olive Sauce 79
Pot-roasted Quinces 132
preserved lemons
    ~ in vinaigrette 157
    Fig and Preserved Lemon
        Salad with Walnuts and
        Goat's Curd 37
    Pasta with Caramelised
        Fennel, Preserved
        Lemon and Garlic 30
prosciutto
    Fresh Fig and Prosciutto
        Salad 36
    Onion, Garlic and Prosciutto
        Sofregit 54
    Saskia's Walnut, Mushroom
        and Prosciutto Tart 164
Proudfoot, Aileen 80
prune plums
    ~ D'Agen prune plum 94
    Chocolate Sweetmeats 166
    Quince and Prune Tart 128, 133
    Trifle of Pears, Prunes and
        Sauternes Custard 93
puddings
    Chocolate Orange Brownie
        Pudding with Rhubarb
        and Mascarpone 139
    Jane's Persimmon Pudding 102
    Rice Pudding with Poached
        Rhubarb and Orange 138
pumpkin 117–23
    ~ baked 118
    ~ barbecued 118
    ~ flowers, stuffed 117–18
    ~ Queensland Blue 117, 118
    ~ soup 118
    Chickpea and Roasted
        Pumpkin Salad 119
    Pumpkin Picnic Loaf 119
    Pumpkin Pizza with Olives
        and Bocconcini 122
    Pumpkin, Verjuice and
        Extra Virgin Olive Oil
        Risotto 118, 122

Q
Quatre Épices 172
quinces 124–34
    ~ baking 128
    ~ colour change 132
    ~ harvesting 126–7
    ~ jelly 126, 127, 128
    ~ paste 126, 127
    ~ pickled 127
    ~ pineapple quinces 133
    ~ purée 127
    ~ Smyrna 124

    ~ storing 128–9
    ~ wine 126
    Flo Beer's Pickled Quinces 130
    Lamb Neck with Quinces 132
    Pot-roasted Quinces 132
    Quince Allioli 130
    Quince Paste 129
    Quinces and Pears Poached
        in Verjuice 134
    Quince and Prune
        Tart 128, 133
    Smoked Duck Breast Salad
        with Pickled Quince and
        Vino Cotto Dressing 127, 131

R
rabbit 52, 59, 78
raspberries
    Peter Wall's Raspberry
        Vinegar 157
Red-wine Sauce 56
Renner, Jane 43
rhubarb
    ~ adding sugar 135–6
    ~ poisonous leaves 135
    ~ stringiness and acidity 135
    Chocolate Orange Brownie
        Pudding with Rhubarb
        and Mascarpone 139
    Rhubarb, Strawberries and
        Crème Fraiche 136
    Rhubarb Crumble 139
    Rice Pudding with Poached
        Rhubarb and Orange 138
rice
    ~ al dente 185
    ~ arborio 185
    Rice Pudding with Poached
        Rhubarb and Orange 138
    see also risotto
rillettes
    ~ spice mixture 172
    Rillettes de Canard (Compote
        of Shredded Duck) 173
risotto
    ~ cheese for 186
    ~ rice for 185
    Pumpkin, Verjuice and
        Extra Virgin Olive Oil
        Risotto 118, 122
    Risotto with Mushrooms 73
riverfish
    ~ Murray cod 69, 147
rocket
    Baby Beets in Vino Cotto
        with Rocket, Walnuts
        and Goat's Cheese 158
Rough Puff Pastry 179

S
sabayon
    Verjuice Sabayon with
        Grilled Figs 149

sage
  Kathy Howard's Wild
    Crabapple and Sage Jelly 24
sago
  Sherri's Rotegrütze 50
salads
  ~ dressing 157
  ~ drying lettuce 157
  Baby Beets in Vino Cotto
    with Rocket, Walnuts
    and Goat's Cheese 158
  Chickpea and Roasted
    Pumpkin Salad 119
  Dried Pears Poached
    in Verjuice 93
  Fig and Preserved Lemon
    Salad with Walnuts and
    Goat's Curd 37
  Fresh Fig and Prosciutto
    Salad 36
  Persimmon and Fennel Salad 100
  Salade Niçoise 79
  Salad with Walnut Oil
    Vinaigrette 165
  Smoked Duck Breast Salad
    with Pickled Quince and
    Vino Cotto Dressing 127, 131
  Walnut and Pomegranate
    Salad 115
  Warm Salad of Smoked
    Pheasant 108
salad dressings see
  mayonnaise; vinaigrette
salad spinner 157
salsa
  ~ fennel 27
Sandor Palmai's Persimmon
  Tarts 103
Santich, Barbara 141, 145
sardines with caramelised
  fennel 29
Saskia's Walnut, Mushroom
  and Prosciutto Tart 164
sauces, savoury
  ~ tomato 187
  Green Olive Sauce 79
  Pomegranate Sauce
    (Savoury) 114
  Orange Sauce 169
  Red-wine Sauce 56
  Verjuice Butter Sauce 146
  Wine Sauce 169
sauces, sweet
  Pomegranate Sauce
    (Sweet) 115
  Pomegranate-caramel
    Sauce 86
sausages, pork 26, 45
Sauternes Custard 94
Schiacciata 48
Schubert, Sherri 44
Schulz's Butcher 156
seafood
  Seared Razorfish on Spinach
    with Verjuice Butter Sauce 146

Seared Razorfish on Spinach
  with Verjuice Butter
  Sauce 146
Seared Tuna with Persimmon
  and Fennel Salad 100
Searle, Phillip 60
Sedgley, Margaret 77
shallots
  Guinea Fowl with Cèpe Butter
    and Golden Shallots 57
  Sherri's Rotegrütze 50
slices see cakes and slices
Slow-braised Beef Cheeks
  in Barossa Shiraz 16
Slow-roasted Oyster Blade
  with Onion Cream and
  Braised Cavolo Nero 19
Smith, Penny 100
Smoked Duck Breast Salad
  with Pickled Quince and
  Vino Cotto Dressing 127, 131
sofregit
  ~ basic mixture 54
  ~ with game 54
  Onion, Garlic and
    Prosciutto Sofregit 54
sorbet
  Lime Sorbet 103
soup
  ~ almond 6
  ~ cold 48
  ~ pumpkin 118
  Almond and Garlic Soup
    with Grapes 48
  Gerard Madani's
    Mushroom Soup 72
Sour Cream Pastry 177
South Australian Field and
  Game Association 168
Sparkling Ruby Cabernet 47,
  142, 144
spices
  ~ pâté spice mixture 172
  Quatre Épices 172
  Spiced Crabapples 23
spinach
  Seared Razorfish on Spinach
    with Verjuice Butter
    Sauce 146
Stephanie's Lard Pastry 64
Stephanie's Partridge Pies 87
sterilising bottles and jars 186
stock
  ~ jellied 182
  ~ straining and cooling 182
  Chinese Master Stock 86
  Golden Chicken Stock 181
strawberries
  ~ with balsamic vinegar
    or vin cotto 156
  Rhubarb, Strawberries
    and Crème Fraiche 136
Stuffed Guinea Fowl with
  Red Wine Sauce 56
sugar syrup 186

sultanas
  Hare with Pine Nuts,
    Lemon and Sultanas 63
Sun-dried Pears Farm
  Follies Style 91
sweetbreads
  ~ deglazed with verjuice 145
  ~ with grapes 47
Syllabub 94
syrup
  ~ grenadine 114
  ~ sugar 186

T
tapenade
  Dried Fig Tapenade 37
  Olive Tapenade with
    Red-wine Vinegar 158
tarts (savoury)
  Fig and Gorgonzola Tart 38
  Saskia's Walnut, Mushroom
    and Prosciutto Tart 164
tarts (sweet)
  Figs in Puff Pastry with
    Crème Anglaise 39
  Fig and Walnut Tart 41
  Quince and Prune
    Tart 128, 133
  Sandor Palmai's
    Persimmon Tarts 103
Tea-smoked Ocean Trout
  with Fennel 30
terrine spice mixture 172
terroir 3–4
The Cook and The Chef 118, 144
Tolley, Noëlle 5, 139, 148
tomatoes
  ~ passata 187
  ~ sugo 187
  Duck Egg Pasta with
    Smoked Kangaroo,
    Sun-dried Tomatoes
    and Pine Nuts 179
Trifle of Pears, Prunes and
  Sauternes Custard 93
truffles 71
tuna
  Salade Niçoise 79
  Seared Tuna with
    Persimmon and
    Fennel Salad 100

V
veal, grilled, with verjuice 145
verjuice 141–9
  ~ commercial production 141–2
  ~ in drinks 142
  ~ flavour 141
  ~ grapes for 142, 144
  ~ poached fruit 142
  ~ sorbets and jellies 144
  Dried Pears Poached in
    Verjuice 93

Kangaroo Carpaccio
with Cumquats,
Green Peppercorns
and Verjuice 148
Ocean Trout in Verjuice
Jelly 147
Partridge with Savoy Cabbage,
Pancetta, Walnuts and
Verjuice 85
Partridge 'Puddings' with
Sultanas and Verjuice 84
Pheasant with Sultana
Grapes and Verjuice 109
Pumpkin, Verjuice and
Extra Virgin Olive Oil
Risotto 118, 122
Quinces and Pears Poached
in Verjuice 134
Seared Razorfish on Spinach
with Verjuice Butter Sauce 146
Verjuice Butter Sauce 146
Verjuice Hollandaise 144, 148
Verjuice Jelly 147
Verjuice Sabayon with
Grilled Figs 149
Verjuice Vinaigrette 144, 145
Vietch, Trish 60
vinaigrette 119
~ anchovy 83, 157
~ mustard 157
~ tips 157
~ with vin cotto 157
~ vinegars 150
~ warm 114
Verjuice Vinaigrette 144, 145
Walnut Oil Vinaigrette 165
vine leaves
~ game birds parcels 83, 145
~ mushrooms baked in 70–1
~ pickling walnuts 161
vinegar 150–8
~ aged 152, 153
~ containers for 153
~ making your own 153–4,
156–7
~ malt 150
~ Orléanais method 153
~ oxidation 153
~ red-wine/sherry 150, 152–3
~ tasting 152
~ uses 156
Olive Tapenade with
Red-wine Vinegar 158
Peter Wall's Raspberry
Vinegar 157
see also balsamic vinegar;
vinaigrette
vinegar 'mother' 154
vino cotto 150, 156, 157, 187
Baby Beets in Vino Cotto
with Rocket, Walnuts
and Goat's Cheese 158
Fillet of Beef in Balsamic
Vinegar or Vino Cotto 17
von Bremzen, Anya 100

W

Wall, Eloise and Cressida 13
Wall, Judith and Peter 13, 66,
68, 69, 88, 141–2, 161, 167–8
Peter Wall's Raspberry
Vinegar 157
walnuts 169–66
~ dry roasting 161
~ freshness 162
~ green 159, 161
~ harvesting 161
~ leaves 159, 161
~ pickled 159, 161
~ rancid 161–2
~ storage 162
~ uses 162
~ 'wet' 159
Baby Beets in Vino Cotto
with Rocket, Walnuts
and Goat's Cheese 158
Chocolate Sweetmeats 166
Fig and Preserved Lemon
Salad with Walnuts and
Goat's Curd 37
Fig and Walnut Tart 41
Oxtail with Orange, Olives
and Walnuts 18
Partridge with Savoy Cabbage,
Pancetta, Walnuts and
Verjuice 85
Saskia's Walnut, Mushroom
and Prosciutto Tart 164
Walnut Flatbread 165
Walnut and Parsley
Pesto 162, 183
Walnut and Pomegranate
Salad 115
walnut oil 161
~ rancid 163
~ uses 163–4
Walnut Oil Vinaigrette 165
Wark, Alf 168
Wark, James 168
Warm Salad of Smoked
Pheasant 108
Waters, Alice 27
Welchman, John 100
wild duck 167–73
~ black duck 167, 169
~ duck season 167
~ flavour 167
~ giblets 169
~ mallard 167
~ 'preen' glands 169
~ slow-cooking 167
~ teal 167
Black Duck and Orange
Sauce 169
Wild Duck Poached in
Wine Sauce 169
Wine Sauce 169
Wolfert, Paula 3, 127, 170, 173

LANTERN

UK | USA | Canada | Ireland | Australia
India | New Zealand | South Africa | China

Penguin Books is part of the Penguin Random House group of companies whose
addresses can be found at global.penguinrandomhouse.com.

Penguin
Random House
Australia

First published by Penguin Group (Australia), 2015
This material was originally published as a section of *Maggie's Harvest* by Maggie Beer

1 3 5 7 9 10 8 6 4 2

Text copyright © Maggie Beer 2015
Photographs copyright © Mark Chew 2015
Author photograph © Earl Carter 2015

The moral right of the author has been asserted.

Cover and text design by Daniel New © Penguin Group (Australia)
Design coordination by Hannah Schubert
Typeset in Cochin by Post Pre-Press Group, Brisbane, Queensland
Colour reproduction by Splitting Image, Clayton, Victoria
Printed in China by 1010 Printing International Limited

National Library of Australia
Cataloguing-in-Publication data:

Beer, Maggie.
Maggie Beer's Autumn Harvest Recipes.
Notes: Includes bibliographical details and index
ISBN 9781921384257 (pbk.)
Subjects: Seasonal cooking
Other Creators/Contributors:
Chew, Mark, photographer.
641.564

penguin.com.au/lantern

MAGGIE'S HARVEST
Maggie Beer

This landmark book from one of Australia's best-loved cooks
was first published in 2007 and is now available
as four seasonal paperbacks.

ISBN 9781921384226   ISBN 9781921384233   ISBN 9781921384240